PERSECUTION AND TOLERATION IN PROTESTANT ENGLAND, 1558–1689

STUDIES IN MODERN HISTORY

General editors: John Morrill and David Cannadine

This series, intended primarily for students, will tackle significant historical issues in concise volumes which are both stimulating and scholarly. The authors combine a broad approach, explaining the current state of our knowledge in the area, with their own research and judgements: and the topics chosen range widely in subject, period and place.

PERSECUTION AND TOLERATION IN PROTESTANT ENGLAND, 1558–1689

JOHN COFFEY

Longman

An imprint of **Pearson Education**

Harlow, England · London · New York · Reading, Massachusetts · San Francisco
Toronto · Don Mills, Ontario · Sydney · Tokyo · Singapore · Hong Kong · Seoul
Taipei · Cape Town · Madrid · Mexico City · Amsterdam · Munich · Paris · Milan

Pearson Education Limited
Edinburgh Gate
Harlow
Essex CM20 2JE
England

and Associated Companies throughout the world

Visit us on the World Wide Web at:
www.pearsoneduc.com

First published 2000

ISBN 0 582 30464 4 PPR
      0 582 30465 2 CASED

British Library Cataloguing-in-Publication Data
A catalogue record for this book is available from the British Library

Library of Congress Cataloging-in-Publication Data
Coffey, John, 1969–
      Persecution and toleration in Protestant England, 1558–1689 / John Coffey.
         p.   cm. — (Studies in modern history)
      Includes bibliographical references and index.
      ISBN 0–582–30464–4 (pbk.) — ISBN 0–582–30465–2 (cased)
         1. Persecution—England—History—16th century.   2. Religious tolerance—
      England—History—16th century.   3. England—Church history—16th century.
      4. Persecution—England—History—17th century.   5. Religious tolerance—
      England—History—17th century.   6. England—Church history—17th century.
      I. Title.   II. Studies in modern history (Longman (Firm))

BX1492.C56   2000
272′.7—dc21   00–059805

10 9 8 7 6 5 4 3 2 1
04 03 02 01 00

Typeset by 35 in 11/13pt Baskerville

Printed and bound by Antony Rowe Ltd, Eastbourne

For John and Emma

CONTENTS

CONTENTS

LIST OF TABLES

PREFACE

A Free Disputation against Pretended Liberty of Conscience (1649) has been described by Owen Chadwick as 'the ablest defence of religious persecution
during the seventeenth century'.[1] Its author was the Scottish Covenanter
Samuel Rutherford, the subject of my first book, *Politics, Religion and the
British Revolutions: The Mind of Samuel Rutherford* (Cambridge University Press,
1997). Ironically, Rutherford's treatise introduced me to the tolerationist
pamphlets he had condemned, and led to the writing of this book. It tries to
provide the first survey of persecution and toleration in early modern England since W. K. Jordan, *The Development of Religious Toleration in England*, 4
vols (London, 1932–40). Readers will be relieved to hear that it is almost
ten times shorter than Jordan's *magnum opus*.

The idea for the book was suggested by John Morrill, and like so many
others I am deeply indebted to him for his enthusiasm and support. In the
midst of a formidably busy life he has somehow found time to read my
work and offer much wise advice. It is also a pleasure to say thanks to my
former supervisor Mark Goldie, who offered invaluable comments on several of my chapters, and who has contributed so much to our understanding of persecution and toleration in later Stuart England. I am grateful to
Michael Davies, Terry Hartley, Aubrey Newman and David Wykes, who
read and commented upon sections of the book. They cannot be held
responsible for any of my blunders or misinterpretations, but their help was
much appreciated. The students who took my Cambridge University History Summer School course on persecution and toleration in early modern
Europe also contributed a great deal to my thinking.

Several institutions have supported me during the course of my research
and writing. Most of the work was done at Churchill College, Cambridge,
where I was a Junior Research Fellow from 1994 to 1998. Churchill provided an ideal environment for research and writing, and I am indebted to
the Master, the Fellows, and the staff for the very happy years I spent there.
The completion of the book was made possible through the award of a
Postdoctoral Fellowship from the British Academy. I am grateful to David
French, Rebecca Spang, Nicholas Tyacke and other colleagues for their
support during my year at University College London. The final chapters

were written at the University of Leicester, and I wish to thank everyone at the Department of History for helping me to settle in.

I am especially grateful to my uncle and aunt, John and Emma Parker, who gave me vital support at an important stage in my career. Without them, this book would probably not have been written. My parents have also given me lots of encouragement, even if research for this book did not take me to Scotland as did my work on Rutherford. Finally, my wife Cate has helped me far more than she knows by being herself and by tolerating my frequent musings on toleration.

Note

1   O. Chadwick, *The Reformation* (Harmondsworth, 1964), p. 403.

Publisher's Acknowledgements

The publishers are grateful to Cambridge University Press for permission to reproduce a Table from Braithwaite, *The Second Period of Quakerism*, Second Edition (1961), p. 114 and a Table from G. Nuttall, 'The English martyrs 1535–1680: a statistical review', *Journal of Ecclesiastical History* 22 (1971), pp. 191–7.

CHAPTER 1

Introduction

The Whig history of toleration

Historians of Stuart England have often been impressed by its modernity. Although their emphases differ, Whigs, Marxists, and Weberians alike have maintained that the modern world was forged in the furnace of seventeenth-century England. It was here, argued Marxist and Weberian writers, that one must look for the rise of the bourgeois mentality, the first of the great modern revolutions, the birth of modern science and modern capitalism.[1] Here too, suggested Whig historians, was the seedbed of modern political liberalism, with its twin ideals of popular sovereignty and religious toleration.[2]

For nineteenth-century Whigs, the Act of Toleration in 1689 was a liberal landmark. In the words of Lord Macaulay, the Act

> put an end, at once and for ever . . . to a persecution which had raged during four generations, which had broken innumerable hearts, which had made innumerable firesides desolate, which had filled the prisons with men of whom the world was not worthy, which had driven thousands of those honest, diligent, godfearing yeomen and artisans, who are the true strength of a nation, to seek a refuge beyond the ocean among the wigwams of red Indians and the lairs of panthers.

Yet Whig historians were by no means as naive in their celebration of the Toleration Act as is often supposed. Macaulay freely confessed that its provisions were 'cumbrous, puerile, inconsistent with each other, inconsistent with the true theory of religious liberty'. But its genius lay in the fact that it 'removed a vast mass of evil without shocking a vast mass of prejudice'.[3]

As well as emphasising the achievement of 1689, Whig historians of freedom also accorded an important role to the 'Puritan Revolution'. The great Victorian scholar S. R. Gardiner argued that 'the idea [of toleration] had been laid before the world' during the 1640s and 1650s, and 'could not be buried out of sight'. Oliver Cromwell and John Milton had prepared the ground for the Act of Toleration.[4] The American historian William Haller began his study of the period in order to contextualise Milton's famous defence of the liberty of the press, *Areopagitica* (1644). Haller hailed Milton as an 'apostle of freedom',[5] and agreed with Gardiner that the 1640s were of 'the greatest significance'. 'Here, in a word', he wrote, 'are revealed the beginnings of democracy, of economic individualism, and of modern English prose'.[6] A. S. P. Woodhouse took the same view in the introduction to his collection of texts, *Puritanism and Liberty*. 'Puritans of the Left', he suggested, had laid down the key principles of modern liberal democracy, including individualism, egalitarianism, and the separation of church and state.[7]

But the most ambitious attempt to chronicle the rise of religious toleration in the seventeenth century was W. K. Jordan's monumental work *The Development of Religious Toleration in England, 1558–1660*, 4 vols (London, 1932–40). Like Haller and Woodhouse, Jordan wrote as the shadow of fascism fell across Europe, and his *magnum opus* was an apologia for the fragile values of humanity and tolerance. In over 2000 pages of text, he described the rise of toleration in England and lovingly catalogued the opinions of hundreds of writers. Fifty years on, his books remain essential reading for anyone working on the subject of toleration in early modern England.

Yet despite its admirable qualities, Jordan's work is more problematic than that of Haller and Woodhouse. The sheer scale of his four volumes makes it exceedingly difficult to see the wood from the trees. Rather than synthesising his reading in a digestible form, Jordan compiled an exhaustive list of everyone who had anything to say about toleration, and his lengthy descriptions of their pamphlets are often tediously repetitive. More seriously, Jordan illustrates the cardinal failings of Whig historiography. His is a strongly teleological narrative, one which seems to progress inexorably (though rather laboriously) towards a predetermined end, the triumph of the ideal of toleration in England by 1660.[8]

The dangers of this kind of historical writing are well known. The contingency of historical developments is forgotten and the story takes on a certain inevitability; 'reactionary' aspects of the past are overlooked as the historian focuses on the winners, those who had 'history on their side' and successfully 'anticipated' modern ideals; anachronism strikes with a vengeance. In his desire to discover and celebrate tolerationist heroes, for example, Jordan tends to turn his subjects into modern, secular liberals. Whereas

Haller and Woodhouse had edited valuable collections of primary texts and shown real sensitivity to the theological context of seventeenth-century tolerationism, Jordan persistently secularises his subjects. Milton is pigeon-holed with the 'rationalists and sceptics', and described as 'only vaguely religious',[9] something that will come as a surprise to most readers of his poetry and prose. We are told that Sir William Cecil was a man who 'discounted the importance of religion in public affairs',[10] though a recent historian informs us of Cecil's firm belief that the Pope was the Antichrist.[11] The same tendency to paint things in modern colours can be detected in Jordan's broader conclusions. He claims, for instance, that the Elizabethan settlement 'was a long step towards toleration',[12] even though the Act of Uniformity made it possible to prosecute individuals for failing to attend church. When he suggests that by 1660 'responsible opinion in England was . . . persuaded of the necessity, if not of the positive virtue, of religious freedom',[13] he ignores the mass of evidence which suggests that much 're-sponsible opinion' in Restoration England was far from convinced of the need for toleration.

The revisionist reaction

The strongly teleological and anachronistic tendencies of Whig historians like Jordan have provoked a revisionist reaction. Instead of modernising the past, recent historians have been intent on recapturing its strangeness, and understanding mentalities radically different to our own. Political historians have been stressing the centrality of religious *intolerance* to the history of early modern England. In particular, they have identified anti-popery as perhaps the most powerful and visceral force in English politics, one which helped to topple Charles I and his son James II. The most famous events of this period – the Spanish Armada, the Gunpowder Plot, the English Civil War, the Popish Plot, the Glorious Revolution – were events driven along by religious intolerance. Indeed, it is tempting to say that the fear of popery was almost the ground bass in the nation's political life between the Act of Uniformity in 1559 and the Act of Toleration in 1689.[14]

Besides emphasising the power of anti-Catholicism, historians have high-lighted the mutual hostility between different sorts of Protestants. Accord-ing to John Morrill and Conrad Russell, religion was the crucial polarising factor in the months leading up to the English Civil War, a conflict which Morrill has described as the last of the European wars of religion.[15] For most of the seventeenth century the prospects for toleration looked bleak, not least after 1660, and historians of the Restoration period have argued that the bitter rift between church and Dissent was at the heart of political conflict in the period.[16] Moreover, when legal toleration was finally achieved, it fell far short of religious equality, and was the result of fortuitous circumstance rather than the triumph of an ideal in the minds of the English. Even after 1689, strident voices deplored the concessions made to Dissenters and the Act of Toleration seemed vulnerable. According to Jonathan Clark, England remained a confessional state whose Protestant Dissenters were second-class citizens.[17] The triumph of tolerance was neither assured nor complete.

In this new revisionist paradigm, historians have also emphasised the limits of seventeenth-century tolerationism. Blair Worden, for example, has highlighted the limits of Cromwellian toleration, and argued that when Puritans like Cromwell and John Owen talked about 'liberty of conscience' they meant liberty for conscientious Protestants, not licence for ungodly and false religions.[18] William Lamont has suggested that Puritans like Roger Williams and John Milton were 'not interested in wishy-washy nineteenth-century concerns such as personal freedoms and equality', and J. C. Davis has examined the conception of freedom held in the 1640s, and concluded that Puritans longed for a godly rather than a liberal society, and sought not the freedom of the sinner, but the freedom of Almighty God.[19] Others have pointed out that England's most famous tolerationist, John Locke, explicitly excluded Roman Catholics and atheists from toleration, and have compared him unfavourably to more radical figures like the Huguenot Pierre Bayle. More importantly, historians have demonstrated the relative isolation of seventeenth-century tolerationists, and the continuing vitality of theories of persecution.[20] Richard Ashcraft emphasises that even the Latitudinarians, the 'liberal' Anglicans of their day, usually opposed toleration for groups outside the established church.[21] In place of Jordan's vision of a nation bustling with earnest progressives, we have a picture of a land still dominated by traditional defenders of religious uniformity.

Historians of European religion have also questioned the simplicity of the traditional Whig narrative. In *Toleration and the Reformation*, the Jesuit scholar Joseph Lecler destroyed any idea of a simple dichotomy between a tolerant Protestantism and an intolerant Catholicism. By 1600, Lecler pointed out, the Catholic lands of Poland and France had established toleration, whilst most Protestant countries still enforced uniformity.[22] Despite its rather Whiggish title, Henry Kamen's *The Rise of Toleration* also offered a more complex picture of Catholic attitudes and argued that 'toleration has pursued not a linear but a cyclic development; it has not evolved progressively but has suffered periodic and prolonged reverses'.[23] A recent collection of essays on *Tolerance and Intolerance in the European Reformation* casts further doubt on the Whig identification of Protestantism and liberty, and on the traditional opposition between a persecutory medieval period and an increasingly tolerant early modern era. Several contributors argue that early modern tolerationists were interested in Christian concord rather than in modern religious liberty, and they replace grand narratives centred on rising tolerationist conviction with detailed case studies of particular cities and territories.[24]

But the most iconoclastic assault on the traditional Whig story has been mounted by John Laursen and Cary Nederman. They criticise the grand narrative 'describing a unilinear progression from darkness to light, from persecution to toleration, from all that was old and backward to all that is new and modern'. They set out to debunk liberal myths: 'the Inquisition cliché', which portrays medieval Europe as a benighted, persecuting society; the 'Enlightenment stereotype' of a benevolent modernity; and 'the Locke obsession', which attributes the rise of toleration to the intellectual achievements of a great and lonely thinker. By contrast, they argue that toleration was practised and theorised in medieval and early modern Europe on a scale few have realised. The history of toleration, it is implied, should focus on continuities rather than on a dramatic break with the past in the late seventeenth and eighteenth centuries.[25]

A post-revisionist approach

Thus the revisionist scholarship of the past generation has created a far richer and more complex picture of the history of persecution and toleration. Yet despite the provocative presence of Jordan's massive work, there has been no revisionist survey of persecution and toleration in Tudor and Stuart England. My goal, therefore, is to close that gap by providing a synthesis of some of the most significant historical research undertaken on the topic since the 1930s. Obviously, this book cannot hope to rival Jordan in terms of comprehensiveness; as Blair Worden once remarked, 'any subsequent account can be no more than a footnote'.[26] But this footnote should prove more accessible than Jordan's tomes, and it will temper his Whiggish optimism with a dose of revisionist realism. This book has more to say about persecution than about toleration, and it emphasises the power of religious intolerance in early modern England. However, it also reasserts the unfashionably Whiggish claim that seventeenth-century England did indeed witness a dramatic movement from persecution to toleration and from religious uniformity to pluralism.

This claim is still widely accepted by scholars who do not specialise in the period. In his book *Liberalism*, for instance, the political theorist John

Gray argues that the liberal tradition was born in seventeenth-century England, in the debates of the English Civil War, the work of Locke, and the period of Whig ascendancy following the Glorious Revolution.[27] Historians of the period, however, are more reticent about making broad claims for the significance of their subject, and many have spent their careers fleeing from the exaggerated modernisation narratives of earlier Whig and Marxist writers. Yet in reacting against Whiggish excesses, it is possible to lose sight of the major transformations which did occur in seventeenth-century England. Recently, historians have begun to recognise this. In *From Persecution to Toleration*, Ole Grell, Jonathan Israel and Nicholas Tyacke have argued that for all its limitations, 1689 was a 'very real milestone'.[28] Other scholars have argued that the origins of the liberal political tradition can be found in seventeenth-century England. David Wootton has made a vigorous case for the liberalism of the Levellers and John Locke,[29] and Annabel Patterson has studied the development of what she calls 'early modern liberalism'.[30] Even one of England's leading revisionist historians, Conrad Russell, traces the roots of English liberalism to seventeenth-century Whigs like Locke and Sidney.[31] Indeed, with regard to persecution and toleration it seems hard to deny that the period did constitute a major turning point. Two great religious changes occurred in seventeenth-century England. Firstly, the monopoly of the national church was broken, and a plurality of sects and denominations became firmly entrenched beyond its walls. Secondly, the consensus in favour of religious uniformity backed by coercion – which had been the orthodoxy in Christian Europe for many centuries – began to crumble.

To reassert the turning point thesis is not to deny that religious tolerance could exist in theory and practice in medieval Christendom. In medieval Europe, infidels and Jews were marginalised and subjected to disapproval, but they were often tolerated.[32] Yet this is 'toleration' in its meanest and narrowest sense, and it does not invalidate the traditional narrative describing the transition from persecution to toleration in early modern Europe. Although medieval theorists allowed for a certain degree of toleration within the Catholic church and for non-Christian minorities outside it, almost all refused to extend this to heretics (who denied Catholic orthodoxy) and schismatics (who separated themselves from the church). The classic theory of religious coercion expounded by St Augustine was almost universally accepted in the medieval period, and hardly anyone held to the standard modern position that the magistrate must not punish individuals for their religious beliefs. Although toleration was sometimes implemented as a political necessity, religious uniformity remained the ideal. The Augustinian consensus in support of the persecution of heretics and schismatics was only widely challenged in the sixteenth and seventeenth centuries.

The problem with Laursen and Nederman's approach is that the question they pose is too vague. They ask, 'Can we find tolerance of diversity in medieval life and thought?', and rightly conclude that we can. Yet this is not surprising. Every society has a theory of toleration; societies simply differ over what is tolerable. In this sense the dichotomy between a tolerant modernity and an intolerant Middle Ages is misleading, and Laursen and Nederman are right to criticise the popular image of medieval Europe as a totalitarian 'persecuting society'. But we need to sharpen the question by asking, 'Did intellectuals and magistrates have a principled commitment to the toleration of heretics and schismatics?' Once we do this, the gulf between medieval and modern opens up again, and the early modern period reappears as a critical era of transition. For it is during this period that tolerationists emerge who provide principled opposition to the persecution of heretics and schismatics and argue for a frank acceptance of a plurality of churches and religions within one society. Although their ideas take a long time to win general acceptance, they do mark a significant break with the past.

This book tries to illustrate this with reference to England. It argues that the traditional consensus concerning persecution and the ideal of uniformity was still in place in Tudor and early Stuart England. But the 1640s witnessed a dramatic change, and in my view Haller and Woodhouse were correct to argue that the initial impetus towards religious toleration came from radical Puritanism. The fragmentation of English Puritanism laid the groundwork for pluralism, and radical Puritans launched a sustained attack on the use of coercion for religious purposes. Rejecting the ideal of religious uniformity, they envisaged a pluralistic society in which the magistrate concentrated on civil tasks and ceased to meddle in religious affairs. This new theory was not a uniquely English development, but it differed starkly from traditional assumptions, and laid the foundation for modern Christian and secular attitudes. In many respects, the worldview of these tolerationists was still very different from that of modern secular liberals, but this should not obscure their significance. Isaac Newton, after all, laid the foundations for modern physics whilst pursuing his researches in alchemy and apocalyptic.[33] The strangeness of the seventeenth century does not cancel out its status as a turning point which saw the emergence of distinctively modern ideas.

Relating past and present

Indeed, it is all too easy to miss the striking similarities between early modern Europe and the contemporary world. Seventeenth-century England is by no means as alien as historians sometimes suggest, and the story of persecution and toleration in the period is far from irrelevant to contemporary concerns. It is no doubt true that the study of the period introduces us to a world very different from our own, one as fascinating and unfamiliar as the worlds explored by anthropologists. Yet it would be a mistake to draw too bold a contrast between a devout past and an irreligious modernity, or to tie modernisation too closely to secularisation. This is a mistake made by both Whigs and revisionists. Working on the assumption that to be modern is to be secular, W. K. Jordan described a seventeenth century populated by rationalists, whilst revisionists have rediscovered the power of religion in the period and concluded that it is pre-modern. Yet the fact that early modern tolerationists, for instance, thought in profoundly theological terms does not make them distant and irrelevant; it places them in the good company of modern liberal–democratic leaders like Martin Luther King. Ironically, in claiming to repudiate strongly teleological narratives, revisionists have often uncritically accepted one of the grandest teleological stories of all, the secularisation thesis, which in its classic Marxist and Weberian versions suggests that modernisation leads inevitably to the decline of religion.

Yet secularisation theory is in something of a crisis. Peter Berger, who was once among its foremost proponents, has recently edited a book entitled *The Desecularization of the World*. He argues that 'the assumption that we live in a secularised world is false: The world today, with some exceptions . . . is as furiously religious as it ever was, and in some places more so than ever'.[34] Since the Iranian revolution of 1979, fundamentalist movements within Islam, Christianity, Judaism, Hinduism and other religions have become a major political phenomenon.[35] The religious militancy and violence that characterised early modern Europe have returned to haunt the modern world.[36] Three decades ago, religious terrorism was almost non-existent; since 1980, Shi'a extremists alone have probably been responsible for more than half of all terrorist killings. Indeed, Professor Christopher Andrew has argued that the 'new generation of religious terrorists has more in common with the bloodthirsty fanatics of the age of religious warfare than with most of their 20th-century predecessors'.[37]

Indeed, in many countries of the world today, religious persecution is a major human rights problem, with Christian minorities being particularly vulnerable.[38] While I have been writing this book, the British press has carried numerous tales of persecution and religious violence: in Pakistan, a Catholic bishop shoots himself dead in protest against the blasphemy trials being brought against his fellow Christians; in China, the government bans the Falun Gong sect and imprisons Catholic priests and Protestant pastors in the name of public order and atheistic orthodoxy; in Russia, a new Orthodox-inspired law on religion arouses anxiety among religious minorities and secular liberals; in Indonesia, Muslim–Christian riots result in the destruction of churches and many fatalities; in India, a Protestant missionary and his two young sons are burned to death by Hindu extremists; in the Balkans, ethnic conflict is exacerbated by the contrasting religious identities of Catholic Croatians, Orthodox Serbians and Muslim Kosovans; in Bangladesh, the novelist Taslima Nasreen is threatened with death for alleged blasphemies against the Koran.

Yet this revival of persecution and religious violence is only half the story, for the recent resurgence of religion has also contributed to the growth of pluralism and democracy. In eastern Europe, the Catholic and Orthodox churches played a critical role in the downfall of Communist regimes, whilst in South Africa, clerics like Desmond Tutu figured prominently in the transition to black majority rule and the struggle for justice and reconciliation thereafter. Meanwhile, popular versions of evangelical Protestantism (uncannily reminiscent of movements that flourished during the Puritan Revolution) have grown explosively in Latin America, Africa and mainland China, attracting tens of millions of converts. Even in western Europe and North America, the relationship between religious conviction and politics is being debated with renewed vigour. The presence of immigrant communities, the growth of new religious movements, and the continuing influence of the traditional Catholic and Protestant churches ensure that religion still retains a significant place on the cultural landscape.[39] Thus modern societies are profoundly *pluralistic* rather than simply *irreligious*, and as scholars like Alasdair Macintyre have argued, contemporary people do their moral thinking from within very different traditions, secular and religious.[40]

The political philosopher John Rawls has recently highlighted one of the most important implications of this ineradicable pluralism. Rawls realises that if liberal principles like freedom of religion are to be firmly established across the contemporary world, they will need to be embraced from within different worldviews and traditions. If political liberalism is to be successful, people must find justification for it within their own 'reasonable comprehensive doctrines'.[41] As Rawls recognises, something like this happened in early modern Europe, where tolerationist ideals developed as a response to the disastrous wars of religion. 'The historical origin of political liberalism (and of liberalism more generally)', argues Rawls, 'is the Reformation and its aftermath, with the long controversies over religious toleration in the sixteenth and seventeenth centuries'.[42]

Here, then, is one important reason why our subject is so significant. Contrary to what revisionists often imply, early modern England is not completely alien territory. In a world where religious extremism is rampant, this historical example is as pertinent as it ever was. Holy wars, fundamentalist terrorism, godly assassins, book burnings, blasphemy trials and religious persecution are with us once again. In an age of multi-faith soci-eties when many religious traditions are witnessing a struggle over questions of tolerance, seventeenth-century England provides a revealing case study. It helps us to consider the reasons for the demise of persecution in one particular culture, and takes us to the origins of the Western tolerationist tradition.

This book, therefore, tries to reclaim some of the positive aspects of Whig historiography, including its curiosity about the origins of modern ideals and its conviction that the study of the past is of some practical value. To revisionist historians this may seem reprehensibly present-minded.[43] But present-mindedness in historians is both inevitable and potentially fruitful; the recent interest in women's history and in 'the British problem', for example, is clearly inspired by contemporary concerns. Yet this book does take on board the key findings of revisionist scholarship. In particular, it takes to heart revisionist warnings against anachronism; an entire chapter is devoted to the Protestant theory of persecution, and the text as a whole seeks to give full weight to the force of religious intolerance in early modern England. Revisionists have been right to insist that as we approach the past we must be on the lookout for mentalities, practices and institutions rad-ically different to our own. In order to make sense of the phenomenon of religious persecution, we will need to work hard to understand early mod-ern religion in its own terms. To begin with we need to unpack the concept of toleration and investigate its applications in the sixteenth and seven-teenth centuries.

The concept of toleration

For all its familiarity, the concept of toleration is more complex than it seems. It may be defined as 'the policy of patient forbearance towards that which is not approved'.[44] Properly understood, toleration has two major components: objection and acceptance. Those who tolerate disapprove of an opinion, act, or lifestyle, and yet choose to exercise restraint towards it.[45]

The element of *disapproval* is important, because toleration is often con-fused with indifference or approval. The concept of toleration loomed large in early modern discourse precisely because people took religion very seri-ously indeed, and religious diversity aroused strong feelings. Early modern Christians experienced distress when confronted with those whom they regarded as idolatrous, superstitious, heretical or schismatic. Thus the deci-sion to exercise *restraint* involved acceptance of the mental pain caused by dissenters. Toleration was a paradoxical policy, for tolerationists had to explain why it was appropriate to accept the presence of a religion to which one objected. Their concept of tolerance was closely connected to notions of patience, forbearance, and longsuffering. Tolerant persons were pent-up rather than laid-back, restraining themselves in the face of something of which they disapproved.

But defining tolerance is only half the problem. Confusion abounds in this field because many writers fail to distinguish the different contexts in which the concept of tolerance can be used. A good example is Katherine Moore's 1964 anthology *The Spirit of Tolerance*, which includes excerpts from a host of seventeenth-century English authors. The foreword vaguely defines tolerance as 'fellow-feeling with all humanity' and 'the spirit of respect for personality'.[46] Tolerance is presented as a warm personal attitude which one either possesses or lacks, rather than as a tough practical policy adopted in the face of something one finds alienating or problematic. No attempt is made to probe the extent and limits of the tolerance of particular authors in the anthology, or to explain the various contexts in which tolerance can apply. The present book, by contrast, attempts to be far more rigorous when speaking about tolerance and toleration. It will use the terms interchangeably, rather than using 'tolerance' to refer to an attitude, and 'toleration' to a policy. But it will try to be precise about the extent and limits of the toleration advocated by various authors, and carefully distinguish between the various contexts in which tolerance could operate. These contexts need to be described in more detail before we begin.

When English pamphleteers spoke of toleration they were usually thinking of *civil* tolerance – of the policy of the state towards religious dissent. The debate over persecution and toleration was a debate about what the civil magistrate ought to do about dissent, and it is on this issue that the book will focus. For most of the period between 1558 and 1689, the English state can be described as a persecuting state. It was committed to securing religious uniformity, and to achieve that end it was prepared to employ coercive measures. Its laws and statutes penalised those outside the established church, and although executions for heresy or dissent were rare, fines and imprisonments were common. As we shall see, the enforcement of the penal statutes varied considerably across time and place, but the legitimacy of the state's coercive action against Catholics and nonconformists was widely accepted. From the 1640s, however, a vigorous debate over the question of toleration saw the publication of numerous pamphlets attacking persecution and calling for civil tolerance of religious diversity.

Yet civil tolerance itself could mean different things. At its most minimal, toleration merely entailed relief from persecution, allowing dissenters to worship without government harassment, either in private or in public. Toleration in this sense was a generous grant of 'indulgence' by the state, rather than a natural right of religious dissenters.[47] Such a toleration could be either a tacit, *de facto* acceptance of the existence of dissent, or an explicit legal statute (such as the Act of Toleration of 1689). This mere toleration, however, would still leave religious dissenters on the margins of society, as second-class citizens subject to heavy discrimination. Radical tolerationists were looking for something more than this, something closer to what we now mean when we speak of 'religious liberty'. They wanted the government to recognise the right of dissenters to worship when and where they pleased and possess the full privileges of citizenship. For Locke, 'toleration' or 'liberty of conscience' meant the natural right or entitlement of religious dissenters to worship freely and enjoy civil equality. The most radical tolerationists went a stage further and advocated what was later called 'disestablishment', or 'the separation of church and state', a development that we tend to associate with the American and French Revolutions, but one which has never taken place in England itself.

The second context for toleration was the *ecclesiastical*. Ecclesiastical tolerance concerned the degree of diversity tolerated within a particular church. The distinction between civil and ecclesiastical tolerance was one used by seventeenth-century writers.[48] From the late 1660s, 'toleration' or 'indulgence' (i.e. civil tolerance) was often contrasted with 'comprehension' (i.e. ecclesiastical tolerance), but even in this period the term toleration was often used to refer to both 'indulgence' and 'comprehension'.[49] There were basically four different positions with regard to civil and ecclesiastical tolerance. The first position, adopted by Anglicans like John Locke and a few liberal Dissenters, favoured both civil and ecclesiastical tolerance; they wanted the state to tolerate a variety of religious groups, but also favoured broad and internally tolerant churches. A second group, including the Laudians and Restoration High Anglicans, was hostile to both ecclesiastical and civil tolerance. They were unwilling to accommodate nonconformists within the Church of England, and they steadfastly opposed any toleration for Dissenting denominations outside it. A third group of Anglicans, the so-called 'Latitudinarians', agreed with ecclesiastical tolerance but was wary of civil tolerance. Whilst they worked hard to create a comprehension scheme which would reincorporate most Protestant Dissenters into a broad Church of England, they saw this as an alternative to the toleration of a plurality of denominations. Finally, sectarian Protestants often favoured a combination of civil tolerance and ecclesiastical intolerance. They wanted the state to tolerate a wide variety of religious sects and denominations, but they believed that godly congregations should impose strict ideological and moral discipline on their members. Internally, Separatist churches were often more intolerant and exclusive than the Church of England, but as voluntary communities they relied on willing submission to their discipline rather than on coercive measures. Indeed, their emphasis on the voluntary nature of the church was as modern as their demand for toleration. In contrast to the situation in the established church, excommunication from these congregations did not entail exclusion from public office and social marginalisation.

Thirdly, we need to consider the *social* context of tolerance. In recent years there has been considerable historical research on the interaction of religious groups in England, so that we now have a much clearer understanding of how religious minorities were treated by local communities. Surprisingly, perhaps, this research has often uncovered a great deal of informal neighbourly tolerance in towns and villages throughout England. However, local communities had the power to make life very unpleasant for dissenters. In early modern France, Huguenots who fell into the hands of the mob were far less likely to survive than those who fell into the hands of the magistrate. In England, the situation was nowhere near as dangerous, but religious minorities could still experience intense communal hostility. From the seventeenth through to the nineteenth centuries, Catholics and Dissenters were victims of mob attacks.

The fourth context is the *polemical*. Confronted by an alternative set of beliefs and practices of which they disapproved, early modern believers had to choose between showing restraint and engaging in polemical argument. For most this was no choice at all; they felt they had a solemn duty to assail false religion with arguments. Moreover, in theory at least, this was a mild and acceptable form of intolerance, one which broke no bones. Even the most ardent advocates of civil tolerance insisted that false religion must be attacked with words (not with force). But in early modern religious debate words could be deployed in the most aggressive fashion. Preachers and pamphleteers could throw restraint to the wind and pour vitriol on their opponents. In Archbishop Whitgift's phrase, this was 'persecution of the tongue'.[50] In its turn, this heated rhetoric aroused passions which could erupt into physical violence. Words were sometimes followed by sticks and stones.[51] It was for this reason that moderates pleaded for a lowering of the polemical temperature. Disagreement, argument and some degree of polemical intolerance were inevitable, but there had to be restraint.

Behind these four contexts stood the grand theme of *divine* tolerance. The patience and longsuffering of God were continually emphasised in the Bible, and those who called for tolerance frequently appealed to the love and compassion of God. Yet the Scriptures also spoke of the wrath and intolerance of the Lord. They warned that one day God's patience would run out, that the wicked would receive their come-uppance. Some tolerationist writers felt acutely uncomfortable with this teaching, and muted the theme of divine intolerance, but many turned it to their own advantage. They argued that believers should not persecute the ungodly because vengeance belonged to the Lord, who would judge all people at the end of time. They also warned the persecutors that if they continued to hound the saints, they would experience the torments of hell. Those who supported persecution, on the other hand, felt that their actions were in accord with God's character. The Lord displayed just severity against human evil, and the state was his agent of wrath against the wrongdoer. In punishing heretics, schismatics and recusants, the magistrate was acting on God's behalf.

The distinctions between these five contexts of tolerance are worth bearing in mind as we proceed, for many historians persist in confusing them. It is a mistake to assume that those who called for greater polemical restraint or ecclesiastical tolerance were necessarily committed to the civil tolerance of religious dissent. Often this was not the case; the Latitudinarians within the Restoration church sounded sweet and reasonable and called for a broad church, but they could also be staunch defenders of persecution. Conversely, aggressive sectarians could be intolerant in polemical and ecclesiastical contexts and yet be firm supporters of civil tolerance. In the seventeenth century, as in the present, the divide between the tolerant and the intolerant was far from neat.

Aspects of the history of toleration

A satisfactory history of religious tolerance is one that weaves together three major strands.[52] Traditionally, historians of toleration have focused on the *ideological* dimension. They have described the intellectual debates over persecution, and devoted particular attention to the champions of religious tolerance. Although the contemporary trend is to focus on the political and social history of toleration, there are still good reasons for giving intellectual history a high profile. Over the past generation, historians have become far more willing to acknowledge the importance of beliefs and mentalities in generating political and social action, and in order to explain persecution we need to pay close attention to what persecutors said they were doing. Moreover, what makes seventeenth-century England stand out to the historian of persecution and toleration is the sheer wealth of the pamphlet literature on the subject. After 1643–4, in particular, hundreds of books and tracts were published either for or against religious toleration. Few countries in early modern Europe saw such a deluge of tolerationist literature, and it seems only reasonable for the historian of England to take it seriously. Consequently, chapters 2 and 3 will be devoted to a detailed consideration of the arguments deployed in defence of persecution and toleration.

Since historians have often been more interested in the secular case for persecution or toleration – whether it be philosophical or political and economic – both chapters take time to redress the balance by emphasising the importance of the theological arguments used by early modern thinkers.

The second aspect of the history of toleration is the *legal* or *political*. Again this is a dimension which has received a good deal of attention from historians who have analysed the laws, statutes and proclamations of central government, and their enforcement at a local level in different areas of the country. For England, this includes important pieces of parliamentary legislation such as the Elizabethan penal laws against Catholics, the Clarendon Code, and the Act of Toleration itself, and the application of these laws by JPs and local magistrates. In recent years, historians have argued that the enforcement of penal laws was patchy and spasmodic, varying considerably from place to place and from time to time. In particular, the practice of persecution intensified when the political threat from Catholics and Dissenters was at its height. And the passing of the Act of Toleration itself owed more to political contingencies than to any rising tide of tolerationist sentiment. Thus the politics of persecution and toleration will be a central concern of the narrative chapters of this book.

The third way of approaching the history of toleration is by exploring the *social* dimension. How did different religious groups interact in towns and villages throughout England? Did religious minorities experience social tolerance, or did they encounter abuse, ostracism and even violence? How well were such minorities integrated into society? As we have already noted, social historians have recently begun to provide satisfying and sometimes surprising answers to these questions. Their work suggests that we need histories of tolerance in early modern Europe to set alongside the more familiar histories of intolerance. In this relatively brief book it is impossible to provide a detailed survey of the social experience of Catholics and Dissenters in different localities, but local examples are used in order to paint a more vivid picture of what life was like for those who refused to conform to the Church of England.

Certain themes that lie adjacent to my topic are not tackled in detail in this book. The persecution of witches was one of the most remarkable manifestations of religious intolerance in the early modern period, but it is such a vast subject in its own right that it is impossible to integrate into this study.[53] Censorship is another theme closely related to persecution which is mentioned only in passing.[54] Another related subject which I have not covered is that of international ecumenical relations. The leaders of the Church of England continually discussed what stance they should adopt towards other Christian communions, including the other Reformed churches, the Lutherans, the Roman Catholics, and the Greek Orthodox.

Anthony Milton has recently provided us with a magisterial study of these discussions within the early Stuart church, and he reveals a complex mixture of tolerance and intolerance. Calvinist theologians within the church could be tolerant toward Lutherans and Orthodox yet profoundly intolerant toward the Roman Catholic church, which they identified with Antichrist. Laudians, on the other hand, were far more tolerant toward the Roman Catholic church, whilst being more suspicious of the thoroughly Reformed bodies.[55] James I, as W. B. Patterson has demonstrated, was deeply committed to the cause of ecumenical reunion, and worked tirelessly for the reunion of Christendom.[56] Ecumenical relations, therefore, is obviously a major theme in itself, but my central focus will be on the treatment of religious minorities in England itself: Catholics, Protestant Dissenters, heretics, and Jews.

In the main part of the book (chapters 4 to 8) I will concentrate on the fluctuating fortunes of these groups following the Elizabethan Settlement. By attempting to weave together the ideological, legal, and social dimensions of the story, I hope to create a coherent narrative history of persecution and tolerance in Protestant England from 1558 to 1688. Chapter 8 will also include a sketch of developments after 1689, tracing the steps taken from mere toleration to full religious liberty and civil equality. I am aware that this is a rather ambitious (some would say foolhardy) undertaking, particularly given the constraints of space. However, persecution and toleration remains one of the grand themes of early modern English history, and it deserves to be the subject of renewed attention.

Notes

1   See M. Weber, *The Protestant Ethic and the Spirit of Capitalism* (1904); R. H. Tawney, *Religion and the Rise of Capitalism* (London, 1926); R. K. Merton, *Science, Technology and Society in Seventeenth-Century England* (1938; New York, 1970); M. Walzer, *The Revolution of the Saints: A Study of the Origins of Radical Politics* (Cambridge, MA, 1965); C. Hill, *Intellectual Origins of the English Revolution* (Oxford, 1965); Hill, *The Century of Revolution, 1603–1714* (London, 1961).

2   See R. C. Richardson and G. M. Ridden, eds, *Freedom and the English Revolution* (Manchester, 1986), ch. 1.

3   Lord Macaulay, *History of England*, 4 vols (London, 1967), II, p. 466.

4   S. R. Gardiner, *The First Two Stuarts and the Puritan Revolution* (New York, 1970), p. 208, *passim*.

5   W. Haller, *The Rise of Puritanism* (New York, 1938), p. 289.

6 W. Haller, ed., *Tracts on Liberty in the Puritan Revolution, 1638–47*, 3 vols (New York, 1933–4), I, p. vii.

7 A. S. P. Woodhouse, ed., *Puritanism and Liberty* (London, 1938), pp. 51–60.

8 On teleological history see G. Burgess, 'Revisionism, politics and political ideas in early Stuart England', *Historical Journal* 34 (1992), 465–78.

9 W. K. Jordan, *The Development of Religious Toleration in England*, 4 vols (London, 1932–40), IV, p. 203.

10 Ibid., I, p. 89.

11 M. Thorp, 'William Cecil and the Antichrist', in Thorp and A. J. Slavin, eds, *Politics, Religion and Diplomacy in Early Modern Europe* (Kirksville, Miss., 1994), pp. 289–304.

12 Jordan, *The Development of Religious Toleration*, I, p. 96.

13 Ibid., IV, p. 9.

14 See R. Clifton, 'Fear of popery', in C. Russell, ed., *The Origins of the English Civil War* (London, 1973), pp. 144–67; Clifton, 'The popular fear of Catholics during the English Revolution', *Past and Present* 52 (1971), 23–55; C. Hibbard, *Charles I and the Popish Plot* (Chapel Hill, NC, 1983); P. Lake, 'Anti-popery: the structure of a prejudice', in R. Cust and A. Hughes, eds, *Conflict in Early Stuart England* (London, 1986), pp. 72–106; J. Kenyon, *The Popish Plot* (London, 1972); and J. Miller, *Popery and Politics in England, 1660–1668* (Cambridge, 1973).

15 J. Morrill, *The Nature of the English Revolution* (Harlow, 1993), pp. 33–90; C. Russell, *The Causes of the English Civil War* (Oxford, 1990), pp. 58–130.

16 T. Harris, P. Seaward and M. Goldie, eds, *The Politics of Religion in Restoration England* (Oxford, 1990).

17 J. C. D. Clark, *English Society, 1688–1832* (Cambridge, 1985).

18 B. Worden, 'Toleration and the Cromwellian Protectorate', in W. J. Sheils, ed., *Persecution and Toleration* (Oxford, 1984), pp. 199–233.

19 W. Lamont, 'Pamphleteering, the Protestant consensus and the English revolution', in Richardson and Ridden, eds, *Freedom and the English Revolution*, pp. 72–92; J. C. Davis, 'Religion and the struggle for freedom in the English Revolution', *Historical Journal* 35 (1992), 507–30. See also C. Condren, 'Liberty of office and its defence in seventeenth-century political argument', *The History of Political Thought* 18 (1997), 460–82.

20 M. Goldie, 'The theory of religious intolerance in Restoration England', in O. P. Grell, J. Israel, and N. Tyacke, eds, *From Persecution to Toleration* (Oxford, 1991), pp. 331–68.

21 See R. Ashcraft, 'Latitudinarianism and toleration: historical myth versus political history', in R. Kroll, R. Ashcraft and P. Zagorin, eds, *Philosophy, Science and Religion in England, 1640–1700* (Cambridge, 1992), pp. 151–73.

22   J. Lecler, *Toleration and the Reformation*, 2 vols (London, 1960).

23   H. Kamen, *The Rise of Toleration* (London, 1967), p. 7.

24   O. P. Grell and R. Scribner, eds, *Tolerance and Intolerance in the European Reformation* (Cambridge, 1995), pp. 35–8.

25   J. C. Laursen and C. J. Nederman, eds, *Beyond the Persecuting Society: Religious Toleration before the Enlightenment* (Philadelphia, 1997), pp. 1–10. See also C. J. Nederman and J. C. Laursen, eds, *Difference and Dissent: Theories of Toleration in Medieval and Early Modern Europe* (Lanham, MD, 1996).

26   Worden, 'Toleration and the Cromwellian Protectorate', p. 199.

27   J. Gray, *Liberalism* (London, 1986), ch. 2, p. 11.

28   Grell, Israel and Tyacke, eds, *From Persecution to Toleration*, p. 16.

29   D. Wootton, 'Leveller democracy and the puritan revolution', in J. H. Burns and M. Goldie, eds, *The Cambridge History of Political Thought, 1450–1700* (Cambridge, 1991), ch. 14; D. Wootton, ed., *John Locke: Political Writings* (London, 1993), pp. 7–16.

30   A claim developed in A. Patterson, *Early Modern Liberalism* (Cambridge, 1997).

31   C. Russell, *An Intelligent Person's Guide to Liberalism* (London, 1999), *passim*.

32   I. Bejczy, ' "Tolerantia": a medieval concept', *Journal of the History of Ideas* 58 (1997), 365–84.

33   J. Brooke, 'The God of Newton', in J. Fauvel *et al.*, eds, *Let Newton Be! A New Perspective on his Life and Works* (Oxford, 1988), pp. 169–83.

34   P. Berger and J. Sacks, eds, *The Desecularization of the World: Resurgent Religion and World Politics* (Grand Rapids, 1999). Quotation from Berger, 'Secularism in retreat', *The National Interest* 46 (1996/7), 3.

35   M. Marty, ed., *The Fundamentalisms Project*, 5 vols (Chicago, 1991–5); and D. Westerlund, ed., *Questioning the Secular State: The Worldwide Resurgence of Religion in Politics* (London, 1996).

36   M. Juergensmeyer, *The New Cold War? Religious Nationalism Confronts the Secular State* (Berkeley, CA, 1993).

37   C. Andrew, 'Guardian agents', *Times Higher Educational Supplement*, 14 Nov 1997, p. 15.

38   K. Boyle and J. Sheen, eds, *Freedom of Religion and Belief: A World Report* (London, 1997); P. Marshall, *Their Blood Cries Out: The Worldwide Tragedy of Modern Christians who are Dying for their Faith* (Dallas, TX, 1997).

39   See O. Chadwick, *The Christian Church in the Cold War* (London, 1992); J. De Gruchy, *Christianity and Democracy* (Cambridge, 1995), chs 5–7; D. Martin, *Forbidden Revolutions: Pentecostalism in Latin America, Catholicism in Eastern Europe*

(London, 1996); G. Parsons, ed., *The Growth of Religious Diversity: Britain from 1945* (London, 1993).

40 See A. Macintyre, *Whose Justice? Which Rationality?* (London, 1988), ch. 1.

41 J. Rawls, *Political Liberalism* (New York, 1993), pp. xvi–xix; lecture 4.

42 Ibid., p. xxiv.

43 See Blair Worden's recent critique of Quentin Skinner, which draws a sharp contrast between historical-mindedness and present-mindedness. Worden, 'Factory of the Revolution', *London Review of Books*, 5 Feb 1998, pp. 13–15.

44 R. Scruton, *A Dictionary of Political Thought* (London, 1982), p. 464.

45 See P. King, *Toleration* (London, 1976), ch. 1. See also S. Mendus, *Toleration and the Limits of Liberalism* (London, 1989).

46 K. Moore, *The Spirit of Tolerance* (London, 1964), p. 9.

47 See G. Schochet, 'From persecution to "toleration"', in J. R. Jones, ed., *Liberty Secured? Britain before and after 1688* (Stanford, CA, 1992), p. 127.

48 See P. J. Morman, *Noel Aubert de Versé: A Study in the Concept of Toleration* (Lewiston, NJ, n.d.), p. 218.

49 See J. Marshall, *John Locke: Resistance, Religion and Responsibility* (Cambridge, 1994), p. 57.

50 *The Works of John Whitgift*, ed. J. Ayre, 3 vols (Cambridge, 1851–3), III, p. 320.

51 See R. Scribner, 'Preconditions of tolerance and intolerance in sixteenth-century Germany', in Grell and Scribner, eds, *Tolerance and Intolerance in Reformation Europe*, pp. 45–6.

52 I am indebted to the analysis of P. Benedict, 'Un roi, une loi, deux fois: parameters for the history of Catholic–Reformed co-existence in France, 1555–1685', in ibid., ch. 5.

53 Readers who want to know more about this aspect of religious intolerance should start with J. Sharpe, *Instruments of Darkness: Witchcraft in England, 1550–1750* (London, 1996).

54 See C. S. Clegg, *Press Censorship in Elizabethan England* (Cambridge, 1997); C. Hill, 'Censorship and English literature', in Hill, *The Collected Essays of Christopher Hill*, 3 vols (Brighton, 1985–6), I, ch. 2; S. Lambert, 'State control of the press in theory and practice', in R. Myers and M. Harris, eds, *Censorship and Control of Print in England and France, 1600–1910* (Winchester, 1992), pp. 1–32; A. Milton, 'Licensing, censorship and religious orthodoxy in early Stuart England', *Historical Journal* 41 (1998), 625–51; A. Patterson, *Censorship and Interpretation: The Conditions of Writing and Reading in Early Modern England* (1984); A. B. Worden, 'Literature and censorship in early modern England', in A. C. Duke

and C. A. Tamse, eds, *Too Mighty to be Free: Censorship in Britain and the Netherlands* (Zutphen, 1987).

55   A. Milton, *Catholic and Reformed: The Roman and Protestant Churches in English Protestant Thought, 1600–40* (Cambridge, 1995).

56   W. B. Patterson, *James VI and I and the Reunion of Christendom* (Cambridge, 1997).

CHAPTER 2

The Protestant Theory of Persecution

Will any man deny that the Church doth need the rod of corporal
punishment to keep her children in obedience?
(Richard Hooker, *The Laws of Ecclesiastical Polity*, VIII.iii.4)[1]

The rise of persecution

To understand the persecutory mentality of early modern intellectuals, we
need to take a step back and look briefly at how religious coercion came to
be seen as a legitimate weapon in the armoury of the Christian church. The
magistrates and theologians of Tudor and Stuart England were profoundly
conscious of standing within a tradition which extended for many centuries
into Europe's past. When they sat down to justify their policies of coercion,
they appealed repeatedly and extensively to the historical example of Christian kings and emperors. In using coercion, they insisted, they were doing
nothing new. They were simply following precedent. Tolerationists took
issue with this appeal to precedent and delivered a radically different verdict on the church's tradition of coercion, but they did not deny that the
tradition existed. In early modern England, Christian history was a polemical battlefield.

The controversy centred on the church's first four centuries. In the first
three centuries, Christians had not persecuted their enemies. They had
been a minority sect, lacking any support from the state, persecuted rather
than persecuting. Yet in the fourth century, everything changed. In the
words of one historian, 'The century began with a systematic effort to
stamp out the upstart faith as a threat to established values. By its end,

21

roving bands of Christian vigilantes, supported at the highest level of imperial government, destroyed temples and assaulted with virtual impunity believers in the old gods.' The persecuted lambs had turned into persecuting lions.[2]

The reason for this momentous change was simple. In the early years of the century, the Emperor Constantine had converted to the young faith. For the first time, therefore, imperial power was on the side of the church rather than against it. The Emperor was soon intervening in theological disputes and issuing edicts against the heretical Arians. Arian books were burnt and Christian sects like the Novatians and the Gnostics were banned from holding assemblies. Yet although Constantine had set the tone for the treatment of heretics, he had tolerated pagans, and encouraged their peaceful coexistence with the Christians. Only after the short reign of Julian the apostate (361–3) did Christian emperors sanction attacks on pagan worship. Julian seems to have terrified Christians, for although he did not persecute the church, his flamboyant state paganism reminded them of the early years of the century, when a dynamic pagan emperor, Diocletian, had turned against the Christians after a long period of tolerance. When Christian emperors regained the throne after Julian's death, pagans quickly became victims of persecution. In the decades around the turn of the fifth century, numerous laws were passed against both heretics and pagans. Christianity had become a persecuting religion.

Christianity's fourth-century transformation lay at the heart of the quarrel between persecutors and tolerationists. Many tolerationists pointed to the fourth century as the time when everything had gone wrong, when the church had fallen from grace. The supporters of coercion, on the other hand, looked to the fourth and fifth centuries to justify their programme of repression. Most of all, they looked to the writings of St Augustine, who had done more than anyone else to legitimise the use of force in religion. In the 390s, Augustine had been decidedly sceptical about the value of religious coercion, but a few years later he wrote a series of famous letters justifying the persecution of the Donatists. The Donatists were a purist, schismatic sect who had separated from the Catholic church in North Africa because some of its bishops had compromised during Roman persecutions. Augustine's change of mind over the issue of coercion came about when he witnessed the Donatists in his own town being 'brought over to the Catholic unity by fear of the imperial edicts'.[3] Convinced of the effectiveness of mild forms of persecution, Augustine developed a principled defence of their use. His arguments carried the day, or rather the millennium, for his position became the established orthodoxy of Western Christendom, both Catholic and Protestant.[4] In early modern England the champions of religious coercion appealed repeatedly to the great 'St Austin'. Elizabethan bishops, mid-seventeenth-century Puritans and Restoration Anglicans all justified their drive for uniformity by referring their readers to Augustine's famous epistles against the Donatists.[5]

However, Augustine's notoriety as the 'father of the Inquisition' is not entirely deserved; according to Henry Chadwick, 'Augustine would have been horrified by the burning of heretics'.[6] Fines, imprisonment, banishment and moderate floggings were one thing, but the death penalty was an illegitimate weapon for Christians to wield in their war against error. To use early modern terminology, Augustinian persecution was 'medicinal' rather than 'exterminative'; it treated the heretic as a patient to be healed, rather than a cancer to be excised. In the first Christian millennium, the execution of heretics appears to have been very rare indeed. When the heretic Priscillian and his followers were burned in 383, their persecutors were roundly condemned by bishops like Ambrose, Augustine's mentor.

Not until 1022, when fourteen people were burned at Orleans, do we come across another case of the execution of heretics in western Europe, though this may simply be due to the lack of sources for the earlier period. Yet the Orleans case certainly signalled a turning point, for in the next two centuries the capital punishment of heretics was to become widespread across the continent.[7] In large part, this was because of the challenge of popular heretical movements like the Waldensians and Cathars in Italy and France. The medieval Inquisition was established to counter the threat of these groups, and the fourth Lateran Council of 1215 codified the theory and practice of persecution. The greatest medieval theologian, Thomas Aquinas, summed up the standard medieval position when he declared that obstinate heretics deserved 'not only to be separated from the Church, but to be eliminated from the world by death'.[8] The condition of the Jews also worsened dramatically in these years, as massacres occurred in a number of areas of Europe, and vicious anti-semitic stereotypes developed. Eventually, in 1478, an Inquisition was established in Spain which aimed to destroy all remnants of Jewish faith in the land.[9] Finally, from the mid-fifteenth century, we find the first outbreaks of the witch-hunts that were to claim more than 30,000 lives over the next three centuries.[10]

The sixteenth-century Reformation did little to end these persecutions. Indeed, by presenting a new and more powerful threat to the unity of Christendom than the medieval heresies, the Reformation served to intensify persecution by Catholic regimes. Moreover, the magisterial Reformers themselves fully embraced Augustine's vision of the coercive role of the Christian magistrate, and many shared Aquinas's belief in the legitimacy of the death penalty for heresy. Luther did write against persecution in the early 1520s, but after 1525 his position hardened, and he returned to the conviction that the temporal authorities should root out false religion by force from Protestant lands. Having demonstrated genuine sympathy towards the Jews in his early writings, he later wrote a violently anti-semitic tract, *On the Jews and their Lies* (1543). In Geneva, the second most influential Reformer, John Calvin, worked to establish a godly regime which would not tolerate heresy, idolatry or immorality. In 1553, he helped to secure the execution of the anti-Trinitarian heretic Michael Servetus by the Genevan authorities, an action that won the approval of many other Protestants including the great Lutheran theologian Philip Melancthon.[11] If Protestantism was all about religious freedom, no one told the Reformers.

The intolerance of the Church of England

Despite its later reputation for moderation and tolerance, the early Church of England was as firmly committed to religious persecution as any other Protestant church. Magistrates and theologians followed the lead of Calvin and the magisterial Reformers and bowed to the wisdom of Augustine. Indeed, an Augustinian consensus on the legitimacy of religious coercion held firm until the 1640s, and had very few critics, as Richard Hooker's rhetorical question at the head of this chapter suggests. Even the Separatists and Presbyterians who condemned the liturgy and government of the church did not question the duty of the Christian magistrate to punish heresy.[12] Moreover, even after the practice of coercion had come in for heavy criticism during the Puritan Revolution, the Augustinian view remained dominant among Presbyterians and conservative Independents. It was the orthodoxy of the Church of England after the Restoration[13] and it retained its hold on many conservative Anglicans beyond 1689.

Within this Augustinian consensus, however, there were certain disagreements. Although hardly anyone before 1640 condemned outright the use of coercion in religion, there were many who felt uneasy about the use of the death penalty in cases of heresy. The martyrologist John Foxe, for example, seems to have deplored all executions for religion, and he lodged a serious protest against the sentence of burning passed against a group of Dutch Anabaptists in 1575.[14] The influential Elizabethan bishop Thomas Bilson followed Chrysostom and Augustine in arguing that men ought to be 'corrected, not murdered'.[15] John Hales, the early Stuart writer who is often mistakenly identified as a firm tolerationist, praised Augustine as 'a man of as mild and gentle spirit as ever bare rule in the church', and followed the great Latin Father in defending mild forms of religious coercion, but rejecting capital punishment. The church must not forget that heretics were 'the sons of her womb', and that to kill them would be 'to send them quick dispatch to hell'.[16] Similarly, Richard Perrinchief, during the Restoration period, insisted that the Church of England would not proceed against Dissenters 'in some violent way of Terror'. He cited with approval Augustine's rejection of the death penalty for heresy and dissent, and associated the killing of heretics with 'Roman-tyranny'.[17] Henry Thorndike agreed, arguing that the judicial law of Moses was no guide for Christians, and that the execution of heretics was incompatible with the meekness of Christianity.[18] Locke's critic Jonas Proast adopted the same line, suggesting that whereas 'Fire and Sword' were counter-productive, mild penalties were more successful at getting Dissenters to rethink their position.[19] Indeed, although Restoration churchmen usually backed the persecution of Dissenters, few showed any willingness to endorse the death penalty for religious offences.

The major reason for this reluctance was that most Dissenters were orthodox Trinitarian Christians who only differed from the church on matters of worship and ecclesiology. Although their separation or 'schism' from the established church was viewed as a serious sin, Anglicans and Presbyterians still shared a great deal in common, and even Independents and Baptists preached a Protestant gospel that many within the Church of England could recognise and endorse. Although a number of Separatists were executed under Elizabeth for attacking the Church of England in their preaching and pamphlets, few seventeenth-century writers believed that schism was serious enough to justify the death penalty.

Heresy, however, was a different matter, and a surprising number of intellectuals in early modern England were prepared to defend the death penalty for 'gross' or 'blasphemous' heresy. They included figures as significant as King James I and John Jewel, the greatest early apologist of the Church of England, both of whom defended the execution of Servetus. In his *Defence of the Apology of the Church of England,* Jewel responded aggressively to the claim of a Catholic opponent that many of the Protestant martyrs were actually heretics like Servetus and David George, who had been accused of Messianic delusions. 'As for David George, and Servete the Arian', wrote Jewel, 'You brought them up, the one in Spain, the other in Flanders. We detected their heresies, and not you. We arraigned them. We condemned them. We put them to the execution of the laws . . . we burnt them.'[20] James I also seemed to condone the execution of Servetus, when he wrote that the Spanish heretic had been 'powerfully conuicted by Gods word, and lawfully condemned by the ancient General Councils'.[21] Even the Independent theologian John Owen, well known for his writings on toleration, offered a guarded defence of Calvin's action; the 'atheism and blasphemy' of Servetus was so great, wrote Owen, 'that I must say he is the only person in the world, that I ever read or heard of, that ever died upon the account of religion, in reference to whom the zeal of them that put him to death may be acquitted'.[22]

Heresy executions had other defenders. Thomas Bilson did not condemn the Christian emperors for executing Manichaeans for 'monstrous blasphemies',[23] and Sandys used the Old Testament to prove that in the judgement of God 'open and public maintainers of errors and heresy . . . are thought unworthy to live'.[24] We shall see in chapter 6 that when the case of the Quaker James Nayler was debated in Parliament in 1656, a sizeable minority of MPs enthusiastically called for him to be executed for 'horrible blasphemy'. During the Restoration, Richard Perrinchief rejected the death penalty for heresy and schism, but supported it for atheism and blasphemy, both of which he believed to be contrary to natural law,[25] and the aptly named Henry Savage adopted the same position.[26]

Yet although capital punishment for heresy and blasphemy was defended in this period, it was very rarely implemented. During Elizabeth's reign only six people were executed for heresy or blasphemy, and only two under James, both in 1612. There were, however, many other executions of religious dissidents, though these were for secular rather than religious offences. More than 300 Roman Catholics were put to death by English governments between 1535 and 1681 – but for treason, not for heresy. The same was true of the small number of Separatists executed in the 1580s and 1590s. Both Catholics and Separatists protested that they were martyrs for their religion, and there can be no doubt that almost all were executed simply for 'seditious' religious activities – there was no evidence that they had plotted the overthrow of the government. Yet these executions were implicitly supported by eminent Jacobean intellectuals. The moderate early Stuart bishop Joseph Hall was quite clear that no blood should be shed for 'mere heresy'; but he also argued that when heresy was mixed with blasphemy, schism, 'infectious divulgation', sedition or plotting, it 'may be well worthy of a faggot'.[27] Francis Bacon was adopting the same position when he wrote that it was wrong to use 'sanguinary persecutions to force consciences; except it be in cases of overt scandals, blasphemy, or intermixture of practice against the state'.[28]

Bacon's aversion to 'sanguinary persecutions to force consciences' was widely shared, but there was far less reticence with regard to fines, loss of civil office, imprisonment and exile. Those opposed to the Inquisition model of persecution could still endorse the milder measures suggested by the original Augustinian model. Before 1640, there was overwhelming support for the Elizabethan Act of Uniformity and associated penal legislation. Even after 1662, when the Augustinian consensus had broken down, the Restoration Act of Uniformity and the Clarendon Code had majority backing among churchmen, who continued to follow the lead of the great Latin

Father. Nearly all of them believed that the magistrate had both the right and the duty to establish true religion in his territory, order the church, and punish those who refused to conform.

Emphasising the milder forms of persecution also had great polemical advantages, for it allowed Protestants to present English persecution in the softest, most flattering light, and to contrast it sharply with the harsh brutalities of Roman tyranny. Even those who supported the death penalty for serious heresy emphasised the moderation of their proceedings in contrast to what Joseph Hall called the 'bloodthirsty cruelty' of the Roman church.[29] The Scottish Presbyterian George Gillespie characterised the mainstream Protestant position on coercion as a middle way between the licentious tolerance advocated by heretics, and the brutality of the papists. Whereas Catholic theologians talked crudely of extirpating all heretics and opposers of their church, Protestants punished people as 'the nature and degree of the error, schisme, obstinacy, and danger of seducing others, doth require'.[30] Others pursued the same line. In a speech to the English Parliament, James I declared: 'it is a sure rule in Divinitie, that God never loves to plant his Church by violence and bloodshed'.[31] Bishop Bilson told English Catholics that they were simply being subjected to 'fatherlie chastisement' which 'sucketh not your blood',[32] and moderates like John Hales praised the edicts and statutes of the English government for their restraint and balance, since they avoided cruelty without licensing error.[33] Like Augustine before them, Protestant persecutors continually emphasised the mildness and clemency of their measures, and reacted with genuine horror when their critics made comparisons with the legendary Spanish Inquisition. They would all have agreed with the response of Roger L'Estrange to critics of English religious policy: 'That which you call Persecution, I translate Uniformity'.[34]

Yet it remained the case that English legislation effectively criminalised everyone who refused to conform to the national church. Foreign diplomats and merchants were exempted from these Acts, and allowed to worship in embassies or in a few Protestant 'Stranger Churches', but everyone else had to conform. Aware of the problems of criminalising large segments of the population, the defenders of government policy took pains to differentiate between various levels of religious error, some more serious than others.

The offence which was subject to the most severe penalties was religiously inspired *sedition*. Contemporaries were careful to distinguish this from purely religious offences. Religious zealots who were punished for sedition and treason were not persecuted martyrs. They suffered for their political crimes, not for their religious faith. The worst purely religious offences were *blasphemy* and *atheism*. Both of these were viewed as a profound insult to the Almighty, whose honour the magistrate was bound to protect. But they were also commonly seen as violations of natural religion, offences that undermined the fabric of human community and would be punished in any reasonable society, Christian or otherwise. As we shall see in the next chapter, even many tolerationist writers could not come to terms with toleration for the blasphemer or the atheist.

Close behind blasphemy and atheism came *gross heresy*, or the denial of traditional Christian doctrines, such as biblical infallibility or the Trinity. Many theologians saw little difference between heresy and blasphemy. The rejection of the Trinity was viewed as a blasphemous insult to God, no matter how devout and sincere the heretic happened to be. Minor heresy, or the denial of secondary truths of Christian doctrine, was often classed as error rather than full-blooded heresy, and could therefore be treated with far more tolerance. As with blasphemy and gross heresy, however, the line between fundamental heresy and *secondary error* was a pretty blurred one, and many theologians did not attempt to sharpen it. An exception was John Owen, who in the 1650s proposed a list of fifteen fundamentals, the denial of which would lead to prosecution. Owen did not include infant baptism among his fundamentals, and he clearly regarded the Calvinistic Baptists, at least, as orthodox brethren who had fallen into error on a secondary matter. Socinians, by contrast, were heretics pure and simple, and they should be punished by the state.

Significantly, even the most hardline advocates of religious coercion insisted that they had no intention of persecuting people simply for erroneous or heretical *opinions*. Roger L'Estrange, a leading defender of the Clarendon Code, claimed that Nonconformists enjoyed full liberty of conscience under the Act of Uniformity, since it only regulated actions not thoughts,[35] and Samuel Rutherford promised in a major defence of persecution that Presbyterians would not interfere with the individual's 'internal liberty . . . to think, understand, judge, conclude'.[36] The profoundly heterodox Thomas Hobbes also only guaranteed internal intellectual liberty; in *Leviathan* he gave the state a licence to meddle in everything else, though his concern was for public order, not for doctrinal orthodoxy.[37] However, even the orthodox emphasised that individuals would only suffer if they revealed their gross heresies, actively propagated them, and stubbornly refused to recant. Thus persecutors continually stressed their longsuffering toward heretics. Rather than being promptly dispatched, erroneous individuals were handled with great patience. Inquisitors maintained that they were more interested in reclaiming a damaged person by persuasion than in hounding them to prison. They were also keen to point out that they were not demanding complete intellectual conformity. They accepted that orthodox Christians would differ about many minor matters, such as the exegesis of particular texts of Scripture. Indeed, Latitudinarians like Edward Stillingfleet combined a call for wider tolerance within the church with support for the penal laws against Dissenters who remained without.[38] They felt hurt that people were not satisfied with the generous degree of latitude already offered by the church. It was churlish to complain of civil intolerance when ecclesiastical tolerance was so considerable.

But heretics were not the only, or even the main, target of penal legislation. Above all, the Acts of Uniformity were intended to prevent *schism*. Although some of those who separated from the Church of England could be classed as heretics or even blasphemers, many were orthodox. To contemporaries, these Protestant sectarians were the new Donatists, orthodox in doctrine but schismatic in practice. In its own way, their schism was as serious as heresy. Archbishop Whitgift quoted St Chrysostom, who had written that 'To divide the church is as great a fault as to fall into heresy'.[39] A century later, Edward Stillingfleet defended the penal legislation against Dissenters by arguing at length than schism was a terrible sin.[40]

Roman Catholicism was a rather different matter. Theoretically, the papists' offence was a terrible one, since many English Protestants, certainly before 1640, regarded them as idolaters, who worshipped the host at mass.[41] Since idolatry was punishable by death in the Old Testament, one might have expected Catholics to experience terrible persecution. In fact, according to William Monter, 'there were no Catholic martyrs in Reformation Europe outside England',[42] not least because such a policy of wholesale persecution would have provoked reprisals from foreign Catholic powers. Even in England, the Catholic martyrs were only executed for treason or sedition. As we shall see in chapter 4, early modern Europeans rarely if ever applied the death penalty for heresy to those who were more theologically conservative than themselves. Yet most Protestants were willing to defend a milder persecution of Catholics on purely religious grounds. Thomas Bilson, for example, wrote that Roman Catholics could be 'compelled of Christian magistrates, for dread of punishment, tempered with good instruction, to forsake their heresies and forbeare their idolatries'. Protestant magistrates had a solemn duty to purge their lands of Catholic idolatry and falsehood; even Catholic worship in private places was intolerable.[43] The fact that almost all Protestants before the Laudians believed that the Pope was the Antichrist reinforced their commitment to harsh anti-papal policies. In 1603–5, the establishment divines Gabriel Powell and Robert Abbott wrote expositions of the book of Revelation to ensure that the new Jacobean regime would not yield to Catholic pressure for toleration. 'If the Pope is Antichrist', wrote George Downame, 'it followeth necessarily, that Christian princes are not to tolerate either the religion of papists or their persons within their dominions'.[44]

Non-Christian religion, by contrast, usually met with a more generous attitude. Many writers did not even bother to consider the case of pagans and infidels, since hardly any actually lived in early modern England. Those who did take the trouble to consider them were ambivalent. On the one hand they agreed that a Christian magistrate could not tolerate pagan or 'Turkish' (i.e. Muslim) worship. The magistrate should follow the example of Constantine and other godly emperors who had closed pagan temples. Yet on the other hand, they argued that the Christian magistrate could not have the same kind of hold over those who had been raised within another religion as he had on professing Christians. The Protestant ruler could compel Christians to follow the Scriptures since they had already pledged themselves to obey God's Word, but compelling Jews or Muslims to embrace Christianity was something different. Bishop Bilson agreed with his Catholic opponents that Jews, Muslims and pagans should not be forced to abandon their faith, though he also noted that this had been done in a number of European countries.[45] The Covenanter Samuel Rutherford also took the view that non-Christians like the American Indians could not be compelled to convert by sword and fire, though he was in two minds over whether it was legitimate to remove their children and train them up in Christian religion.[46] Others were more clear-cut. Richard Perrinchief, for example, was emphatic that infidels could not be compelled to embrace Christianity, and argued that force could only be used against those who claimed to be Christians.[47] The theorists of persecution were deeply uncomfortable with the idea of an anti-heathen crusade. Their concern was simply to justify the use of religious coercion against deviants within the fold of the Christian church.

The theology of persecution

In putting their case for persecution, mainstream Protestants drew heavily on the arguments of Augustine. The magisterial Reformers were convinced that Old Testament Israel was a model for other times and places. Following the great Latin Father, they repeatedly cited two scriptural passages which promised that the rule of God would be established over other nations too. They pointed to Psalm 2, which declared that 'the Son' would inherit the nations of the earth, and called on kings to 'serve the Lord with fear', and to 'kiss the Son lest he be angry'. And they quoted Isaiah 49.23, where the prophet predicted that kings would be nursing fathers to the people of God. Like Augustine, English Protestants argued that this had happened even in the Old Testament era, when Darius, Nebuchadnezzar and the king of Nineveh had commanded their people to worship the God of Israel. But the fulfilment of these prophecies had begun in earnest in the fourth century, when the mighty Roman empire had bowed to the authority of Christ. Before Constantine, the church had received no help from the rulers of the world; after Constantine, godly emperors like Theodosius, Justinian and Charlemagne had devoted themselves to serving the church and crushing its enemies. Through godly princes, the Lord was extending his rule throughout the earth.[48]

Thus Protestant princes and magistrates were seen as walking in the illustrious footsteps of the kings of Israel and the holy emperors. Like their great predecessors, they had a duty to purge their lands of idolatry and heresy, and to establish the true religion. In defending Elizabeth's royal supremacy over the church and her demand for religious uniformity, John Jewel cited Augustine and declared that 'queen Elizabeth doth as did Moses, Josua, David, Salomon, Josias, Jehosaphat, as Constantine, Valentinian, Gratian, Theodosius, Arcadius, Honorious, and other godly emperors have done'. For good measure he also added those Old Testament Gentile rulers Darius, Nebuchadnezzar, and the king of Nineveh.[49] Edwin Sandys agreed, and reminded his hearers that Hezekiah and Josiah 'could not abide idolatry to be committed, or God to be blasphemed, within their dominions'.[50] Bilson declared that 'the godly kings of Israell and Judah . . . removed idols, razed [hill] altars, slue false prophets, purged the land fro al abominations', and set up the true worship of God.[51] James I was adamant that the kingdom of the Jews 'ought to bee a patterne to all Christian and well founded Monarchies, as being founded by God himselfe'. In the Old Testament', he noted, 'kings were directly Governors over the Church within their Dominions; [they] purged their corruptions; reformed their abuses . . . destroyed all idoles and false gods'. Christian kings were no different. Like their ancient Jewish counterparts they were '*custos utriusque Tabulae*', custodians of both tables of the Ten Commandments; responsible for enforcing both the second table, concerning man's duties to other people, and the first table, concerning man's duties to God.[52]

After 1640, the Israel model remained central to the case for persecution. Indeed, for orthodox Puritans it was if anything more important than it was for others, because Puritans were more likely to hold that the Mosaic judicial law was still binding on Christian magistrates. The Elizabethan Puritan Thomas Cartwright had advocated the death penalty for heretics and those who refused to attend established services on the basis of Exodus 22, Deuteronomy 13 and Zechariah 13, which ordered the death of idolaters, and even of their parents. Whitgift claimed that Cartwright was a bloody man who was far too willing to 'play the Jew'.[53] The influential Scottish commissioner to the Westminster Assembly, George Gillespie, also appealed to Deuteronomy 13, and cited the examples of Moses slaying idolaters, Elijah killing the prophets of Baal, and Josiah destroying the priests of Samaria.[54] The English Westminster divines adopted similar arguments. In their sermons to Parliament they constantly reiterated the teaching that magistrates were keepers of both tables of the law. Edmund Calamy, for example, warned against those 'that would blot out halfe your commission'.[55] The divines insisted on the paradigmatic character of godly Old Testament kings like Josiah and Asa. Arthur Salwey declared that the prophet Elijah was 'an admirable pattern' for magistrates, and Calamy recalled Isaiah's prediction that magistrates were to be 'nursing fathers' to the church.[56] John Cotton, the Congregationalist Puritan who participated in the English toleration debate after his emigration to New England, called on the testimony of Augustine, Bernard, Calvin and Beza in support of coercion, and praised 'famous princes' like Constantine, Valentinian, Gratian, Theodosius, and Elizabeth I.[57] In 1659, Richard Baxter answered Puritan tolerationists by pointing to 'the Kings of Israel and Juda', and particularly to the days of King Asa, when the people had covenanted 'to put him to death that would not seek the Lord God of Israel'.[58]

Even in the Restoration period, when secular arguments for religious coercion became popular, theorists of persecution continued to appeal to the precedents of Old Testament kings and Christian emperors. Samuel Parker, perhaps the leading defender of uniformity during the Restoration, was no exception:

> Nothing can be more unquestionable than the Precedents of David, Solomon, Hezekiah, Jehu, Jehosaphat, Josiah &c, who exercised as full a legislative Power in Affairs of Religion, as in Affairs of State. They alone restrain'd and punish'd whatever tended to the subversion of the Publick and establish'd Religion; they suppress'd Innovations, reform'd Corruptions, ordered the Decencies and Solemnities of publick Worship, instituted new Laws and Ceremonies, and conducted all the concerns of Religion by their own Power and Authority.[59]

Henry Savage was aware that tolerationists refused to listen to Old Testament examples, but he still reminded his readers of holy princes like Moses, Joshua and Josiah, who in accordance with the instructions for rulers in Deuteronomy 17 had read the book of the law of God and put it into practice.[60]

It is difficult, therefore, to exaggerate the significance of the Israel model to the case for persecution. For mainstream Protestants the rule which the Lord had established over Israel was now being spread to the nations of the earth. It was only natural that the great toleration debate from the 1640s onwards was to revolve around the relationship between Old Testament Israel and the New Testament church.

Yet the case for persecution was not built exclusively on the examples of ancient Israel and the Christian emperors. Augustine's New Testament arguments were also pressed into the service of persecution. Most notoriously, Augustine had justified coercion through his idiosyncratic exposition of Christ's parable of the banquet, in which a rich man throws a party to which none of the invited guests turn up. Infuriated, the man sends his servants to 'go out into the highways and hedges, and compel them to come in [*compelle intrare* in Latin]' (Luke 14.23). The banquet, Augustine argued, was a figure for the communion of the church, and the highways and hedges were 'schisms and heresies'. Christ was teaching that heretics and schismatics were to be coerced back into fellowship with the church. This interpretation was widely accepted by English churchmen, including Bilson and Restoration Anglicans,[61] and other Augustinian arguments were popular too. Augustine had justified religious coercion by appealing to the case of Jesus throwing the money-changers out of the temple. This was a particular favourite with Edwin Sandys, who preached a sermon on the incident and reminded his hearers that 'godly princes' had always been willing to use force to purge the temple of God.[62] Sandys also repeated Augustine's argument from St Paul's conversion: 'Paul never embraced the gospel until he was cast off his horse flat upon the earth', Sandys wrote.[63] For Bilson, too, Paul had been 'compelled to Christianitie by corporal violence'.[64] In the face of this example, how could anyone claim that force had no role to play in conversion?

The few New Testament texts that referred to the political authorities were also believed to support religious coercion. Romans 13 taught that rulers were God's agents who executed wrath on the evildoer. Persecutors argued that since heretics and schismatics were undoubtedly evildoers, they should feel the blast of the ruler's vengeance.[65] The Covenanter Samuel Rutherford took this view and also pointed to 1 Timothy 2, which commanded prayer for kings so that Christians could live quiet and godly lives under them. This, suggested Rutherford, was a clear call to pray for the conversion of kings, 'that they may promote godliness in a politicke way by their sword'.[66]

More frequently, however, the defenders of persecution reasoned from the ecclesiastical intolerance of the New Testament church to the civil intolerance of the Christian state. Joseph Hall highlighted New Testament texts which said that heretics were to be avoided and rejected by the church, and took them as evidence that heretics were to be suppressed by Christian kings.[67] Thomas Thorowgood argued that because Paul did not tolerate schism and heresy in his churches, the Christian magistrate should not tolerate them in his nation.[68] Behind these arguments lay the deep-rooted assumption stated so crisply by Hooker: 'there is not any man of the Church of England but the same man is also a member of the commonwealth; nor any man a member of the commonwealth, which is not also of the Church of England'.[69] The rigorous ecclesiastical intolerance of the primitive church had now been translated onto a larger stage. Since the entire population of a Christian nation constituted a church, its standards of belief and practice must be just as demanding as those of the early church. But there was an added twist in the tale. Whereas the primitive congregations had only had the weapon of excommunication at their disposal, church-commonwealths could now call on temporal force.

Because intolerance was perceived as flowing from concern for true religion, tolerance was associated with relativism and indifference. 'The evil which others do by our sufferance, is ours', maintained Sandys. 'We do it, when we suffer it to be done.'[70] Matthew Newcomen went further: 'it is most certaine [that] he that admits contrary Religions, believes neither of them'.[71] Rutherford, in particular, identified tolerance with relativism and uncertainty. Deeply disturbed by the tolerationist stress on human fallibility, he caricatured Roger Williams as saying: 'dear brother Atheist, you are a godly pious hereticke, and have no God but your conscience; and doe not for feare of your conscience believe that there is a God, and I dare not rebuke you, but be going on in your Divinity; I have as little infallible assurance there is a God, as you have there is no God, and neither you nor I are to be punished for our consciences'.[72]

Such a view of conscience, Rutherford believed, was utterly mistaken. Tolerationists made conscience 'a free borne absolute Princesse' which could 'no more incur guiltinesse in its operations about an infinite Sovereigne God, and his revealed will . . . then can fire in burning'. As long as people were sincere in their beliefs, tolerationists were satisfied. Rutherford and other traditionalists felt that this was to capitulate to a hopeless subjectivism. The objectivity of truth was lost to view, and only subjective opinions remained. Thus it was vital to reassert the orthodox view that 'A conscience void of knowledge is void of goodnesse'. Conscience was neither 'God nor Pope, but can reele, and totter and dream', and thus it had to be seen as 'an under-Judge onely', subordinate to the objective standard of God's truth as understood by the orthodox.[73] Only the rightly informed conscience had to be respected. Erroneous conscience had no rights.

Furthermore, the Christian magistrate had a solemn duty to re-educate the erroneous conscience, if necessary by means of force. This did not mean that faith could be produced by mere force apart from rational persuasion or the work of the Spirit. But like Augustine, persecution theorists pointed to the example of St Paul to show that God could use a short, sharp shock to open up hard-hearted minds to the rational arguments for orthodox faith. They also followed the Latin Father in pointing out that heretics and schismatics often had pretty poor reasons for their position which would only be exposed when they were forced to reconsider. Augustine had argued that many Donatists remained in the sect 'merely because ease had made them too listless, or conceited, or sluggish, to take pains to examine Catholic truth!' Civil penalties could provide them with the necessary incentive to think again about their poorly grounded position.[74] As one Restoration Anglican put it, 'Heresie is not seated so solely and altogether in the Mind, but St Paul thinks fit to rank it among the works of the Flesh; it hath often times no sublimer Motives, then many other of the most sensual Transgressions; outward considerations are very frequently its Cause, and may sometimes be its Cure.'[75]

To fail to employ all the means at one's disposal to re-educate erroneous consciences was to allow one's neighbours to persist in soul-destroying heresy. In seeking to be kind, tolerationists were simply being cruel. To grant 'the publique freedome of heresies', suggested Bilson, was to countenance the 'murder of souls'.[76] Augustine, Thomas Case noted, had declared that those who called for liberty of conscience only gained ' "Libertatem perditionis", liberty to destroy themselves'.[77] Instead of shepherding their subjects along the path to heaven, towards true freedom, irresponsible magistrates allowed them the liberty to choose hell. In contrast, the godly ruler should compel the lost to come in to the banquet. 'Mercy is cruel', said Sandys, 'and why should not the church compel her abandoned children to return, if her abandoned children compel others to perish?'[78]

Besides the destruction of souls, there were other terrible consequences of failing to suppress heresy. In a letter to the Westminster Assembly in 1645, the London Presbyterian clergy declared that toleration would lead to the multiplication of schisms, confusion in the minds of the people, 'bitter heart-burnings' among brethren, the despising of the ministry, acrimonious disputes which would drown out true piety, the end of godly reformation, and the spread of heresies.[79] In the following year, Thomas Edwards's *Gangraena* seemed to provide the empirical evidence to support their claims. Roger L'Estrange later complained that during the Interregnum the church had been devoured, heresies had flourished, and blasphemy had been 'hunted out the Tavern into the Pulpit'.[80] Edward Stillingfleet was convinced that if a toleration of Protestant sectarianism were granted again, it would prepare the way for the authoritarian rule of Rome; a 'Wilderness of Confusion' would push the nation into the 'Abysse of Popery'. Besides thinking it likely that the Jesuits had been major promoters of Protestant separatism, he also believed that priests would creep in under cover of the toleration and that the anarchy of Protestant division would make people turn to popery as the best means to re-establish unity.[81]

As if these consequences were not enough, tolerance of false religion would also be judged by God. Nations which turned a blind eye to gross heresy would experience the wrath of the Lord. Bishop Bilson declared that it would be foolhardy to tolerate that which God 'with sore plagues revengeth'.[82] When responding to those who praised the combination of tolerance and prosperity in the United Provinces, one Puritan preacher warned ominously that God was not yet done with judging nations for their sins: 'God hath not spared such State Polities, which have sought their own rise by the ruine of God and his Truth'.[83] Thomas Edwards also feared that the writing might be on the wall for an England which tolerated heresy and blasphemy: 'I tremble to thinke lest the whole Kingdom should be in Gods Black Bill'.[84] 'Of all the arguments for religious unity', suggests Conrad Russell, 'this need to avoid earthly punishment for sin was repeated most often.'[85] The political intolerance of heresy and schism was motivated by fear of divine intolerance.

The abhorrence of schism needs to be underlined. Early modern Protestants did not take a relaxed view of denominational plurality. Instead, most regarded the existence of separate churches and sects as a scandal. Even the great majority of Dissenters (i.e. all Presbyterians and many Independents) cherished the ideal of a national and established church. At the Restoration, these Dissenters had no desire to leave the Church of England, but they felt that they were forced out by a rigid policy of uniformity. Anglicans, on the other hand, compared Dissenters to the Donatists, arguing that though they agreed with the church theologically, they had separated from it over trivial issues. For Anglicans, the church was always a mixed body containing both the godly and the sinful. By separating from it in order to form pure congregations, Dissenters were abandoning the historic principle of catholicity, and opting for schismatic sectarianism.

Anglicans did not simply respond to the Dissenter challenge by reiterating the arguments of Augustine – though they did see the penal laws as a means to restore the unity of the English church. They also offered a newer line of argument, which was less clerical and more Erastian.[86] Like the Swiss theologian Thomas Erastus (1524–83), they championed the authority of the civil magistrate over the church. In a country where the monarch was the supreme governor of the established church, Erastianism had a powerful appeal, and it was used very effectively against the Puritans by Richard Hooker in his *Laws of Ecclesiastical Polity*, written in the 1590s. Yet it was in the Restoration period that this argument for uniformity really came into its own. It was central to the most notorious defences of persecution, Samuel Parker's *Ecclesiastical Polity* (1670) and Edward Stillingfleet's *Unreasonableness of Separation* (1680). Parker's work was influenced by the writings of Hobbes, and by stressing the power of the magistrate to order the church as he saw fit, Anglican theorists did incur charges of Hobbism. Yet the Erastian argument drew on the traditional Christian idea that certain aspects of Christian practice had not been determined by Scripture and were not necessary for salvation. These *adiaphora*, or 'things indifferent', included clerical dress, the time and place of worship, and the gestures used by worshippers. Erastians argued that the Church of England had to decide on each of these matters, and that for the sake of peace, order and decorum they should be determined by the magistrate.

Ironically, one of the clearest expressions of this adiaphorist argument comes from John Locke. Locke eventually became England's leading tolerationist, but in the early 1660s, he welcomed the reimposition of religious uniformity as the surest way to end the chaos of the Puritan Revolution. In his *Two Tracts* (1660–1), he defended the magistrate's power to determine 'things indifferent'. Whilst freely acknowledging that the magistrate did not have the authority to command things contrary to natural law or the essentials of Christianity, he argued that God had given magistrates the power to impose a pattern of uniformity in 'things indifferent' for the sake of good order and national unity. Thus the English monarch was quite within his rights in determining 'the circumstances of time, place, behaviour, appearance' which accompanied religious worship. He could, for example, command ministers to wear vestments, and command worshippers to kneel at communion. Those who objected to such orders had no legitimate grounds for complaint, for they were not being required to do anything that might jeopardise their salvation and they were not being asked to conscientiously approve these practices as Christian essentials. All they had to do was to recognise that the magistrate had a duty to ensure order by determining things indifferent, and to obey his laws. To do otherwise was to place one's own ego above the public good, and to risk returning the nation to chaos and anarchy. In Locke's words, 'our only hope lies in punctilious obedience'.[87]

The paradox of this argument for uniformity is that it was often favoured by churchmen of more liberal theological attitudes. Whereas many Puritans claimed that the Bible offered detailed regulations for every aspect of Christian worship, Anglicans like Hooker and Locke argued that in many cases God allowed people to decide what was most appropriate for their circumstances. To Anglican eyes, Puritans and Dissenters were legalistic fundamentalists, who protested at the violation of their conscience every time a minor ceremony offended their narrow principles. 'Numerous are the complaints of this sort that they raise', bemoaned Locke, 'for these foolish men imagine all sorts of things which horrify their simple minds.'[88] Because Latitudinarians did not believe that the forms of Anglican worship were *jure divino* (divinely ordained), they were far more flexible, and willing to make certain alterations to Anglican worship to satisfy Puritan scruples. What they could not understand was the intransigence of Puritans, who were willing to breach the unity of the established church over a few minor differences. The vehemence with which Latitudinarians like Stillingfleet attacked Dissenters arose from their horror of schism and their passion for religious unity.

The politics of persecution

Yet the theorists of uniformity were not just concerned about religious truth and church unity, but also about political order. Indeed, Gordon Schochet has suggested that Samuel Parker 'basically had no *theological* position. He was much more concerned with political power and the preservation of stability than he was with religious *principles*.'[89] This may be an exaggeration, but there can be no doubt that defenders of uniformity were convinced that religious pluralism would have disastrous political consequences.

As Conrad Russell has demonstrated, most early modern Englishmen assumed that some form of religious uniformity was absolutely essential for the unity of a nation.[90] 'Religion being the chief band of human society', wrote Francis Bacon, 'it is a happy thing when itself is well contained within the true band of unity.'[91] In a confessional state, withdrawal from the national church was effectively withdrawal from the commonwealth itself – an intolerable offence in the eyes of most commentators. 'Schism in the church, begets a Schism in the State', averred Matthew Newcomen.[92] 'Divisions whether they be Ecclesiasticall or Politicall in Kingdomes, Cities and Families, are infallible causes of ruin', claimed Edmund Calamy.[93] Roger L'Estrange agreed: 'Uniformity is the Ciment of both Christian, and Civil Societies. Take away that, and the parts drop from the body; one piece falls from another.'[94] To tolerate different religions, therefore, was to commit political suicide. So strong was this assumption, that Christian writers generally accepted the right of heathen magistrates to order religion as they saw fit. The historical lesson of Europe's recent religious wars was not that persecution caused strife, but that it was highly dangerous to allow two religions in one territory.

Those who supported persecution constantly stressed the seditious character of religious deviants. Sir William Cecil was emphatic in his assertion that Catholics were only executed for sedition, not for their religion. He argued that Catholicism was a highly politicised imperialistic religion, committed – by Pius V's 1570 bull of excommunication against Elizabeth – to the overthrow of the English Protestant regime. Far from being religious quietists, the missionary priests who entered England were basically the secret agents of a foreign power, sent to undermine the government. Like the extremist Islamic clerics who today provide inspiration for terrorist campaigns, the priests could not be treated like men who only sought the spiritual nourishment of their flock. They were dangerous and seditious.[95]

Nothing did more to lend credibility to these fears than a growing cata-logue of real and imagined Catholic plots and rebellions: the revolt of the Northern Earls in 1569, the Ridolfi Plot of 1571, the Throckmorton Plot of 1583, the Babington Plot of 1586, the Spanish Armada in 1588, the Main and Bye plots of 1603, the Gunpowder Plot of 1605, the Irish uprising of 1641, and finally the Popish Plot concocted in the fevered mind of Titus Oates and 'revealed' to a horrified nation in 1678. Together, these events (or in some cases, non-events) helped to settle any qualms which English Protestants felt about punishing Catholics. 'The horrible Powder-treason', for example, struck fear into the heart of James I, and he was outraged that Catholic polemicists could not see that *he* was the victim, not the Catholics who had been justly executed for the most abominable crimes.[96]

Similar charges of political subversion were also thrown at Protestant Dissenters. Archbishop Bancroft maintained that under a godly pretence, Presbyterians 'seditiously endeavour to disturb the land'. His exhibits were Puritan plots like those of Hacket, and the English Puritan enthusiasm for the resistance theory of Knox, Buchanan, and Beza.[97] After the Puritan Revolution, this line of argument carried even greater force. Restoration Anglicans laid the blame for the appalling bloodshed of the civil wars squarely on the shoulders of the Dissenters. As they demonstrated by lengthy quota-tions, Puritan clergy had justified the execution of Charles I, 'one of the most execrable acts of Cruelty and Injustice that ever was committed upon the face of the Earth since the Crucifixion'.[98] The young Locke believed that the Puritan refusal to acknowledge the power of the magistrate in religion had been a prime cause of England's civil wars. By insisting on their Christian liberty and 'the rights of their consciences', militant Puritans had shown 'contempt for the magistrate and disrespect for the laws'. In-stead of quietly submitting to the magistrate's authority in matters of reli-gion, they had howled in protest and ignited 'a fire capable of devastating everything'. Only with the Restoration had order been restored, and Locke hoped that 'nobody will now be so pig-headed and obstinate as to try once again to destabilise society, or to question the magistrate's authority to legislate on indifferent things'.[99]

Locke's hopes were not realised, and the involvement of Dissenters in a whole series of plots after the Restoration simply reinforced their reputation for disloyalty and sedition. Besides Venner's Fifth Monarchist Rising in 1661, Nonconformists were implicated in the northern rising of 1663, the Rye House Plot of 1683, Monmouth's rebellion in 1685, and numerous minor conspiracies. To many Anglicans, therefore, Dissenters were danger-ous hotheads. The very thought of them provoked a torrent of vitriolic abuse from Samuel Parker. They were 'Zealots', 'Brain-Sick People', 'Madmen' purveying 'Religious Lunacies', 'Seditious Preachers', 'Villains' and 'Vermin'.[100] Richard Perrinchief warned that Dissenters simply could not be trusted; they might seem tame at present, but given a taste of power they would turn wild. Pliny had wisely said that you can train a lion to be gentle, but if he licks you with his rough tongue and draws blood, he will be 'so ravisht with the savoriness of it, that he is put into rage and fury'.[101] The practice of persecution was underpinned by a mixture of hostile stereotype, painful experience, and genuine fear.

The knowledge of what the persecuted had done when they were in charge lent indignation to their oppressors. Advocates of uniformity felt that Catholic and Dissenter complaints were pretty rich coming from groups who themselves specialised in persecution. Bishop Bilson reminded the Catholics of 'your inquisiting, your burning, your murdering of thousands, without any respect of innocent or ignorant'.[102] Outraged by the hypocrisy of Catholic critics, John Jewel recalled the unspeakable horrors of the Marian persecution:

> Ye have imprisoned your brethren, ye have stript them naked, ye have scourged them with rods, ye have burnt their hands and arms with flaming torches, ye have famished them, ye have drowned them, ye have summoned them being dead to appear before you out of their graves, ye have ripped up their buried carcasses, ye have burnt them, ye have thrown them out into the dunghill; ye took a poor babe falling from his mother's womb, and in most cruel and barbarous manner threw him into the fire.[103]

King James was equally frank with his Catholic critics, reminding them that when they were in power, 'no sorts of cruell deathes were spared vnexecuted upon men, women, and children professing our Religion'. Like Jewel, both James and William Cecil recounted Foxe's tale of the woman who had given birth at the stake, only to have her baby hurled sadistically back into the flames. To Cecil, the persecutions of Mary's reign afforded 'examples beyond all heathen cruelty'.[104] To tolerate and encourage a religion as ruthless as Catholicism would be sheer folly. The Church of Rome was a wild animal, commonly identified with the Beast of Revelation 13, a fierce, persecuting creature with sharp claws and bloody teeth. Like all dangerous animals, popery had to be caged, not liberated.

After the Restoration, Anglicans used the same argument against Dissenters. Defenders of the Clarendon Code felt that Puritans were now getting a richly deserved taste of their own medicine. The Anglican tract *Persecutio Undecima*, first published in 1648 and reprinted during the royalist reaction in 1682, recorded the sufferings of Anglican clergy during the civil wars, and declared that they constituted the eleventh great persecution of the church, following the ten great persecutions experienced by the primitive Christians. In the 1630s, the Puritan faction had styled themselves 'the meek of the Earth', and moaned about persecution, but after 1640 they had become 'the only and most bloody persecutors, having slain more thousands of Protestants in England, under colour for fighting for the Protestant Religion, then Queen Mary condemned scores, within the like compass of years'.[105] In the face of such belligerence, Anglicans felt that they must strike back if they had any interest in self-preservation. Dissenters were dangerous, and they had to be suppressed. The Clarendon Code was not merely an expression of spite, but of fear. A pluralistic 'live and let live' policy would be suicidal.

Thus the case against the toleration of religious dissent was a multi-faceted one. Most of its facets were captured by the Scottish Presbyterian George Gillespie when he castigated the English sectaries for promoting a 'pernicious, God-provoking, Truth-defacing, Church-ruinating, & State-shaking toleration'.[106] Many early modern Europeans shared Gillespie's conviction that the toleration of open heresy and schism would destroy Christian society. But the fact that they did hold to this belief is largely explained by its great longevity and respectability. For more than a millennium, Christian Europe had followed a path marked out by St Augustine. His authority and subsequent tradition weighed very heavily indeed on the minds of Tudor and Stuart Protestants. The theory of religious coercion only came under sustained attack from the 1640s onwards.

Notes

1   *The Works of Richard Hooker*, 2 vols (Oxford, 1885), II, p. 513.

2   H. A. Drake, 'Lambs into lions: explaining early Christian intolerance', *Past and Present* 153 (1997), 3–36.

3   The quotation comes from Letter 93, written to Vincentius in 408. It is reprinted in D. Mullan, ed., *Religious Pluralism in the West: An Anthology* (Oxford, 1998), pp. 39–50, quotation at p. 47. Further excerpts from Augustine's seminal letters justifying the persecution of the Donatists can be found in *The Political Writings of St Augustine*, ed. H. Paolucci (Chicago, 1962), pp. 184–240.

4   See, for example, P. Biel, 'Bullinger against the Donatists: St Augustine to the defence of the Zurich reformed church', *Journal of Religious History* 16 (1991), 237–46.

5   See, for example, Thomas Bilson, *The True Difference between Christian Subjection and Unchristian Rebellion* (1585), pp. 19–20, 28–9; *The Sermons of Edwin Sandys*

(Cambridge, 1841), pp. 42, 46; 'The Answer of Mr John Cotton', in Roger Williams, *The Bloudy Tenent of Persecution*, ed. E. B. Underhill (London, 1848), pp. 28–9. See also M. Goldie, 'The theory of religious intolerance in Restoration England', in O. P. Grell, J. Israel, and N. Tyacke, eds, *From Persecution to Toleration* (Oxford, 1989), esp. pp. 335–45.

6   See H. Chadwick, *Augustine*, in *Founders of Thought* (Oxford, 1991), pp. 264–5.

7   See R. I. Moore, *The Formation of a Persecuting Society: Power and Deviance in Western Europe, 950–1250* (Oxford, 1987).

8   *Aquinas: Selected Political Writings*, ed. A. P. D'Entreves (Oxford, 1959), p. 77. The quotation comes from the *Summa Theologica*.

9   See H. Kamen, *The Spanish Inquisition: An Historical Revision* (London, 1997).

10   See B. Levack, *The Witch-Hunt in Early Modern Europe*, 2nd edn (Harlow, 1995).

11   The key documents from the Servetus case are reprinted in G. R. Potter and M. Greengrass, eds, *John Calvin* (London, 1983), pp. 102–9.

12   See S. Brachlow, *The Communion of the Saints: Radical Puritan and Separatist Ecclesiology, 1570–1625* (Oxford, 1988), ch. 7.

13   See Goldie, 'The theory of religious intolerance in Restoration England'.

14   See G. R. Elton, 'Toleration and the Reformation', in W. J. Sheils, ed., *Persecution and Toleration* (Oxford, 1984), pp. 171–80.

15   Bilson, *Christian Subjection*, pp. 20, 384.

16   *The Works of John Hales*, 3 vols (Glasgow, 1765), II, pp. 98–103.

17   Richard Perrinchief, *A Discourse of Toleration* (1668), p. 32; [*idem*], *Samaritanism; or, A Treatise of Comprehending, Compounding and Tolerating several Religions in one Church* (n.d.), pp. 38–9.

18   Henry Thorndike, *A Discourse of the Forbearance or the Penalties which a Due Reformation Requires* (1670), pp. 145–9.

19   See R. Vernon, *The Career of Toleration: John Locke, Jonas Proast and After* (Montreal, 1997), p. 18.

20   *The Works of John Jewel*, ed. J. Ayre, 4 vols (Cambridge, 1840–50), III, p. 188.

21   *The Political Works of James I*, ed. C. H. McIlwain (Cambridge, MA, 1918), p. 232.

22   John Owen, *Vindiciae Evangelicae* (1655) in *Works*, ed. W. Goold, 16 vols (Edinburgh, 1850–3), XII, pp. 40–1.

23   Bilson, *Christian Subjection*, p. 19.

24   *The Sermons of Edwin Sandys*, p. 40. See also pp. 72–3.

25   [Perrinchief], *Samaritanism*, pp. 25–9.

26 H[enry] S[avage], *Toleration with its Principal Objections Fully Confuted* (1663), p. 62.

27 *The Works of Joseph Hall*, ed. P. Wynter, 10 vols (Oxford, 1863), VI, pp. 649–50.

28 Francis Bacon, 'Of Unity in Religion', *Essays* (London, 1992 edn), p. 11.

29 *The Works of Joseph Hall*, VI, p. 641.

30 George Gillespie, *Wholesome Severity Reconciled with Christian Liberty* (1645), pp. 1–4.

31 *The Political Works of James I*, p. 322.

32 Bilson, *Christian Subjection*, p. 28.

33 *The Works of John Hales*, II, pp. 100–3.

34 Roger L'Estrange, *Toleration Discuss'd* (1663), p. 100.

35 Ibid., pp. 5–6.

36 Samuel Rutherford, *A Free Disputation against Pretended Liberty of Conscience* (1649), p. 46.

37 On Hobbes's 'extraordinarily narrow' toleration see G. Burgess, 'Thomas Hobbes: religious toleration or religious indifference', in C. J. Nederman and J. C. Laursen, eds, *Difference and Dissent: Theories of Toleration in Medieval and Early Modern Europe* (Lanham, MD, 1996), ch. 8.

38 See R. Ashcraft, 'Latitudinarianism and toleration: historical myth versus political history', in R. Kroll, R. Ashcraft and P. Zagorin, eds, *Philosophy, Science and Religion in England, 1640–1700* (Cambridge, 1992), pp. 151–73.

39 *The Works of John Whitgift*, ed. J. Ayre, 3 vols (Cambridge, 1851–3), III, p. 595.

40 Edward Stillingfleet, *The Unreasonableness of Separation* (1681).

41 On the theme of idolatry in Protestant thought see C. Eire, *War against Idols: The Reformation of Worship from Erasmus to Calvin* (Cambridge, 1986).

42 W. Monter, 'Heresy executions in Reformation Europe, 1520–1565', in O. P. Grell and R. Scribner, eds, *Tolerance and Intolerance in the European Reformation* (Cambridge, 1996), p. 54 n. 11.

43 Bilson, *Christian Subjection*, pp. 16, 26–8.

44 Quoted in Anthony Milton, *Catholic and Reformed* (Cambridge, 1995), p. 100.

45 Bilson, *Christian Subjection*, pp. 16–17.

46 Rutherford, *Free Disputation*, pp. 249–50.

47 [Perrinchief], *Samaritanism*, pp. 24–5.

48 See the profound examination of this central theme in Christian political thought in O. O'Donovan, *The Desire of the Nations: Rediscovering the Roots of Political Theology* (Cambridge, 1996), esp. ch. 6.

49 *The Works of John Jewel*, IV, p. 145.

50 *The Sermons of Edwin Sandys*, p. 42.

51 Bilson, *Christian Subjection*, p. 130.

52 *The Political Works of James I*, pp. 59, 107, 39.

53 *The Works of John Whitgift*, I, pp. 204, 331–2, 271.

54 Gillespie, *Wholesome Severity*, pp. 5, 9.

55 Quoted in *Toleration Disapprov'd and Condemn'd* (1670), p. 35, an Anglican compilation of Puritan testimonies against toleration.

56 See ibid., pp. 27, 35, 53.

57 'The Answer of Mr John Cotton', in Williams, *The Bloudy Tenent*, pp. 24–30.

58 Richard Baxter, *A Holy Commonwealth*, ed. W. Lamont (Cambridge, 1994), p. 25.

59 Samuel Parker, *A Discourse of Ecclesiastical Politie* (1670), pp. 32–3.

60 S[avage], *Toleration . . . Confuted*, p. 34.

61 Bilson, *Christian Subjection*, p. 33.

62 *The Sermons of Edwin Sandys*, Sermon XIII, and pp. 42, 59, 234.

63 Ibid., p. 46.

64 Bilson, *Christian Subjection*, p. 17.

65 Gillespie, *Wholesome Severity*, pp. 12–13.

66 Rutherford, *Free Disputation*, chs. 17 and 18; quote at p. 231.

67 *The Works of Joseph Hall*, VI, p. 613.

68 Quoted in *Toleration Disapprov'd*, pp. 24–5.

69 *The Laws of Ecclesiastical Polity*, VIII.i.2, in *The Works of Richard Hooker*, II, p. 485.

70 *The Sermons of Edwin Sandys*, p. 43.

71 Quoted in *Toleration Disapprov'd*, p. 43.

72 Rutherford, *Free Disputation*, p. 339.

73 Ibid., sig. A3, pp. 5, 8, 10.

74 Augustine's Letter 93. In *Religious Pluralism*, ed. Mullan, p. 47.

75 *The Inconveniences of Toleration* (1667), p. 23. For a lucid examination of this line of argument see Goldie, 'The theory of religious intolerance in Restoration England', pp. 345–68.

76 Bilson, *Christian Subjection*, p. 22.

77 Quoted in *Toleration Disapprov'd*, p. 29.

78 *The Sermons of Edwin Sandys*, p. 441.

79 *A Letter of the Presbyterian Ministers in the City of London* (1645; 1668), pp. 6–7.

80 L'Estrange, *Toleration Discuss'd*, pp. 84–5.

81 Stillingfleet, *The Unreasonableness of Separation*, xciv, xi, lxxix–lxxx.

82 Bilson, *Christian Subjection*, p. 21.

83 Quoted in *Toleration Disapprov'd*, pp. 32–3.

84 Thomas Edwards, *Gangraena* (1646), I, A2.

85 C. Russell, 'Arguments for religious unity in England, 1530–1650', *Journal of Ecclesiastical History* 18 (1967), 222.

86 What follows draws on Goldie, 'The theory of religious intolerance in Restoration England', pp. 332–4.

87 J. Locke, *Political Writings*, ed. D. Wootton (London, 1993), pp. 156, 153.

88 Ibid., p. 176.

89 G. Schochet, 'Samuel Parker, religious diversity and the ideology of persecution', in R. Lund, ed., *The Margins of Orthodoxy: Heterodox Writing and Cultural Response, 1660–1750* (Cambridge, 1995), p. 135.

90 See Russell, 'Arguments for religious unity in England', 201–26.

91 Bacon, *Essays*, p. 8.

92 Quoted in *Toleration Disapprov'd*, p. 43.

93 Quoted in ibid., p. 33.

94 L'Estrange, *Toleration Discuss'd*, p. 86.

95 *'The Execution of Justice in England' by William Cecil and 'A True, Sincere and Modest Defense of English Catholics' by William Allen*, ed. R. M. Kingdon (Ithaca, NY, 1965).

96 *The Political Works of James I*, p. 96.

97 Richard Bancroft, *Dangerous Positions and Proceedings* (1593), pp. 183, 141–83.

98 Roger L'Estrange, *Dissenters Sayings, The Second Part* (1681), p. 79.

99 Locke, *Political Writings*, p. 153.

100 Parker, *A Discourse of Ecclesiastical Polity*, iii, iv, l–li.

101 [Perrinchief], *Samaritanism*, pp. 79–80.

102 Bilson, *Christian Subjection*, p. 29.

103 *The Works of John Jewel*, III, p. 189.

104 *The Political Works of James I*, p. 158; 'The Execution of Justice' by William Cecil, p. 20.

105 *Persecutio Undecima, The Churches Eleventh Persecution; or, A Briefe of the Puritan Persecution of the Church of England* (1648; 1682), p. 2.

106 Gillespie, *Wholesome Severity*, A3.

CHAPTER 3

The Protestant Theory of Toleration

The Christian church doth not persecute; no more than a lily doth scratch
the thorns, or a lamb pursue and tear the wolves, or a turtle-dove hunt the
hawks and eagles, or a chaste and modest virgin fight and scratch like
whores and harlots.

(Roger Williams, *The Bloudy Tenent of Persecution*, 1644)[1]

the Gospel frequently declares that the true Disciples of Christ must suffer
Persecution; but that the Church of Christ should persecute others, and
force others by Fire and Sword, to embrace her Faith and Doctrine, I
could never yet find in any of the Books of the New Testament.

(John Locke, *A Letter concerning Toleration*, 1689)[2]

1644 was a decisive moment in the history of English Protestantism, for in
that year the Augustinian consensus concerning persecution was irrepar-
ably fractured. There had been a few attacks on the whole concept of religious coercion earlier in the century, particularly from General Baptists,
but theirs were isolated voices drowned out by the chorus of intellectuals
who defended uniformity.[3] 1644 was a fundamental turning point. It was a
year which saw the publication of some of the most eloquent critiques of
religious coercion in the English language: John Milton's *Areopagitica*, William
Walwyn's *The Compassionate Samaritane*, Henry Robinson's *Liberty of Conscience*,
and Roger Williams's *The Bloudy Tenent of Persecution*. Milton argued for the
liberty of the press, Walwyn took up the cause of the despised and persecuted sects, Robinson presented the economic case for toleration, and
Williams called for the toleration of heretics, blasphemers, Catholics, Jews,
Muslims and pagans.[4] From this year onwards, England was to be the scene
of one of the most vigorous and protracted debates over persecution in
early modern Europe.

The toleration debate intensified at particular moments, as another flurry of pamphleteering was provoked by a new development: the drive for Presbyterian uniformity in the mid-1640s; the Whitehall debates of 1648; the Humble Proposals of 1652; the renewed excitement over the 'Good Old Cause' in 1659–60; the Restoration and the passing of the 'Clarendon Code' in the early 1660s; the publication of Parker's *Ecclesiastical Politie* (1670); the issuing of the Declaration of Indulgence in 1672; Stillingfleet's *Unreasonableness of Separation* (1680); James II's sudden conversion to toleration in 1686–7; and the Glorious Revolution of 1688–9.[5] The most famous contribution to the debate, John Locke's *Letter concerning Toleration*, was actually written in Latin in 1685–6 when Locke was living in Holland, and was as much concerned with the Revocation of the Edict of Nantes as it was with events in England. But it was first published in 1689, both in Latin and in English translation, and became forever associated with that other landmark, the Act of Toleration. However, far from marking the end of debate over toleration, the events of 1689 simply perpetuated the argument, as High Churchmen attempted to overturn or limit the toleration already achieved.[6]

Nevertheless, the very fact that the toleration of religious pluralism was being openly debated was of immense significance. In 1600, almost no one in England would have taken issue with Augustine's theory of religious coercion. As the French scholar Jean Delumeau has noted, 'Augustine's authority [was] undisputed and pervasive in Latin culture'. He was 'the common denominator of Catholicism and Protestantism', and 'The elite culture of early modern Europe can be understood only by allotting Augustine the full influence he held at that time'. Erasmus quoted Augustine more than any other author in his *Enchiridion*, More was deeply imbued with Augustinian ideas, Luther called the Latin Father 'the best interpreter of Scripture', Calvin cited him no less than 4100 times.[7] As we have seen in chapter 2, every one of these authors followed Augustine by accepting that the Christian magistrate could punish heretics and schismatics. When faced with a choice, the More who wrote *Utopia* and the Luther who composed *On Secular Authority* set aside wild notions of toleration and bowed to the superior wisdom of Augustine.

Yet in seventeenth-century England, the opposite happened. Significant numbers of English Protestants – including many Baptists, Quakers and Socinians, some Independents and some Anglicans – broke decisively with tradition and argued for the toleration of heretics and separatists. The demise of the Augustinian consensus was epitomised by a book published in 1687. It was a translation of a Latin treatise by the church Father Lactantius, *De Mortibus Persecutorum*, which described in lurid detail the horrible deaths of those who persecuted the primitive Christians. The translator was an

Anglican clergyman, Gilbert Burnet, who was in exile in the Netherlands where he was winning the confidence of William of Orange, a man soon to become the king of England. In his preface, Burnet included an off-the-cuff dismissal of Augustine which spoke volumes about the revolution in attitudes since 1644. Burnet described how Augustine's attempt 'to justify Severity in General, when it was employed upon the account of Religion', had successfully overwhelmed the earlier tradition of Christian tolerance. Yet he went on to denigrate Augustine as a man who 'had a heat of Imagination' and preferred to rush into allegorising 'without troubling himself to examine critically what the true meaning' of Scripture might be. Augustine's lazy hermeneutical method had allowed him to misapply New Testament stories like the parable of the banquet in order to justify persecution. The rise of his influence marked the beginning of the church's spiritual decline. 'With that Father the learning of the Western Church fell very low', wrote Burnet, 'so that his works came to be more read in the succeeding Ages, than the writings of all the other Fathers'. The stage was set for 'a Night of Ignorance' ushered in by the barbarian invasions.[8]

To appreciate the remarkable character of Burnet's dismissal of Augustine, we need only look across the Channel to contemporary France. In 1685, Louis XIV had revoked the Edict of Nantes, prompting a mass emigration of Huguenots. According to Geoffrey Adams, 'there was an all but unanimous conviction among the nation's leading minds that the king's decision to restore France's unity by decree was a noble one'. Court, artists, and clergy united to praise the Revocation. The great bishop and intellectual Bossuet saluted Louis as a 'new Constantine'. Even the exiled Jansenist Antoine Arnauld defended the persecution by appealing to Augustine. From 1685 to the end of the century, the Académie Française offered prizes for works celebrating the eradication of heresy. 'The tiny band of people who viewed the Revocation as a moral and political error knew that open criticism of the king's religious policy was out of the question.' Only from 1715 did overt criticism begin to emerge.[9]

In England, by contrast, the theory of persecution had been subjected to vigorous attack since 1644. This is not to say that English attitudes prior to this date were wholly intolerant. There was often a good deal of *de facto* toleration at a local level, and many theologians insisted that Christianity was not a persecuting religion. Moreover, some churchmen wanted an internally tolerant church, which would allow latitude for nonconformists and for theological debate. However, before the 1640s, there was very little debate about toleration for religious minorities outside the Church of England. For intellectuals within the established church, civil tolerance of a plurality of Christian sects and denominations was simply not on the agenda.[10] Although the tolerationists of the 1640s assembled their doctrine using various elements of traditional Christian theology and biblical hermeneutics, the doctrine itself struck contemporaries as dangerously innovative.

The call for toleration came from two distinct groups, who together formed a kind of pincer movement against the theory of persecution. Many, perhaps most, of England's tolerationists were radical Puritans or Dissenters. Milton, Robinson, Williams and, arguably, Walwyn were among the hotter sort of Protestants, idiosyncratic or heterodox in some of their beliefs, but passionately committed to a radical Protestant faith.[11] It was the sheer intensity of their Protestantism that led them to condemn persecution, which they saw as a popish corruption of primitive Christianity. From the 1640s, they and other Puritan and nonconformist tolerationists published scores of tracts in defence of toleration. Among them we can number the Levellers Richard Overton and John Wildman, the radical Independent John Goodwin, the Baptists Samuel Richardson and Thomas Collier, and the Quakers Samuel Fisher and William Penn. These writers were among the most thoroughgoing of seventeenth-century tolerationists.[12]

The second group was comprised of moderate Anglicans, the heirs of Erasmian irenicism and the precursors of Enlightenment politeness. The greatest was John Locke, who despite his Socinian beliefs always remained a devout member of the Church of England. Alongside him we can place his patron, Anthony Ashley Cooper, the first Earl of Shaftesbury, and republicans like James Harrington. Jeremy Taylor's *Liberty of Prophesying* (1647) was by no means the most radical tolerationist book published in the 1640s, but it was one of the most widely read, and the Cambridge Platonist Henry More also wrote against persecution. Latitudinarians like John Tillotson and Gilbert Burnet became advocates of toleration, and were staunch supporters of the 1689 Act. In general, these churchmen were more cautious in their break with the Christian past than their radical Protestant counterparts, and they continued to support the notion of an established national church. Sometimes they were more interested in ecclesiastical tolerance than in civil tolerance of religious pluralism. However, as part of the Latitudinarian stream within the Church of England stemming from William Chillingworth, they undermined the foundations of intolerance by popularising a new religious style, one characterised by openness, ecumenism and 'reasonableness'.

From the 1690s, a third group emerged, one which owed much to the other two but which had stepped decisively outside the Protestant tradition by rejecting biblical authority. The Deists were to be perhaps the most significant advocates of religious tolerance in the eighteenth century; one only has to mention Voltaire and Jefferson, Frederick II and Joseph II, to make the case. In England they were led by indefatigable figures like John Toland, who helped to transmit an expurgated, secular version of the tolerationism of radical Protestants to Enlightened society. However, the Deists lie largely beyond the chronological limits of this book.[13] Before 1689, the English toleration debate was almost wholly conducted within the fragmented tradition of Protestant Christianity.

The European tolerationist tradition

Although the tolerationists of seventeenth-century England were unusually prolific, their ideas were hardly original. Even in the Middle Ages, 'tolerantia' was 'a highly developed political concept'.[14] Christian society tolerated a host of undesirable groups, including Jews, infidels, prostitutes, lepers, beggars and the insane. These outsiders were marginalised and subject to profound discrimination, but they were not exterminated. Heretics and schismatics, on the other hand, were insiders who had apostasised, and as such they were regarded as intolerable. The Augustinian consensus concerning religious coercion remained solid, and had actually hardened.

It is for this reason that we generally associate the concept of toleration with the early modern rather than the medieval period. During the sixteenth and seventeenth centuries, an increasing number of people argued that heresy and schism were tolerable after all. And out of the notion of toleration there began to develop modern ideas of religious freedom which were well-nigh unthinkable in the Middle Ages. Indeed, by the seventeenth century, 'toleration' was often used to mean free and open exercise of religion rather than the mere absence of persecution.[15] This development is often associated with Erasmus, but like his friend Thomas More, the Dutch humanist was profoundly hostile to religious pluralism. In 1516, he wrote in a letter that France was the 'purest blossom of Christianity, since she alone is uninfested with heretics, Bohemian schismatics, with Jews and with half-Jewish marranos'. What he did contribute to the tolerationist tradition was an emphasis on ecclesiastical tolerance, an irenic latitudinarianism which hesitated before labelling anything heretical, and a commitment to work for concord between Christians who agreed on fundamentals but disagreed on secondary matters.[16] When it came to condemning the persecution of heretics, Luther was far more emphatic than Erasmus, particularly in his 1523 work *On Secular Authority*.[17] Though he eventually retracted his views and returned to the Augustinian position, Luther's early polemic against religious coercion was to be quoted repeatedly by later tolerationist writers. A policy of religious toleration was also advocated by *politiques* in both Protestant and Catholic countries, who saw it as the only way to avoid civil war when a nation was divided along confessional lines. However, they usually saw toleration as a necessary evil established to avoid the greater evil of war, and they rarely argued that toleration was always the right policy. The French *politiques*, for example, accepted 'the temporary co-existence of Protestantism as the price to be paid for ending the civil wars', but their long-term aim was to secure the return of the Huguenots to the church, possibly by means of coercion when it once again became feasible. They wished to restore concord, not to perpetuate a policy of toleration, which for them was merely a temporary expedient.[18]

There were, however, unambiguous advocates of toleration for heretics and schismatics in the sixteenth century, particularly within radical Protestantism. Sectarian Anabaptists like Balthasar Hubmaier, Michael Sattler, Menno Simons and Pilgram Marpeck repudiated all religious violence, including the disastrous takeover of the city of Münster by a group of theocratic Anabaptists in 1535. The Anabaptists were the most savagely persecuted Christian minority of the century, partly because of their extremist wing, but the quietists among them survived in communities committed to pacifism. Mystical reformers like Sebastian Franck were equally uncompromising in their rejection of the use of force to promote true faith. A third group, the Socinians, was anti-Trinitarian and largely concentrated in pluralistic Poland. Of all religious minorities, they were probably the most consistent advocates of toleration, and in the seventeenth century John Crell's *Vindiciae pro religionis libertate* presented a powerful case for freedom of religion that went through many editions in several languages. Finally, in the mainstream Reformed churches, humanist intellectuals like Sebastian Castellio, Jacob Acontius, and Dirck Coornhert produced substantial critiques of persecution in the second half of the sixteenth century.[19] In the Netherlands during the 1620s, the Remonstrant theologians Johannes Uyttenbogaert and Simon Episcopius followed in Coornhert's footsteps, and established the Arminian tolerationist tradition.[20]

Some of these authors were little known in early modern England. The Anabaptist calls for toleration remained untranslated and forgotten, though the English General Baptists were moved towards a doctrine of toleration by their contact with the Dutch Mennonites. Sebastian Franck and other mystical tolerationists would have been somewhat more familiar, whilst the Polish Socinians were certainly read by radical Protestants like Milton and Locke. Most influential of all, however, were the tolerationist writings of radical continental Reformed theologians. Acontius's major work was partially translated and published in 1648, and Castellio's writings were also familiar to seventeenth-century English writers. The Dutch influence was particularly significant. Episcopius was highly respected by the Great Tew circle and the Cambridge Platonists, and later Dutch Arminians like Philip van Limborch and Jean LeClerc were close friends of Locke and Burnet. Towards the end of the period, the highly radical tolerationist writings of two thinkers based in the Netherlands – the Huguenot Pierre Bayle and the Jewish freethinker Benedict Spinoza – also began to make an impact in England. English opponents of persecution were thus part of a broad tradition of European tolerationists who were largely found within various branches of radical Protestantism.

The varieties of tolerationism

Tolerationism, of course, came in various shapes and sizes. As we have already suggested, historians have often elided civil tolerance with other forms of tolerance, particularly ecclesiastical. Yet it is crucial to make a clear distinction. Moderate Anglicans were usually more interested in a broad ecclesiastical tolerance than in civil tolerance of a diversity of religious groups. We saw in chapter 2 that although figures like John Hales chided conservative churchmen for casually accusing others of heresy and schism, they still supported the penal laws against real heretics and schismatics, including separatists and recusants. Even William Chillingworth, who laid the groundwork for greater ecclesiastical tolerance within the Church of England, did not develop 'a comprehensive doctrine of toleration, including freedom of practice and expression as well as conscience, in the manner of Episcopius'.[21] Latitudinarians were champions of 'comprehension' within the Church of England, rather than 'toleration' for those outside. John Tillotson, for example, insisted that the Church of England allowed 'private persons to judge for themselves in matters of religion', but he was equally clear that if they broke away from the church because of their 'every scruple and frivolous pretence', the magistrate 'may restrain and punish them'.[22] In the long run the ecclesiastical tolerance of Tillotson and his allies assisted the cause of civil tolerance by generating more open attitudes, but before 1689 they were mostly unwilling to propose an official toleration of sectarian and Catholic dissent.

Even those who did call for some form of civil tolerance were not always willing to break with the Augustinian tradition, and condemn all persecution. We have already seen that there was not an absolute gulf fixed between persecution and toleration. In the medieval period, the two phenomena co-existed: heretics and schismatics were persecuted, whilst Jews and Muslims were granted a mere toleration on the margins of Christian society. In the early modern period too, both coercion and persuasion were often regarded as legitimate strategies which could be used in tandem or in separate situations. Discipline might prepare the way for argument, or coercion might be used against one group and toleration given to another. Toleration could be advocated on purely pragmatic grounds as the lesser of two evils, but as an evil nonetheless, and one to be dispensed with whenever the opportunity arose.

Moreover, many held firmly to a double standard with regard to religious coercion. When their own true religion was on the receiving end of state prosecution they lamented the heinous persecution. But they continued to believe that the true faith itself had every right to employ force against dissenters when it was in power. Such a view was taken by Elizabethan Puritans and Catholics, and neither qualify as tolerationists. The Separatist Henry Barrow and the Jesuit Robert Persons could both request toleration for themselves, but they had not made the break with the Augustinian theory. At best they could only give pragmatic support for policies of toleration. Their ultimate ideal was a godly state which used its civil powers against heretics. It is particularly difficult to find Catholic theologians in sixteenth- and seventeenth-century Europe who argued that it was always wrong for the Catholic church to use coercion against heretics and schismatics. With lay Catholics, the situation may well have been different, and there are indications that some seventeenth-century English recusants moved from pragmatic pleas for their own toleration to principled rejection of all religious coercion.[23] Yet in our period principled tolerationism developed largely within radical Protestantism, where an iconoclastic attitude towards ecclesiastical tradition could be positively *de rigueur*. For Catholics the break with the past was more painful and more difficult to justify. Indeed, not until the Second Vatican Council's *Declaration on Religious Liberty* (1965) did the Catholic church formally repudiate the tradition of persecution.[24]

Yet among those who presented a principled defence of civil tolerance, many were what Pierre Bayle would later describe as 'Demi-tolerationists'.[25] Even Castellio and Acontius had allowed the magistrate to punish atheism, blasphemy and outright apostasy from the Christian faith.[26] During the Interregnum, the Independent divines took an even stricter line, advocating toleration for all Calvinistic Protestants, but refusing to go further. John Owen proposed that toleration should only be granted to those who subscribed to a list of fundamental doctrines, a list that would have excluded Arminians, Socinians and Catholics.[27] John Milton, by contrast, would have granted toleration to all Protestants, regardless of their 'heresies', but he should perhaps be classed as a 'three-quarter' tolerationist since he emphatically excluded Catholics on grounds of their idolatry[28] (a puzzling position given that his close friends Roger Williams and Sir Henry Vane had both argued explicitly for the toleration of idolatrous Catholics). Besides Milton and Owen, many other writers stopped short of endorsing full religious toleration. During the Restoration, Charles Wolseley rejected toleration for Catholics and never contemplated toleration for non-Christians.[29] John Locke also excluded Catholics, but his reason was a purely secular one – that Catholics were disloyal citizens who owed allegiance to a foreign power. Indeed, far from ignoring the limits on Locke's tolerance, some contemporary scholars are in danger of losing sight of his liberalism.[30] They forget the Locke who argued that 'neither Pagan, nor Mahumetan, nor Jew, ought to be excluded from the Civil Rights of the Commonwealth, because of his Religion'. They also overlook his insistence that 'Preaching or Profession' of the doctrine of the Mass should not be forbidden by the magistrate: 'If a Roman Catholick believe that to be really the Body of Christ, which another man calls Bread, he does not injury thereby to his Neighbour.'[31]

Locke, therefore, belongs among the radical tolerationists. These were the thinkers who broke decisively with the Augustinian tradition by insisting that coercion could *never* be used to advance true religion. Like Locke, they called for the toleration of all religions. 'Let them be heretikes, Turcks, Jewes, or whatsoever it appertynes not to the earthly power to punish them in the least measure', declared Thomas Helwys, the founder of the first Baptist church in England.[32] Before 1640 only his fellow General Baptists went so far, but thereafter radical tolerationism was more widely adopted. Roger Williams began his *Bloudy Tenent* with a startling declaration: 'It is the will and command of God that, since the coming of his Son the Lord Jesus, a permission of the most Paganish, Jewish, Turkish, or anti-christian consciences and worships be granted to all men in all nations and countries: and that they are only to be fought against with that sword which is only, in soul matters, able to conquer: to wit the sword of God's Spirit, the word of God.'[33] The Quaker George Fox was equally emphatic:

As touching religion, it is for [a king's] nobility that there be universal liberty for what people soever. Let them speak their minds; let there be places and houses set forth where every man may speak his mind and judgement and opinion forth . . . And let him be Jew, or Papist, or Turk, or Heathen, or Protestant, or what soever, or such as worship sun or moon or stocks and stones, let them have liberty where every one may bring forth his strength, and have free liberty to speak forth his mind and judgement.[34]

Of course, even radical tolerationists believed that some things were intolerable. As Williams pointed out, sincere devotees of Moloch and Quetzalcoatl could hardly expect the state to turn a blind eye to their activities.[35] People whose religion taught them to do unspeakably cruel things would feel the full force of its justice. Moreover, all tolerationists would have agreed with John Locke when he wrote that 'If any thing pass in a Religious Meeting seditiously, and contrary to the publick Peace, it is to be punished in the same manner, and no otherwise, than as if it had happened in a Fair or Market'.[36] This much was, and remains, uncontroversial. When modern states repress violent cults, few accuse them of religious persecution.

However, seventeenth-century tolerationists made more exceptions to their toleration than modern liberals would accept. Few included atheism in their lists of falsehoods to be tolerated. The only exceptions I have come across were the Levellers Walwyn and Wildman and the Baptist Thomas Collier, who wrote: 'It belongs not to man to punish Heresie, Blasphemy, Atheisme.'[37] Yet Collier later retracted his views, and suggested that the magistrate should punish blasphemy because it was contrary to natural reason.[38] His logic was not unusual. Most radical tolerationists felt that though the magistrate could not punish people for failing to accept truths known only by revelation (e.g. the Trinity, or the Incarnation of Christ), he did have a duty to hold people to certain basic principles of natural law which should be obvious to every rational person. Hence atheism, and on some accounts blasphemy, was intolerable, as were gross immoralities such as adultery which violated natural moral law. It was on these grounds that Henry More argued that liberty of conscience should be granted to all religions, but not to those who had 'degenerated into Atheisme and Profaneness'.[39] Richard Overton also took the view that 'the suffering of Religions' was no warrant 'to be of no Religion, much lesse prophaneness'. The magistrate was to 'preserve publike modesty, comlines, and civility . . . so [the people's] carriage and publike demeanours are to be rational and regular and comely, and not openly licentious, prophane, and blasphemous, contrary to common sense, reason and humanity'.[40] This was virtually identical to the view taken by Locke, who sanctioned the prosecution of adulterers.

Yet once tolerationists had argued that only offences against natural reason could be prosecuted, the door had been left open to further liberalisation. In the future it would become increasingly obvious that rational people disagreed about matters which early modern writers took to be utterly plain. Eventually, even the existence of God and heterosexual monogamy would come to be seen as the deliverances of Christian faith rather than of natural reason. Once this had happened, toleration would be naturally extended beyond what even its most radical seventeenth-century proponents had suggested. Conrad Russell is quite right to suggest that 'the debate about the rights of atheists was not joined in Tudor and Stuart times: it was provoked by Mill, *On Liberty* and the election of Bradlaugh'.[41] Yet early modern tolerationists had sowed the seeds of this extended civil tolerance when they insisted that the state could only prosecute actions and beliefs which were manifestly contrary to natural reason and public order. As the philosopher John Rawls pointed out:

> There is . . . an important difference between Rousseau and Locke, who advocated a limited toleration, and Aquinas and the Protestant Reformers who did not. Locke and Rousseau limited liberty on the basis of what they supposed were clear and evident consequences for the public order. If Catholics and atheists were not to be tolerated it was because it seemed evident that such persons could not be relied upon to observe the bonds of civil society. Presumably a greater historical experience and a knowledge of the wider possibilities of political life would have convinced them that they were mistaken, or at least that their contentions were true only under special circumstances.[42]

Moreover, even if no tolerationist intended to prepare the way for the *permissive* society, some certainly envisaged a *multi-faith* society governed by an impartial, secular state. Dissatisfied with mere toleration, and even with religious liberty for all, they called for the abolition of the confessional state. They argued that the public culture of England should be built on an anthropological rather than a religious foundation. Instead of being grounded in both nature and grace, politics should be based on nature alone. The church and the state should be clearly separated and reconceptualised. The state should not be thought of as a body of Christian believers, but as a pluralistic community created by contract between people of different faiths. The church must be reconceived as a private, voluntary and non-coercive community of like-minded believers. Thus Locke defined the Commonwealth in purely secular terms, as 'a Society of Men constituted only for the procuring, preserving, and advancing of their own Civil Interests'; and he defined a church as 'a free and voluntary Society', analogous to a private commercial company.[43] Earlier Puritan tolerationists had adopted the same view. Williams repeatedly insisted that the state ought to be 'meerly civil', and defined a civil government as 'an ordinance of God, to conserve the civil peace of people so far as concerns their bodies and goods'. A church was a private association of 'volunteers', 'like unto a Corporation, Society or Company of East Indie or Turkie merchants'.[44] Following Williams, Samuel Fisher maintained that the magistrate should 'give protection to men, as men, (living honestly, soberly and justly) without respect to their Religions, whether true or false'. The state should be impartial towards Christians, Jews and heathens, for when Christ's disciples receive preferential treatment from the state 'above their fellow subjects', it 'too often choaks the Church'.[45]

The African scholar Lamin Sanneh has recently argued that these seventeenth-century English tolerationists pointed towards the 'demise of territoriality' and triumph of religious voluntarism in the West. For centuries, faith had been closely tied to territory. 'Christendom identified itself with territoriality in the sense of making religion a matter of territorial allegiance. Church membership was coterminous and interchangeable with territorial location, and territorial rule was established on, and made legitimate by, the ruler's professed allegiance.' Tolerationists like Locke, Williams and Overton, however, broke the link between territory and faith and called for a shift from territoriality to voluntarism.[46] For them, Christianity was about voluntary communities of believers, not godly states. Territory was desacralised, and reconceived in secular terms as the homeland of a pluralist people.

Thus the spectrum of opinion concerning persecution and toleration in early modern England was very broad indeed. On one extreme stood the most furious persecutors, those who enthused about the death penalty for heresy and saw coercion as a general solution to the problem of dissent. Then there were men like James I, who accepted the use of the death penalty in cases of serious heresy and blasphemy, but also believed that 'God loves not to plant his church by violence and bloodshed'. Next came those like John Hales who rejected capital punishment for religious crimes altogether, and who only favoured the mildest of penal laws. More generous still were 'demi-tolerationists', who would have allowed dissent outside the established church but reserved the right to punish serious breaches of doctrinal orthodoxy. Then came those like Milton, who would have tolerated all kinds of heresy and schism, but drew the line at popish idolatry. Finally, there were the radical tolerationists like Locke and Williams who repudiated all religious coercion, called for the toleration of all religions, and even developed a secular definition of the state.

Theological and philosophical arguments

In view of the end product, it is paradoxical that the inspiration and arguments of the radical tolerationists were profoundly religious. It is important to stress this, since modern scholars sometimes bypass the specifically theological case for toleration in favour of concentrating on general philosophical arguments which could still be used in secular discussion today. It is as if tolerationist writers are abstracted from their context within seventeenth-century Protestantism, and forced to argue for toleration without using any of the uniquely Christian arguments which were most calculated to influence their devout readers.[47] Inevitably, this approach distorts our picture of the entire early modern debate over religious toleration. We can hardly understand the English toleration debate, for example, if we fail to appreciate that it took place within a Protestant theological tradition. The tolerationist literature of sixteenth- and seventeenth-century Europe was saturated in theological argument and biblical reference. It represented a massive effort on the part of some Christians to persuade their fellow believers of the evil of persecution. Secular arguments were used, and we shall examine them later, but fundamentally the case for toleration was biblical and theological.[48]

As the quotations from Williams and Locke at the head of this chapter suggest, the case for toleration rested on the paradigmatic example of Jesus and the early Christian church. Whereas defenders of uniformity had pointed to prophecies about the kings of the earth binding themselves to the service of Yahweh, tolerationists highlighted prophecies about the peaceable nature of the Messianic kingdom. 'Even in those dark tymes', wrote Edmund Ludlow, there were 'some glymmerings' of the spiritual nature of Christ's rule, in contrast to the 'carnal, violent, & imposing spirit' which characterised Old Testament Israel.[49] Following Luther, tolerationists repeatedly cited the predictions of the Hebrew prophets that in the Messianic age men 'shall not hurt nor destroy in all my holy mountain' (Isaiah 11.9), but 'shall beat their swords into ploughshares, and their spears into pruninghooks' (Isaiah 2.4; Micah 4.3).[50] They appealed to Isaiah's prophecy that the coming Messiah would not break 'a bruised reed' or quench 'the smoking flax' (Isaiah 42.3), and directed their readers to the Psalmist's declaration, 'Thy people shall be willing in the day of thy power' (Psalm 110.3), a clear proof in their eyes that God had no desire for a press-ganged following.[51] Whereas persecutors had celebrated the fourth-century transformation of the church's status and the conversion of the powerful to the truth, tolerationists praised the gentleness of the primitive church and celebrated its political powerlessness.

Above all, the opponents of persecution appealed to the life and teaching of Jesus. They argued that Christ had come to inaugurate an entirely new kind of kingdom, one not characterised by domineering rule (Matthew 20.25–6). He had been meek and lowly, persecuted but never persecuting. He rode into Jerusalem on a donkey, not a charger. He had been led like a lamb to the slaughter. At his trial he had declared, 'My kingdom is not of this world' (John 18.36). In his declaration of his kingdom's principles in the Sermon on the Mount, he had commanded his followers to love their enemies, to turn the other cheek, to do unto others as they would have done to themselves (Matthew 5–7). When his disciples had tried to call down fire on an unbelieving Samaritan village, he had rebuked them (Luke 9); when they had asked him about the Pharisees, he had declared, 'Let them alone: they be blind leaders of the blind' (Matthew 15.14). The most his followers were to do when their message was rejected was to shake the dust off their feet (Matthew 10.14). Christ had encapsulated his teaching on tolerance in the parable of the wheat and the tares, a proof text deployed by hundreds of tolerationist pamphleteers in the sixteenth and seventeenth centuries.[52] The wheat and tares – believers and unbelievers – were to be allowed to grow peacefully together in the field of the world until judgement day, when God himself would separate them and judge the wicked (Matthew 13). As Christ's final words to his disciples made clear (Matthew 28.19–20), 'teaching, not violent compulsion is constituted, and once and for ever ordained the meanes and only way for conversion to the faith of Jesus in all Nations'.[53]

The earliest followers of Jesus had remained true to this ethic. As the General Baptist Leonard Busher stated it, 'We never read, nor ever shall read, that the apostolic church, or such as have derived their faith and discipline of her did ever persecute'. The apostle Paul had taught that the weapons of the Christian's warfare were not carnal but spiritual (2 Corinthians 10), and the only 'artillery' of which he ever spoke consisted of spiritual armaments like the sword of the Spirit (Ephesians 6). Paul had insisted that 'the servant of the Lord must not strive, but be gentle unto all men . . . in meekness instructing those that oppose' (2 Timothy 2). If heretics and schismatics refused to be instructed, all that the church could do was excommunicate them, and leave them in the hands of God (1 Corinthians 5; 1 Timothy 1.20; Titus 3.10). 'Paul did war', wrote Henry Robinson, 'but not according to the flesh, he did not imprison, fine, nor cut off eares, his weapons were only spirituall, the power and might of Jesus Christ'.[54]

The same testimony could also be applied to those whom William Penn described as 'the true Christians, of the first three hundred years'.[55] Tolerationists frequently cited the writings of early Christian Fathers like Tertullian and Lactantius who had taught that persecution was something Christians endured, not something they meted out.[56] 'Till four hundred years after Christ', wrote the Anglican Jeremy Taylor, 'no Catholic persons, or very few, did provoke the secular arm, or implore its aid'; persecution only 'came in with the retinue and train of Antichrist'.[57] Other Anglicans emphasised the tolerance of the earliest Christian emperors. Charles Wolseley pointed out that Constantine had granted liberty of conscience by the Edict of Milan (313), and claimed that all fourth-century Christian emperors had given Jews 'the same Rights with other Christians'.[58] Gilbert Burnet noted that when the empire had become Christian, heathens were tolerated 'for above a whole age', even holding high office in the imperial government, whilst Donatists and Arians had also enjoyed the tolerance of the Orthodox during the same period.[59]

Yet sometime during or after the fourth century, tolerationists agreed, everything had gone wrong. Faced with the temptations of political power and patronage, the church had succumbed, and taken up the weapons of the world. 'The Church in the primitive tymes', wrote Ludlow, 'consisted only of ye willing, & such as were perswaded to it by ye Word, till Antichrist began to prevayle, and then they fell from perswading to forcing.'[60] The precise dating of Antichrist's ascendancy was open to debate, though most sectarians would have agreed with Roger Williams that 'Christianitie fell asleep in Constantine's bosom'.[61] Along with many radical Protestants since the 1520s, they took the view that if Christians had been doing something for the past thousand years there was a fair chance that it was wrong. In their eyes, 1200 years of church history could be written off as 'Antichristian apostasy'.

This was an argument that appealed powerfully to the anti-popery of the English Protestant mind, and it was one that weighed heavily against the practice of persecution. John Foxe had done much to establish cruel and bloodthirsty violence as the stereotypical mark of false religion, and tolerationists exploited this to the full. They turned repeatedly to the book of Revelation, written at the close of the first century to encourage Christians suffering persecution. Here they found powerful images of persecuting power: the Dragon pursuing the true church into the wilderness (ch. 12), the Beast waging war on the Lamb (ch. 13), and the Whore of Babylon, 'drunken with the blood of the saints' (ch. 17). Tragically, tolerationists argued, these images described the established churches of Christendom, their hands dripping with the blood of the godly. The alliance between church and state had proved to be a catastrophic Fall in the history of God's people, and its damage had still to be undone. 'How long Lord', prayed the persecuted Baptist Thomas Helwys: 'when wilt thou come to destroy Antichrists cruel kingdome, and establish Christs meeke and peaceable kingdome?'[62]

For non-sectarian Christians, the argument from apostasy was a bitter pill to swallow. Roman Catholics, with their great respect for tradition, found it particularly difficult to repudiate centuries of Christian practice as bestial and Antichristian. Magisterial Protestants were also reluctant to dismiss such great authorities as Augustine and Calvin. Hence many favoured the ameliorated theories of persecution we looked at in our last chapter. They rejected the death penalty for heresy, emphasised clemency, and insisted that the purpose of coercion was to correct and restore the heretic, not to exterminate him. However, eventually even the bishops and theologians of the established church were to condemn the long tradition of Christian intolerance. In 1687, Gilbert Burnet remarked that it was 'an amazing thing, to see how much the Christian Church has departed from that Pattern [of the primitive church]'. In contrast to Islam, which had begun in violence and then become tolerant, Christendom had 'so far departed from the Meekness of its Author, and of his first Followers, that . . . it is now the cruellest and the most implacable Society that has ever yet appeared in the World'.[63] Yet as we have seen, Burnet and other Anglicans like Jeremy Taylor traced the rise of Christian persecution to the fifth century and later, exonerating Constantine and his immediate successors from responsibility. They had no wish to throw the baby of religious establishment out with the bathwater of religious coercion. For them the apostasy of the church had set in later and cut less deeply than radical Protestants supposed. Yet they agreed with sectarian tolerationists that something had gone terribly wrong with Christianity after its pristine early centuries, and that the corruption of the church had only deepened through the course of the Middle Ages.

In analysing this corruption, tolerationists focused on the character of the persecutors themselves. 'Persecution does extreamly vitiate the Morals of the Party that manages it', claimed Burnet, since they were forced to court 'vicious men' to implement the policy.[64] Perversely, persecution meant that wicked men were rewarded whilst morally impeccable dissenters were hounded. Moreover, all those who belonged to the established religion were also damaged by the coercive support it received from the state. According to Samuel Fisher, Constantine's patronage had promoted Christianity 'in the shell', but killed it 'in the substance'. Suffering and hardship created disciples, preferential treatment produced 'lazy, luxurious Ministers' and 'formall meer nominal Christians'.[65] Persecutors might argue that their 'cruelty' was a kindness to the church. The truth was that they were being cruel to everyone, even themselves.

The causes of the corruption of Christianity were many, and undoubtedly base motives were involved. Yet tolerationists knew that the practitioners of persecution were earnest men, and concluded that they had gone astray because of a terrible hermeneutical and theological error – they had confused the Old Testament dispensation with the New. When Christian rulers had started modelling themselves on the kings of Israel, declared Williams, they had 'lost the path, and themselves'. Once they had made this mistake, 'they conceived themselves bound to make their cities, kingdoms, empires, new holy lands of Canaan, and themselves governors and judges in spiritual causes, compelling all consciences to Christ, and persecuting the contrary with fire and sword'.[66] 'The Inquisitors of these days', wrote Henry Robinson, 'have no better ground for their strict proceedings, then the Old Testament.'[67]

Tolerationists tried to rectify this error by emphasising the great gulf between the ages of the Old Testament and the New. Williams devoted much of his *Bloudy Tenent* to proving that ancient Israel 'was not a pattern for all lands: It was a non-such, unparalleled, and unmatchable'.[68] Many other tolerationists invested similar energy in the task. Their argument was summarised by John Lilburne: 'the Ordinances, Lawes, Rights and Ceremonies of the Church of the Jewes were types and figures, which were only to last and endure till the coming of Christ, which he by his death did abolish'.[69] Israel and its laws had only been intended as a temporary 'type', foreshadowing the spiritual rule of Christ over his people in the new dispensation. By treating Israel as a permanent model for Christians, proponents of uniformity were confusing the Law and the Gospel and revealing their failure to comprehend the great transformation that had occurred with the coming of Christ. They were guilty of Judaising, of 'grosse legality', of 'denying that Christ had come in the flesh'.[70] For the carnal shadows of the Old Testament had now flown away, and the spiritual realities of the New had appeared.

For some radical Protestants this meant that the whole idea of a godly nation was untenable, based as it was on a confusion of dispensations. God's people in the Old Testament had indeed been a political nation, but in the New they were to be a voluntary community of saints quite distinct from the surrounding world. For Anglican tolerationists this was going too far. Instead, the point to be made was that the Old Testament penalties against idolatry and religious error no longer applied. 'What severities soever might have agreed with the Mosaical dispensation, they seem to be all out of doors under the Christian religion', wrote Gilbert Burnet.[71] John Locke agreed. 'No body pretends that every thing, generally, enjoyed by the Law of Moses, ought to be practised by Christians', he argued, 'and there is nothing more frivolous than that common distinction of Moral, Judicial and Ceremonial Law.' The entire Mosaic law was only binding on the people of Israel, and had been abrogated by Christ.[72] A case which rested almost completely on Old Testament foundations was very flimsy indeed, and its critics demanded stronger proof: 'Shew us the patterne in Christs Testament to punish such as hold errors with corporall punishments.'[73]

The recovery of Christ's 'patterne', tolerationists believed, would lead to the dawning of a new age. God would restore his church to its primitive purity, and teach it the lesson of clemency and mercy all over again. For many radical Protestants, this sense of restoration was bound up with apocalyptic expectations. The millennium was nigh, and God was awakening his people from their long slumber. The church was learning afresh that it should be a non-violent institution. But it was also learning other lessons, and if the voice of the Spirit was to be heard, there must be religious liberty. In a striking image in *Areopagitica*, Milton pictured Truth in the apostolic age as a beautiful woman, 'a perfect shape most glorious to look on'. He then declared that she had been hewed 'into a thousand pieces' during the church's apostasy. Yet God was now 'decreeing to bring some new and great period in his church, even to the reforming of the Reformation itself'. If the pieces of Truth were to be recovered and joined together again, people must be free to publish their ideas, for only in this way could 'new light' be shed.[74] Millenarian restorationism, therefore, reinforced the case for toleration, as conservatives like Rutherford and Gillespie realised. Their treatises lamented the sectarian and Independent enthusiasm for 'new light' which seemed to change hour by hour. But for radical Protestants the truth had not been definitively encapsulated in Calvin's *Institutes*; the Lord had yet more light to break forth from his Word. If primitive Christianity was to be restored in all its glory, innovation and experimentation must be tolerated. 'The variety of forms in the world is the beauty of the world', said the New Model Army preacher William Dell, 'external uniformity is a monstrous thing'.[75] Differences among the godly were not to be lamented, they were to be accepted and even celebrated.[76]

The conviction that new light was breaking forth and that truth was being recovered also lay behind the confident tolerationist prediction – most famously voiced by Milton – that truth would prevail in an open fight. 'Let truth alone', declared Samuel Fisher, 'and turn it loose to plead fully for it self, and it will work out its way and live, and thrive.'[77] Henry Robinson shared his optimism: 'if the Gospel had but a free passage, and the true Professors liberty to teach and publish it, this only as a sovereigne remedy and counterpoyson, would prevail against all heresies, unless you will grant that errour may possibly vanquish truth'.[78] The implication was clear: those who relied on worldly weapons to defend the Gospel were lacking in faith. They did not really believe that truth had the intrinsic power to vindicate itself. They had forgotten that 'it is one of the glories of the Christian religion, that it was so pious, excellent, powerful and persuasive, that it came in upon its own piety and wisdom; with no other force, but a torrent of arguments, and demonstration of the Spirit'.[79] Yet even when truth did not prevail, tolerationists urged Christians to leave the matter in the hands of God and not turn it over to the hands of the state. True religion is based on 'the principle of meekness, patience, and long suffering', wrote Overton, 'for its nature is only to persuade, not to compell; if by faire meanes it cannot prevaile, it hath done, committing the issue to God.'[80]

It is important that we grasp the importance of truth to tolerationists, for historians have often overemphasised the role of scepticism in the emergence of religious tolerance.[81] Scepticism does have a place in the story of toleration,[82] but Richard Popkin, the leading historian of early modern scepticism, has recently argued that dogmatic millenarians 'did at least as much to create modern tolerant societies as the deist and nonreligious groups in Europe and America in the seventeenth and eighteenth centuries'. He suggests that a 'benign egalitarian millenarianism' played an important role in promoting tolerance, particularly of Jews and American Indians.[83] Moreover, scepticism itself could foster intolerance,[84] and radical scepticism is nowhere to be found among English advocates of toleration. Indeed, we would do better to speak of 'mitigated' or 'constructive' scepticism,[85] or else distinguish scepticism (the doctrine that one should suspend judgement wherever there is a possibility of error) from fallibilism (the doctrine that one should recognise the possibility that one's present beliefs may be false).[86]

Theological fallibilism did play an important part in the case for toleration. The notion of progressive revelation, of the Spirit leading the church into new truths, counted against the hasty censure of innovative religious ideas. Tolerationists often praised the wisdom of Gamaliel, the Jewish leader who had argued against killing the early Christians on the grounds that if they were wrong their cause would collapse, whilst if they were right their persecutors would be fighting against God (Acts 5.33–40). One of John Goodwin's tracts – *Theomachia; or, The Grand Impudence of men running the hazard of fighting against God* (1644) – took its cue from this very story. It suggests that there was an 'uncertainty principle' underlying the tolerationists' case. Persecutors were taking a risk, for how could they be sure that the earnest heretics they punished were not godly martyrs? The history of the Reformation itself demonstrated that truth was often called heresy, and that persecutors pulled up good wheat along with the tares they sought to destroy.

This argument simply confirmed the suspicion of conservative Protestants that tolerationists were sinking in a swamp of indifference and doubt. Yet this was not exactly true. Tolerationists were certain about many things, including the gentle nature of true Christianity. But their religion did allow room for grey areas. This was true for both Puritans like Milton and Goodwin whose theological beliefs changed quite dramatically in the 1640s and 1650s, and for Anglicans like Locke who had a similar experience. The Baptist Samuel Richardson, who was later to publish a treatise against the doctrine of eternal torment, made much of the argument from human fallibility. No one thinks he is in error, Richardson pointed out, though it is certain that all human beings err. There was no infallible human judge in matters of religion, and the Presbyterian clergy should not be set up as such. Moreover, 'all truth is not among one sort of men', and even error served a purpose, for 'if there were no error, it could not be known what is truth, or [it would] not be so glorious'.[87] Similar arguments came from the father of the Latitudinarians, William Chillingworth. He argued that in matters necessary to salvation made plain in Scripture, certainty was desirable and possible, but in secondary matters things were different:

though we wish heartily that all controversies were ended, as we do that all sin were abolished, yet we have little hope of the one or the other until the world be ended: and in the meanwhile think it best to content ourselves with, and to persuade others unto, an unity of charity, and mutual toleration; seeing God hath authorised no man to force all men in unity of opinion.[88]

This profoundly Erasmian argument for mutual tolerance among Christians was echoed by later sectarian and Latitudinarian writers. It expressed the conviction that the interminable theological arguments between sincere Bible-believing Protestants were unlikely to be resolved on this side of heaven. The Bible itself was not perspicuous enough on secondary matters to solve all disputes, and even the godliest Christian still saw as through a glass darkly (1 Corinthians 13.12). The participants in these controversies ought to resign themselves to living with their differences, and refuse to employ coercion to bring their debates to a quick resolution. To do otherwise would be to employ popish means, to set oneself up as an infallible authority when the only infallible authorities were God and his Word.

The tradition of fallibilism was summed up by John Locke. Locke believed that the debates which had swirled around the doctrine of the Trinity, for example, were difficult and obscure, and that human beings were fallible and fallen. Thus it was wise to be tentative and charitable in one's judgements, instead of imposing them dogmatically on others. In a letter to the Dutch Arminian Philipp van Limborch, Locke wrote: 'May others forgive my mistakes! I declare war on no one on account of difference of opinions, myself an ignorant and fallible manikin. I am an Evangelical Christian, not a Papist.' He went on to explain that there were only two kinds of Christians. Evangelicals were 'those who, seeking truth alone, desire themselves and others to be convinced of it only by proofs and reasons; they are gentle to the errors of others, being not unmindful of their own weakness; forgiving human frailty and ignorance, and seeking forgiveness in turn'. Papists, on the other hand, were those (in whatever denomination) who regarded themselves as infallible, and 'arrogate to themselves dominion over the consciences of others'.[89]

This claim – that persecutors usurped God's own authority over the conscience – was a common strand in tolerationist argument. The Leveller leader and Separatist John Lilburne was also sure that God alone was Lord over conscience. The Father had established the Son as head over his spiritual kingdom, and 'no Parliament, Councell, Synod, Emperor, King, nor Majestrate hath any spiritual authority or jurisdiction over this Kingdome'. It was 'the incommunicable Prerogative of Jesus Christ alone to be King of his Saints'. Yet earthly kings had dared 'to plucke his Crown from his head'; Henry VIII had declared himself head of the church and so 'set himselfe in the throne of Christ'. For all such usurpers, Lilburne had a simple message: 'leave my conscience free to the Law and Will of my Lord and King'.[90] Tolerationists had no time for the claim that the magistrate could determine 'things indifferent' for the sake of religious peace and unity. The rule of Christ over individual consciences was to be direct and unmediated.

Conservative theologians, whether Anglican or Presbyterian, feared that this stubborn insistence on 'my conscience' would lead to subjectivism. They upheld the traditional scholastic distinction between a properly in-formed conscience (which was to be respected) and an erroneous con-science (which had to be instructed by the church and state). Tolerationists, by contrast, were close to the modern notion that one could have a good conscience simply by being sincere (though they often continued to think in terms of sincere readers of the Christian Scriptures). Milton expressed the new view with great clarity in his definition of heresy:

> Heresie is in the Will and choice profestly against Scripture; error is against the Will, in misunderstanding the Scripture after all sincere endeavours to understand it rightly: Hence it was said well by one of the Ancients, *Err I may, but a Heretick I will not be.* It is a humane frailty to err, and no man is infallible on earth. But so long as all these profess to set the Word of God only before them as the Rule of faith and obedience; and use all diligence and sincerity of heart, by reading, by learning, study, by prayer for Illumination of the holy Spirit, to understand the Rule and obey it, they have done what man can do: God will assuredly pardon them . . . though much mistaken . . . in some Points of Doctrine.[91]

Tolerationists' stress on the sincere conscience was backed up by analysis of the nature of belief. They argued that because faith and true belief could only be produced in the conscience by persuasion and the work of God's Spirit, it was futile to try and coerce it. This line of argument did not reckon with the fact that the defenders of persecution never supposed that coercion alone could produce true faith, but it was highly popular nonetheless. At times it took on a distinctly Calvinist hue, as when Stubbe argued that 'Faith is the gift of God, and no man comes unto the Son but whom the Father draws'.[92] Elsewhere, tolerationists argued that people would believe whatever they found convincing, and that no amount of force could change their belief. Samuel Richardson doubted 'Whether it be in the power of any man to believe what he will, as he will', since 'the mind of man being persuaded with great reasons, is captivated, will he, nill he'.[93] Walwyn agreed, arguing that 'what judgment soever a man is, he cannot chuse but be of that judgement', and that because belief was involuntary it should not be punished, 'for punishment is the recompence of voluntary actions'. And punishing people for believing falsely would be doubly cruel given that 'it is misery enough to want the comfort of true beleeving'.[94]

Because it was not within the power of the individual to believe something contrary to his own convictions, moreover, persecution would simply produce hypocrites. Henry Stubbe believed that 'Force, and Terrour may bring men to an outward complyance but not alter their judgments, it doth not abate their wickedness, but heightens it with the aggravation of hypocrisy'. The forcibly converted 'new Christians' of Spain and Portugal were a case in point. 'To believe what appears untrue, seems to me impossible', concluded Stubbe: 'To professe what we believe untrue, I am sure, is damnable.'[95] Forced conversion actually worsened the converted person's standing before a God who demanded pure and sincere worship.

John Plamenatz once observed that liberty of conscience was 'first asserted and cherished in an age of strong beliefs. It was first asserted among peoples who adhered, as the Greeks and Romans did not, to dogmatic religions, among peoples who had been taught for centuries that nothing was more important than to have the right beliefs.' He suggested that though this stress on the importance of right beliefs was the source of fanaticism and persecution, it was also the source of a new conception of freedom. Because of the division of Christendom in the early modern period, one proposition ('Faith is supremely important, and therefore all men must have the one true faith') gradually gave way to another ('Faith is supremely important, and therefore every man must be allowed to live by the faith which seems true to him'). 'Liberty of conscience was born', Plamenatz concludes, 'not of indifference, not of scepticism, not of mere open-mindedness, but of faith.'[96]

Political and economic arguments

But if theological and philosophical arguments were at the forefront of the case for civil tolerance, its exponents were also convinced that their policy made sense for practical reasons. Prudential considerations – both political and economic – reinforced the case from Christian principle. Tolerationists wanted to demonstrate that, contrary to conventional assumption, religious uniformity was not an essential prerequisite of political stability. Andrew Marvell mocked Samuel Parker's 'Push-pin Divinity', which assumed that if a pin was pulled out of the national church the state would immediately totter. 'There is nothing more natural', wrote Marvell, 'than for the Ivy to be of the Opinion that the Oak cannot stand without its support.'[97] On this view, the loss of religious uniformity was not a calamity. Indeed, a frank acknowledgement of diversity could form the basis for peace and prosperity.

The prudential arguments for toleration were rarely presented more cleverly than by Richard Overton in *The Arraignement of Mr Persecution* (1645). The witnesses for the prosecution of 'Mr Persecution' included Mr Unity-of-Kingdomes, Mr Nationall-Strength, Mr Setled-Peace, Mr United Provinces, Mr Desolate-Germany, Mr Publique-Good, Mr Nationall-Wealth, and Mr Domestick-Miseries.[98] By 1645, his readers would have understood his point immediately. European nations had been racked by decades of religious wars, culminating in the Thirty Years War (1618–48) and the English Civil War (1642–6). Instead of underpinning national unity and prosperity, policies of religious uniformity had resulted in seemingly intractable conflict and destruction. In 1649, the Baptist Henry Danvers asked: 'Are not most of the wars now in the world grounded upon or for Religion?'[99] By the mid-seventeenth century, the question was becoming rhetorical.

Ironically, persecutors still seemed oblivious to the implications of Danvers's question. They continued to complain bitterly about the subversive potential of religious nonconformists, but they were blind to the fact that their own policy was the cause of their problems. No one made this point more forcefully than John Locke. Locke acknowledged that religious dissenters could be seditious – he himself may well have had first-hand knowledge of Dissenter plots – but he blamed their sedition on government repression:

> For if men enter into Seditious Conspiracies, tis not Religion that inspires them to it in their Meetings; but their Sufferings and Oppressions that make them willing to ease themselves. Just and moderate Governments are every where quiet, every where safe. But Oppression raises Ferments, and makes men struggle to cast off an uneasie and tyrannical Yoke.

The solution to the problem was simple: 'let those Dissenters enjoy but the same Privileges in Civils as his other Subjects, and he will quickly find that these Religious Meetings will no longer be dangerous'. As we saw earlier, Locke was not simply thinking of Protestant Dissenters; he envisaged a society in which Jews, Muslims and pagans would enjoy full civil rights.[100] Roger Williams was equally radical, arguing that the 'experience in many flourishing cities and kingdoms of the world' demonstrated that Jews, Muslims, Catholics and pagans could be 'peaceable and quiet subjects, loving and helpful neighbours, fair and just dealers, true and loyal to the civil government'.[101]

Williams was speaking from experience: he had lived with American Indians, and written sympathetically about their language and culture.[102] Other tolerationists did not share his cross-cultural experience, but many of them did think globally. As one Quaker petition put it, if magistrates could only persecute because they were *believers*, they were building dominion on grace and contradicting Christ's teaching on Christian gentleness; but if magistrates could persecute simply because they were *magistrates*, then heathen rulers were within their rights in coercing Christians.[103] The practical effect of defending persecution in England was to encourage persecution elsewhere. Mark Goldie has described this as 'the Alpine argument' against persecution. Since 'truth' was different on the other side of the Alps, tolerationists argued, defenders of coercion were simply providing a licence for all magistrates to impose whatever religion they conceived to be 'true'.[104] 'If the true Religion establish it self alone in some states, by forcing men to subject to it', wrote Samuel Fisher, 'it gives a bad example to false religions in other states, that they think themselves in the right, to do the like.' It only took a moment's thought to realise that if the principle of religious uniformity was universally applied, the odds were 'ten thousand to nothing' against the true religion being the one that benefited. It made far more sense to encourage magistrates everywhere to permit religious diversity in their territory.[105]

Societies which tolerated religious pluralism, after all, were viable and peaceful. Even the Old Testament demonstrated that this was so, for the patriarchs and later Israelites had resided quietly among pagans and idolaters in Canaan, Egypt and Babylon.[106] Some tolerationists even claimed that there was 'liberty of Religion' in Israel itself, since resident aliens worshipped in the temple according to different ceremonies than the Jews, and were not required to obey the law of Moses. In the time of Christ, moreover, Palestine had accommodated a multitude of sects enjoying peaceful coexistence, including Pharisees, Sadducees, Scribes and Essenes (the separatists of their day).[107] And in the contemporary world, the Netherlands, Poland, Transylvania and (for most of the century) France could be cited as pluralistic nations which were not disintegrating.

Indeed, one could go further. Tolerant nations were also economically prosperous. 'Behold the Nations where freedome of Religion is permitted', declared the General Baptist Helwys, 'and you may see there are not more florishinge and prosperous Nations under the heavens then they are.'[108] Helwys knew what he was talking about, for he had spent some time in the Netherlands before returning to England. Other tolerationists – including Burnet and Locke – had also lived in the Dutch republic, and its combination of religious pluralism and economic prosperity was one of the strongest cards they had to play. The Dutch example was particularly powerful because toleration had undermined neither the Protestant character of the society nor its military security. As William Walwyn pointed out, 'the Spaniard will witnesse for [the Dutch] that they unite sufficiently in the defence of their common liberties and opposition of their common enemies'.[109]

But as well as pointing to flourishing pluralistic states, tolerationists could also appeal to the statements of famous rulers. This was particularly useful, because they wanted to convince English magistrates that toleration was not just the hare-brained notion of eccentric sectarians, but a practical policy for hard-headed political rulers. John Murton cited the King of Bohemia: 'men's consciences ought in no sort to be violated, urged or constrained'. He also quoted Stephen, King of Poland: 'I am a king of men, not of consciences; a commander of bodies, not of souls.'[110] James I was another favourite. His statement to Parliament in 1609 that 'God loves not to plant his church by violence and bloodshed' was repeated countless times, along with a later declaration that 'it was usually the condition of Christians to be persecuted, but not to persecute'. In 1661 a Quaker pamphlet cleverly drew on Charles I's *Eikon Basilike*, in which the late king lamented the cruelty men practised 'under the colour of Religion', and confessed that God was 'the onely King of men Consciences'.[111]

The wise remarks of political rulers reinforced the prudential argument. Practical wisdom suggested that religious persecution was quite absurd. Its perpetrators always maintained an outrageous double standard, crying out against monstrous persecution when they were 'under the hatches', but employing it with relish on 'coming to the helm'.[112] They always justified this behaviour on the grounds that their religion was the true one, of course, but so did their opponents. As Jeremy Taylor pointed out, 'If he [the persecutor] says that he is to be spared because he believes true, but the other was justly persecuted because he was in error, he is ridiculous. For he is as confidently believed to be a heretic as he believes his adversary such.'[113] Such blinkered ethics led to endless power manoeuvring as competing religious confessions battled to get magistrates on their side. In Tudor England, for example, the monarchy had oscillated wildly between Catholicism and Protestantism under Henry VIII and his three children, and a vicious circle of persecution and counter-persecution had ensued.[114] Only by accepting a reciprocity principle – of doing unto others what you would have them do to you – could Europeans find a way out of their predicament. Christ's Golden Rule made good political sense.

By the second half of the seventeenth century, tolerationist arguments were themselves making sense to an increasing number of intellectuals and politicians. Whereas 'reason of state' had traditionally pointed towards the necessity of religious unity, it began to favour religious toleration, as contemporaries observed the flourishing condition of pluralistic cities and nations.[115] Yet because the tolerationist outlook ultimately prevailed, we tend to exaggerate its influence during the seventeenth century. In the following chapters, we will see that throughout our period support for toleration was always a minority affair.

Notes

1   Roger Williams, *The Bloudy Tenent of Persecution*, ed. E. B. Underhill (London, 1848), p. 162.

2   John Locke, *A Letter concerning Toleration*, ed. J. Tully (Indianapolis, 1983), p. 30.

3   See L. McBeth, *English Baptist Literature on Religious Liberty to 1689* (New York, 1980), ch. 1; and T. George, 'Between pacificism and coercion: the English Baptist doctrine of religious toleration', *Mennonite Quarterly Review* 58 (1984), 30–49.

4   The tolerationist pamphlets of 1644 are surveyed in W. Haller, *Liberty and Reformation in the Puritan Revolution* (New York, 1955), ch. 5.

5   For overviews of the various stages of the toleration debate see W. K. Jordan, *The Development of Religious Toleration in England*, 4 vols (1932–40), III, pp. 17–266; A. A. Seaton, *The Theory of Toleration under the Later Stuarts* (Cambridge, 1911), ch. 3. For detailed studies of particular episodes see C. Polizzotto, 'Liberty of conscience and the Whitehall debates of 1648–49', *Journal of Ecclesiastical History* 26 (1975), 69–82; C. Polizzotto, 'The campaign against "The Humble Proposals" of 1652', *Journal of Ecclesiastical History* 38 (1987), 569–81; A. Woolrych, 'Introduction', in *Complete Prose Works of John Milton*, gen. ed. D. Wolffe, 8 vols (New Haven, CN, 1953–82), I, pp. 1–228; G. S. De Krey, 'Rethinking the Restoration: Dissenting cases for conscience, 1667–72', *Historical Journal* 38 (1995), 53–83; M. Goldie, 'John Locke, Jonas Proast and religious toleration, 1688–1692', in J. Walsh, C. Haydon and S. Taylor, eds, *The Church of England, c.1689–c.1833* (Cambridge, 1993).

6   See Seaton, *The Theory of Toleration under the Later Stuarts*, ch. 5.

7   J. Delumeau, *Sin and Fear: The Emergence of a Western Guilt Culture 13th–18th Centuries* (New York, 1990), pp. 259–65.

8   *A Relation of the Death of the Primitive Persecutors . . . by Lactantius*, tr. G. Burnet (1687), pp. 31–3.

9   G. Adams, *The Huguenots and French Opinion 1685–1787: The Enlightenment Debate on Toleration* (Waterloo, ONT, 1991), ch. 2.

10   See T. Lyon, *The Theory of Religious Liberty in England, 1603–39* (Cambridge, 1937); Jordan, *The Development of Religious Toleration in England*, II, *passim*.

11   On Walwyn's relationship to Puritanism see L. Mulligan, 'The religious roots of William Walwyn's radicalism', *Journal of Religious History* 12 (1982), 162–79.

12   See J. Coffey, 'Puritanism and liberty revisited: the case for toleration in the English Revolution', *Historical Journal* 41 (1998), 961–85; *idem*, 'Restoration Quakers and the theology of tolerance', *Q/W/E/R/T/Y: Arts, Litteratures & Civilisations du Monde Anglophone* 8 (1998), 231–9.

13   See R. Popkin, 'The Deist challenge', in O. P. Grell, J. Israel and N. Tyacke, eds, *From Persecution to Toleration* (Oxford, 1989), ch. 8.

14   I. Bejczy, ' "Tolerantia": a medieval concept', *Journal of the History of Ideas* 58 (1997), 365–84, quotation from 365.

15   See G. Schochet, 'John Locke and religious toleration', in L. G. Schwoerer, *The Revolution of 1688–89* (Cambridge, 1992), p. 150.

16   Quotation from H. Oberman, *The Roots of Anti-Semitism in the Age of Renaissance and Reformation* (Philadelphia, 1984), p. 38. See also Bejczy, ' "Tolerantia" ', 376–82.

17   See *Luther and Calvin on Secular Authority*, ed. H. Hopfl (Cambridge, 1991), pp. 12–13, 23–31.

18   See M. Holt, *The French Wars of Religion, 1562–1629* (Cambridge, 1995), pp. 109, 162–72; Q. Skinner, *The Foundations of Modern Political Thought*, 2 vols (Cambridge, 1978), II, pp. 249–54.

19   See J. Lecler, *Toleration and the Reformation*, 2 vols (London, 1960). On Coornhert see M. van Gelderen, *The Political Thought of the Dutch Revolt* (Cambridge, 1992), ch. 6.

20   See J. Israel, 'Toleration in seventeenth-century Dutch and English thought', in S. Groenveld and M. Wintle, eds, *The Exchange of Ideas: Religion, Scholarship and Art in Anglo-Dutch Relations in the Seventeenth Century* (Zutphen, 1994), pp. 16–21.

21   Israel, 'Toleration in seventeenth-century Dutch and English thought', p. 23.

22   *The Works of the Most Reverend Dr John Tillotson*, 3 vols (London, 1717), pp. 228, 321.

23   See K. Campbell, *The Intellectual Struggle of the English Papists in the Seventeenth Century* (Lewiston, NY, 1986), ch. 6.

24   Reprinted in D. Mullan, *Religious Pluralism in the West: An Anthology* (Oxford, 1998), pp. 329–40. Even this document was the subject of controversy, as shown by O. Chadwick, *The Church in the Cold War* (London, 1992), pp. 119–21.

25   B. S. Tinsley, 'Sozzini's ghost: Pierre Bayle and Socinian toleration', *Journal of the History of Ideas* 57 (1996), 619.

26 See W. Nihenhuis, 'Calvin's life and work in the light of the idea of toler-
    ance', in his *Ecclesia Reformata: Studies on the Reformation* (Leiden, 1972),
    pp. 126–9; Acontius, *Satan's Stratagems* (London, 1648), pp. 100–3.

27 See Jordan, *The Development of Religious Toleration in England*, III, pp. 425–35.

28 Milton, *Areopagitica* (1644) and *A Treatise of Civil Power in Ecclesiastical Causes*
    (1659), in M. W. Wallace, ed., *Milton's Prose* (London, 1925), pp. 320, 426;
    and *Of True Religion, Haeresie, Schism, Toleration* in *Complete Prose Works of John
    Milton*, VIII, pp. 429–32.

29 C. Wolseley, *Liberty of Conscience* (1668), p. 14.

30 See, for example, H. Oberman, 'The travail of tolerance: containing chaos
    in early modern Europe', in O. P. Grell and R. Scribner, eds, *Tolerance and
    Intolerance in the European Reformation* (Cambridge, 1995), pp. 14–17.

31 Locke, *A Letter concerning Toleration*, pp. 49–51, 54, 46.

32 Thomas Helwys, *The Mistery of Iniquity* (1612), p. 69.

33 Williams, *The Bloudy Tenent of Persecution*, p. 2.

34 George Fox, *Doctrinals*, pp. 234–5, quoted in W. C. Braithwaite, *The Second
    Period of Quakerism*, 2nd edn (Cambridge, 1961), p. 19.

35 Williams, *The Examiner Defended* (1652), in *The Complete Writings of Roger Williams*,
    7 vols (New York, 1963), VII, p. 243.

36 Locke, *A Letter concerning Toleration*, p. 54.

37 *The Writings of William Walwyn*, ed. J. McMichael and B. Taft (Athens,
    GA, 1989), p. 164; Wildman's speech at the Whitehall debates in A. S. P.
    Woodhouse, ed., *Puritanism and Liberty* (London, 1938), p. 161; Thomas
    Collier, *A Generall Epistle* (1648), p. 78.

38 Collier, *A Decision and Clearance* (1659), p. 15.

39 Henry More, *An Explanation of the Grand Mystery of Godliness* (1660), quoted
    from Mullan, ed., *Religious Pluralism in the West*, p. 159.

40 Richard Overton, *The Arraignement of Mr Persecution* (1645), pp. 32–3.

41 C. Russell, 'Arguments for religious unity in England, 1530–1650', *Journal of
    Ecclesiastical History* 18 (1967), 211.

42 J. Rawls, *A Theory of Justice* (1971), pp. 215–16.

43 Locke, *A Letter concerning Toleration*, p. 26.

44 Williams, *The Bloudy Tenent*, pp. 214, 46.

45 Samuel Fisher, *Christianismus Redivivus* (1655), p. 537.

46 L. Sanneh, *The Crown and the Turban: Muslims and West African Pluralism* (Boul-
    der, CO, 1997), pp. 206–11.

47 See, for example, the otherwise stimulating book by R. Vernon, *The Career of Toleration: John Locke, Jonas Proast, and After* (Toronto, 1997).

48 See R. Ashcraft, 'Religion and Lockean natural rights', in I. Bloom, J. P. Martin and W. L. Proudfoot, eds, *Religious Diversity and Human Rights* (New York, 1996), pp. 195–209; and J. Mitchell, 'John Locke and the theological foundation of liberal toleration', *Review of Politics* 52 (1990), 64–83.

49 Edmund Ludlow, 'A Voyce from the Watch Tower', Bodleian MSS Eng.hist.c.487, ff. 1194–5.

50 See, for example, the General Baptist John Murton's *An Humble Supplication*, in E. B. Underhill, ed., *Tracts on Liberty of Conscience, 1614–61* (London, 1846), p. 215.

51 See, for example, Thomas Helwys, *Objections Answered* (1615), p. 6.

52 See R. Bainton, 'The parable of the tares as the proof text for religious liberty to the end of the sixteenth century', *Church History* 1 (1932), 67–89.

53 Overton, *The Arraignement of Mr Persecution*, pp. 14–15.

54 Henry Robinson, *Liberty of Conscience* (1644), pp. 16–17.

55 William Penn, *The Peace of Europe, the Fruits of Solitude, and other Writings*, ed. E. B. Bronner (London, 1993), p. 162.

56 See, for example, Murton, *An Humble Supplication*, pp. 202–3.

57 Jeremy Taylor, *The Liberty of Prophesying* (1647), pp. 18–20.

58 Wolseley, *Liberty of Conscience*, pp. 18–19.

59 *A Relation of the Death of the Primitive Persecutors*, tr. Burnet, pp. 27–30.

60 Ludlow, 'A Voyce from the Watch Tower', f. 1200.

61 Williams, *Bloudy Tenent*, p. 154.

62 Helwys, *Objections Answered*, preface.

63 *A Relation of the Death of the Primitive Persecutors*, tr. Burnet, pp. 23–5.

64 Ibid., tr. Burnet, p. 44.

65 Fisher, *Christianismus Redivivus*, p. 545.

66 Williams, *The Bloudy Tenent*, p. 317.

67 Robinson, *Liberty of Conscience*, p. 13.

68 Williams, *The Bloudy Tenent*, p. 278.

69 John Lilburne, *A Copie of A Letter to Mr William Prinne Esq* (1645), p. 3.

70 Thomas Collier, *The Exaltation of Christ* (1646), pp. 93–111, quotes at p. 109.

71 *A Relation of the Death of the Primitive Persecutors*, tr. Burnet, p. 19.

72   Locke, *A Letter concerning Toleration*, p. 44.

73   Samuel Richardson, *An Answer to the London Ministers Letter* (1648), p. 31.

74   *Complete Prose Works of John Milton*, II, pp. 549–53.

75   W. Dell, *Select Works* (London, 1773), p. 65.

76   See G. F. Nuttall, *The Holy Spirit in Puritan Faith and Experience* (1946: Chicago, 1992), pp. 113–17.

77   Fisher, *Christianismus Redivivus*, p. 547.

78   Robinson, *Liberty of Conscience*, p. 61.

79   [John Sturgion], *A Plea for Toleration* (1660), p. 329.

80   Overton, *The Arraignement of Mr Persecution*, p. 24.

81   For a critique of those who have exaggerated Locke's scepticism, see Vernon, *John Locke, Jonas Proast, and After*, ch. 3.

82   See A. Levine, H. Mansfield and T. Mahoney, eds, *Early Modern Skepticism and the Origins of Toleration* (Lexington, 1999).

83   R. Popkin, 'Skepticism about religion and millenarian dogmatism: two sources of toleration in the seventeenth century', in J. Laursen and C. Nederman, eds, *Beyond the Persecuting Society: Religious Toleration before the Enlightenment* (Philadelphia, 1998), pp. 232–50, quotations at pp. 245, 242.

84   See R. Tuck, 'Scepticism and toleration in the seventeenth century', in S. Mendus, ed., *Justifying Toleration* (Cambridge, 1988), pp. 21–35.

85   See R. Popkin, *The History of Scepticism from Erasmus to Spinoza* (Berkeley, CA, 1979), ch. 7.

86   J. Kilcullen, *Sincerity and Truth: Essays on Arnauld, Bayle, and Toleration* (Oxford, 1988), p. 77 n. 92.

87   Richardson, *An Answer to the London Ministers Letter*, p. 31.

88   William Chillingworth, *The Religion of Protestants*, in his *Works*, 3 vols (Oxford, 1838), I, pp. 214–16.

89   *The Correspondence of John Locke*, ed. E. S. Beer, 8 vols (Oxford, 1978–), VI, p. 495.

90   Lilburne, *A Copie of A Letter*, pp. 4–5, 7.

91   Milton, *Of True Religion, Haeresie, Schism, Toleration*, in *Complete Prose Works of John Milton*, VIII, pp. 423–4.

92   Henry Stubbe, *An Essay in Defence of the Good Old Cause* (1659), p. 35.

93   Samuel Richardson, *The Necessity of Toleration in Matters of Religion* (1647), p. 263.

94 *The Writings of William Walwyn*, pp. 103, 274.

95 Stubbe, *An Essay in Defence of the Good Old Cause*, pp. 32–3, 38.

96 John Plamenatz, *Man and Society*, 2 vols (London, 1963), I, p. 50.

97 A. Marvell, *The Rehearsal Transpos'd* (London, 1672), pp. 132–3.

98 Overton, *The Arraignement of Mr Persecution*, pp. 4–6.

99 Henry Danvers, *Certain Quaeries concerning Liberty of Conscience* (1649), p. 3.

100 Locke, *A Letter concerning Toleration*, pp. 52, 54.

101 Williams, *Bloudy Tenent*, p. 112.

102 Roger Williams, *A Key into the Language of America* (1643).

103 *Liberty of Conscience Asserted* (1661), p. 5.

104 M. Goldie, 'Review of R. Vernon, *The Career of Toleration*', *Locke Newsletter* 29 (1998), 175–80.

105 Fisher, *Christianismus Redivivus*, p. 546.

106 Overton, *The Arraignement of Mr Persecution*, p. 31.

107 *A Letter to a Member of this Present Parliament, for Liberty of Conscience* (1668), pp. 4–6.

108 Helwys, *Objections Answered*, p. 31.

109 *The Compassionate Samaritan*, in *The Writings of William Walwyn*, pp. 114–15.

110 Murton, *An Humble Supplication*, pp. 216–17.

111 *Liberty of Conscience Asserted*, p. 7.

112 Williams, *Bloudy Tenent*, p. 174.

113 Taylor, *Liberty of Prophesying*, p. 517.

114 Williams, *Bloudy Tenent*, pp. 107–8.

115 See Grell, Israel and Tyacke, eds, *From Persecution to Toleration*, p. 7.

CHAPTER 4

Elizabeth I and Protestant Uniformity, 1558–1603

Persecution in England before 1558

When it came to persecution, Tudor England was exceptional.[1] In much of Europe, heresy trials and executions had ground to a halt in the mid-fifteenth century, with the crushing of the Albigensians and the containment of the Waldensians. Heresy burnings only restarted again in the 1520s. In England, however, there was no such lull. The first heretics to be burned in England were Albigensians put to death in 1210, but England also had its own home-grown heretical movement, Lollardy. Inspired by the teachings of John Wycliffe (c.1329–84), the Lollards rejected many of the doctrines and practices of the late medieval church in the name of biblical religion. The government responded to the growth of their movement by passing the statute *de haeretico comburendo* (on burning heretics) in 1401. The first Lollard martyr, William Sawtre, was burned in the same year, but the number of Lollards executed during the fifteenth century was relatively low. However, in the decades leading up to the early English Reformation, persecution of Lollards intensified, with hundreds being hauled before the courts and a number being burned at the stake.[2]

Yet what made the English situation even more unusual was the fact that during the reign of Henry VIII, Catholics were executed for defending papal supremacy over the English church. Ironically, the Pope had conferred the title 'Defender of the Faith' on Henry in the 1520s for his writings against Luther, but when the king broke with Rome over the annulment of his marriage with Catherine of Aragon, he declared himself Supreme Head of the English church. A number of Catholics who denied his supremacy were executed, including Sir Thomas More. William Monter has written that 'No Protestant state, and no European ruler except the Anglo-Catholic "Defender of the Faith" ever threatened to behead his subjects for defending the Pope's claim to be head of the church'.[3] There were, however, Catholic martyrs in the Netherlands, where Brad Gregory tells us that 'around 130 Catholic priests perished between 1567 and 1591, with the peak in 1572'. But in contrast to the English Catholics, who were 'judicially tried and put to death for treason', the Dutch Catholic martyrs were either massacred or hanged without a formal trial.[4] Bizarrely, Henry engaged in a 'murderous ecumenism', beheading Catholics for treason and burning Protestants for heresy. On a single day in July 1540, for example, he executed three papalists and three Protestants.[5]

During the brief reign of Edward VI (1547–53), however, England moved decisively in the direction of the Reformed faith. Archbishop Cranmer drew up a new liturgy for the church, embodied in the Prayer Books of 1549 and 1552, and produced the Forty-Two Articles, defining the church's new doctrinal stance. These documents were largely incorporated into the 1559 Book of Common Prayer and the Thirty-Nine Articles of 1563. Persecution declined sharply under Edward, but it did not cease. The new regime was no friend of religious pluralism. Cranmer made this crystal clear in his address to the boy king at his coronation: 'Your Majesty is God's vice-regent and Christ's vicar within your own dominions, and to see with your predecessor Josiah, God truly worshipped, and idolatry destroyed, the tyranny of the Bishops of Rome banished from your subjects, and images removed.'[6] Like the godly kings of Old Testament Israel, Edward was to ensure the monopoly of pure religion by purging the land of religious corruption. The Acts of Uniformity of 1549 and 1552 were intended to begin this process of compulsory reform. They demanded observance of the new liturgy in all parishes, exempting only a few foreign Protestant 'Stranger Churches' from this requirement. The 1549 Act threatened parish clergy who refused to comply with the loss of a year's income and six months' imprisonment. A second offence would result in deprivation and a year's imprisonment, and a third offence would be punished by a life sentence. Those who spoke against the Book would be subject to the same penalties. The 1552 Act went even further, for although it only imposed ecclesiastical punishments for non-attendance at church, it declared that anyone who attended other forms of service would be subject to imprisonment. If deviation was not permissible inside the church, it was not permissible outside it either.

The practice of the Edwardian regime demonstrated that these were not idle paper threats, for both conservative and radical opponents of the new liturgy were imprisoned for their nonconformity. Conservative bishops like Stephen Gardiner and Edmund Bonner who refused to conform to the new church were deprived of their sees and imprisoned. Protestant nonconformists like John Hooper suffered the same fate; despite being a bishop-elect, Hooper was confined in the Fleet prison along with two conservative bishops until he had agreed to wear the officially prescribed clerical dress. Yet Hooper got off lightly in comparison to radical Protestant heretics. In 1550, Cranmer persuaded Edward to sanction the burning of the influential Joan Bocher for her heretical teachings about the nature of Christ. In the following year, a Flemish heretic, George van Parris, was also burned at the stake.[7] These were the only executions for heresy in Edward's reign, but they showed that magisterial Protestants had no objection in principle to the execution of heretics. Although they preceded the burning of Servetus in Geneva by several years, they were overshadowed by it, so much so that one historian has claimed that Servetus was 'the first person ever to be burned as a heretic on the authority of a reformed church'.[8] In reality, the intolerance of Calvin's Geneva was matched by Protestant England.

Yet Edward's persecution paled beside that of his Catholic sister, Mary I (1553–8). Guided by her zeal for Catholicism and hatred of heresy, Mary launched a persecution of ferocious intensity. In the face of it, almost 800 Protestants fled to continental Europe for refuge. In 1554, Parliament passed an act that revived three medieval statutes against heretics.[9] The act came into force in January 1555, and on 4 February, the Protestant divine John Rogers was burned alive at Smithfield for 'heretical pravity and execrable doctrine'. Within the space of three and a half years, almost 300 Protestants were to suffer the same fate.

In order to comprehend the Marian persecution better, we need to place it in a broader context. Early modern governments shared few of our modern inhibitions about capital punishment, and the death penalty was regularly meted out for a wide range of crimes. In Elizabeth's reign, 700 people were sentenced to death for participating in the Northern Rebellion, though many had their sentences commuted. In Jacobean London, an average of at least 140 felons was executed each year. During the entire Tudor period, there were perhaps 600–1200 executions per year, and in the century from 1530 to 1630 it has been estimated that 'a total of perhaps 75,000 people may have met their deaths on the gallows'. Philip Jenkins has calculated that if the modern United States had the same capital punishment rate as Tudor England, it would execute no fewer than 46,000 people per year. 'It is remarkable', he writes, 'that such endemic slaughter has been so little mentioned in accounts of sixteenth- and seventeenth-century England.'[10] Indeed, in view of the frequency of capital punishment and the horror with which heresy was regarded, it is perhaps surprising that so few heretics were executed.

Some historians have gone further and argued that the Marian executions were not unusual when compared to other instances of religious persecution in early modern Europe. Robert Tittler, for example, writes that 'some 290 martyrs in four years seems a small number compared with the thousands slaughtered in the name of some version of the "true faith" in nearly all other parts of Europe, including Scotland, in the same period'.[11] It is certainly true that the capital punishment of heretics was widely accepted in the period, not least by those who were themselves executed for heresy. Even at his trial, the Marian martyr John Philpot could tell his inquisitor that Joan Bocher, who had been burned under Edward, was 'a vain woman (I knew her well), and a heretic indeed, well worthy to be burnt'.[12] Yet Tittler misleads us by comparing the Marian executions to 'the thousands slaughtered' in religious wars and massacres. Approximately 5000 French Protestants were butchered by Catholics in the wake of the St Bartholomew's Day massacre in 1572, but this was killing by crowds, not judicial execution by the state. If William Monter's estimates are accurate, the Marian persecution accounts for almost 10 per cent of the heresy executions in Latin Christendom between 1520 and 1565. In terms of intensity Mary's campaign was almost unparalleled; in few other cases were so many heretics legally executed in such a short space of time. As G. R. Elton once noted, even by contemporary standards the Marian persecution was 'exceptionally bloody'.[13] The four years of Mary's persecution rank alongside the terrible first decade of the Spanish Inquisition when hundreds of *conversos* were burned for heresy, and the period during the late 1520s and 1530s when hundreds of Anabaptists were put to death in Austria and the Low Countries.

The ferocity of the Marian persecution played into the hands of Protestant apologists. Ever since John Foxe, Protestant historians have juxtaposed the fury of 'Bloody Mary' with the clemency of her siblings, Edward and Elizabeth. At one level the contrast holds up well, for the 300 heresy executions in Mary's reign dwarf those under the Protestant monarchs: only two radicals were executed for heresy under Edward and merely half-a-dozen in the 45 years of Elizabeth's rule. But the contrast between Protestant lenience and Catholic brutality should not be overdrawn. All Tudor governments were committed to a policy of religious uniformity, and had few qualms about employing some form of coercion against those who stepped out of line.

Elizabeth

The accession of Elizabeth, however, did bring a temporary halt to large-scale persecution. The new queen was acclaimed as the contemporary equivalent of Deborah, the female ruler who had delivered the people of Israel from their oppressors. In its first great act of Parliament, the Act of Supremacy (1559), her government repealed the heresy laws revived by Mary.[14]

In stark contrast to her sister, Elizabeth was no religious zealot. As the daughter of Anne Boleyn, she had been given a humanist and mildly Protestant education. Her Protestantism was closer to the evangelical Lutheranism of the 1530s than to the more radical Calvinism that became all the rage among reformers in the 1550s. Although she faithfully attended worship and listened to hundreds of Protestant sermons, Elizabeth's piety was conventional rather than zealous. Under Mary, she had conformed and regularly heard mass. In her own reign, she found herself out of step with her bishops, and even with leading ministers like Burghley, Leicester and Walsingham. These men wished for a more radical break with the Catholic past than did the queen. Her bishops were shocked at her disapproval of clerical marriage, her lack of enthusiasm for the preaching ministry, her habit of swearing 'by God's soul', and her devotion to the crucifix. She was, says Patrick Collinson, 'an odd sort of Protestant'.[15]

The character of Elizabeth's faith helps to explain her own particular blend of tolerance and intolerance. Her religious conservatism makes it easier to see why her government was so lenient to Catholics in the first decade of her reign. Elizabeth was no firebrand intent on purging England of all remnants of popery; she wanted to coax her people from Catholicism to a mild and traditional form of Protestantism. After all, she is famed for saying that she did not like 'to make windows into men's souls'. These were actually the words of Francis Bacon, and they were followed by a crucial rider: 'except the abundance of them [men's secret thoughts] did overflow into overt and express acts and affirmations . . . in impugning and impeaching advisedly and maliciously her Majesty's supreme power, and maintaining and extolling a foreign jurisdiction'.[16] In other words, people could think whatever they liked just so long as they kept it to themselves; to propagate one's beliefs, or to reject the royal supremacy and affirm papal authority, was to incur the queen's wrath. Elizabeth found it hard to tolerate zealous and loud-mouthed nonconformists, precisely because her personal religion was so much quieter. She was a stickler for conformity, and was infuriated by Catholic recusants and Puritan critics. She herself had had the good grace to conform under Mary, and she found it hard to understand why others would not do likewise under her.

Conformity was at the heart of the religious settlement of 1559. It was drawn up on the assumption that both the true Protestant religion and a particular form of worship had to be imposed on the entire nation, without exception. Although W. K. Jordan made the bizarre claim that the settlement was 'a long step towards toleration',[17] Joel Hurstfield was quite right to insist that Elizabeth and her chief ministers were decidedly hostile to such a policy. Lord Burghley expressed the official view when he declared that the 'state cold never be in safety where there was tolleration of two religions. For there is no enmytie so greate as that for religion, and they that differ in the service of God can never agree in the service of theire Contrie.'[18]

To avoid this enmity, the new regime passed an Act of Uniformity in 1559. As Hans Hillerbrand has observed, 'the point of departure [for persecuting regimes] was always a legal act that one might call a "uniformity" statute'.[19] The Elizabethan Act declared that priests who 'wilfully or obstinately . . . use any other rite, ceremony, order, form or manner' of communion or divine service would suffer certain penalties: for the first offence, those with a benefice would forfeit it for one year and receive six months' imprisonment; for the second, they would get one year's imprisonment and deprivation; and for the third, deprivation and imprisonment for life. Laypersons who spoke out against the new prayer book or tried to disrupt parish services would be fined for their first two offences, and imprisoned for life for a third. Finally, and in contrast to the 1552 Edwardian Act of Uniformity, those who failed to attend their parish service on a Sunday or a holy day would be subject to a 12 pence fine for every case of non-attendance.[20]

The Royal Injunctions of 1559 confirmed the government's goal: 'the advancement of the true honor of Almighty God, the suppression of superstition through all her highness realm and dominions, and to plant true religion to the extirpation of all hypocrisy, enormities, and abuses'. After reminding readers of divine intolerance – the 'great threatenings and maledictions of God' against idolatry and superstition – the Injunctions went on to command the queen's subjects to 'take away, utterly extinct, and destroy all shrines, covering of shrines, all tables, candlesticks, trindles, and rolls of wax, pictures, paintings, all other monuments of feigned miracles, pilgrimages, idolatry, and superstition, so that there remain no memory of the same in walls, glasses, window, or elsewhere within their churches or houses'. The outlawing of traditional forms of Catholic worship even within private houses was reiterated elsewhere in the Injunctions;[21] it is a stark reminder of how draconian religious uniformity was in theory, for it not only ruled out a diversity of practices within the church and prohibited the establishment of alternative churches, it also denied the queen's subjects private space in which to pursue voluntarily alternative forms of worship. On paper, the Elizabethan settlement was anything but tolerant.

In practice, too, 1559 was marked by the typical rites of sixteenth-century religious dogmatism. A new wave of iconoclasm hit the country. In various places, popish images were not simply removed from parish churches, they were destroyed. As Margaret Aston explains:

Large bonfires in the capital once again advertised the arrival of a reformist regime. St Bartholomew's day, 1559, was celebrated with great blazes in St Paul's churchyard, in Cheapside by Ironmonger Lane and at St Thomas Acon, in which roods with their statues of the Virgin and St John were 'burned with great wonder'; rood-lofts, sepulchres and censers; copes, vestments and altar-cloths; banners, crosses and books. Such fires continued into September, as the royal commissioners in London and elsewhere interpreted their brief as covering the destruction of imagery in general.[22]

The reformers even removed the crucifix from the royal chapel, though Elizabeth soon had it restored. To committed Calvinists this was deeply disturbing, and in 1562 and 1567, unknown iconoclasts destroyed the cross and candlesticks in the chapel, only to find them quickly replaced. Elizabeth disagreed sharply with those who wanted an imageless church and was determined to stop the destruction of 1559. Many of England's parish churches had changed dramatically – images had been removed and walls had been whitewashed.[23] But Elizabeth ensured that iconoclastic teaching never became the law of the land.

Elizabeth's conservative distaste for radical reform matched that of her people. As revisionist historians have demonstrated, the Reformation did not come to town by popular demand, and the pace of religious change was slow. England became a Protestant state in 1559, but it would take decades before its population became a Protestant people. This was partly due to the fact that almost all the early Elizabethan parish clergy had been Catholic priests under Mary. These men often maintained the old ways alongside the new, mixing Latin prayers with the vernacular Prayer Book service, and following certain Catholic rituals. In a fair proportion of England's 9000 parishes, the traditional images, vestments, ornaments and books survived for years. As Alexandra Walsham puts it, 'in many districts, iconoclasm was paradoxically a gradual process'.[24] Committed Protestants were a distinct minority in 1559, and the majority conformed to the new church out of obedience not enthusiasm.[25]

Those who refused to conform were a surprisingly small minority, but they included virtually the entire bench of Marian bishops. Although all these men were removed from their sees for refusing to endorse the Act of Supremacy, none of them suffered the fate of Latimer, Ridley or Cranmer. 'Let us not follow our sister's example', Elizabeth is reported to have said, 'but rather shew that our reformation tendeth to peace, and not to cruelty.' Thus the bishops were treated with some consideration; they were moved from London during an outbreak of plague, allowed to lodge with the new bishops and even permitted to dine together.[26]

The treatment of the Marian bishops set the tone for the first decade of Elizabeth's reign. Although the Act of Uniformity required everyone to attend church, the queen had no intention of resorting to violent means to secure conformity. The theory was that though it would take time, the English people would gradually become attached to the new religion. In most cases, this was just what happened. As Judith Maltby has argued, historians have tended to concentrate on the disaffected and ignore the great mass of 'conformists from conviction', those who grew to respect and even love the Church of England and the Book of Common Prayer.[27] If the tale we are about to tell is one of resistance and repression, we must not forget that the story of Elizabethan religion is also one of compliance and even satisfaction.

Catholics

Resistance and repression, however, did become the norm for England's Catholics.[28] In the 1560s, the government believed that the old faith would gradually wither away when deprived of state support. The level of prosecution for non-attendance at church in the first decade of Elizabeth's reign was patchy, but it is clear that the government was not particularly active in encouraging repression. Parliament was more aggressive, and in 1563 it passed an Act which prescribed severe punishments for those who defended the pope's authority or refused the oath of allegiance. In 1564, the Privy Council ordered an investigation of the religious opinions of JPs, but though this revealed a high proportion of traditionalists and neutrals, there was no purge. In the diocese of York, at least, there was an intensive campaign to root out traditionalist clergy, but the Catholic laity were let off more lightly. In later years, Catholics looked back on the 1560s with nostalgia.

The relative tranquillity of the 1560s was shattered by a series of developments which served to convince the new regime that Catholicism was too dangerous to be left alone. The arrival of the Catholic Mary Queen of Scots in 1568 provided a focus for plots against the Protestant regime; the Northern Rebellion of 1569 was marked by open celebrations of the mass; and the papal bull *Regnans in Excelsis* (1570) suggested that committed Catholics were potential traitors to the crown. Issued by the reactionary Pius V (1566–72), the bull declared that Elizabeth had 'seized the crown and monstrously usurped the place of supreme head of the Church in all England'. It excommunicated Elizabeth, deprived her of 'her pretended title' to the crown, and absolved Catholics from their obligations to the government.[29] English

Catholics were placed in an impossible situation. From this point on, loyalty to Rome became identified with disloyalty to Elizabeth. Instead of fulfilling its intended goal of precipitating the overthrow of the Protestant regime, the bull merely succeeded in provoking greater persecution of Catholics.

The government was particularly worried because by 1570 there was growing evidence of widespread recusancy. Catholicism was not withering away as anticipated, and it was feared that disaffected Catholics could form a fifth column for a foreign Catholic invasion. In reality, the vast majority of Catholics were loyal to the crown,[30] but the actions of militants brought the whole community under suspicion. In 1568 William Allen had founded an English seminary at Douai in the Spanish Netherlands, and from 1574 missionary priests began to arrive in England. They were followed in 1580 by the first Jesuit missionaries, and together they encouraged a more militant attitude, advocating a 'sweeping spiritual apartheid' between true Catholics and corrupt conformists.[31] Although most priests were simply involved in pastoral work among the Catholic community, some were up to their necks in plotting for a Catholic invasion. William Allen and the Jesuit Robert Persons, in particular, were tireless in their efforts to prod the papacy and the Catholic powers towards military action against England's heretical government.[32] The Ridolfi, Throckmorton and Babington plots, together with the far greater threat posed by the Spanish Armada, convinced Elizabeth and her Council that Catholicism constituted the greatest single threat to her regime.

The official reaction to the rising Catholic threat was unequivocal. Between 1571 and 1593, Parliament passed a raft of draconian legislation aimed at Catholic recusants and missionary priests.[33] In 1571 an Act against Papal Bulls made it an act of high treason to import papal bulls, and the Act against Fugitives over the Sea declared that anyone who left England without permission for over six months could be deprived of his lands. Following the arrival of the Jesuits, Parliament passed an Act to Retain the Queen's Majesty's Subjects in their True Obedience (1581). This targeted the missionaries by making it treason to draw English subjects away from their loyalty to the queen or the Church of England, and it also raised the fine for failing to attend Common Prayer for a month from 12d. to a crippling £20. The Act against Jesuits, Seminary Priests and such other like Disobedient Persons (1585) was passed in response to new fears of Catholicism prompted by the assassination of William of Orange in 1584 and the alliance between the Catholic League in France and Philip II. The Act declared that the purpose of the missionaries was 'to stir up and move sedition, rebellion and open hostility within her Highness' realms and dominions, to the great endangering of the safety of her most royal person to the utter ruin, desolation and overthrow of the whole realm'. It became an act of treason simply to be a Jesuit or seminary priest, and even those who sheltered priests were guilty of felony and might be put to death. Of 146 Catholics executed between 1586 and 1603, 123 were indicted under this statute.[34] Finally, the Act against Popish Recusants (1593) determined that convicted adult recusants were to be confined to within a 5-mile radius of their homes. Ironically, this statute was significantly less harsh than the legislation proposed by the government; for once, Parliament was taking a softer line on Catholics than the queen. Yet taken together, the anti-Catholic laws were formidable and frightening.

'On paper', observes Eliot Rose, 'Catholicism ought not to have survived the reign of Elizabeth I.'[35] Yet Catholicism did survive, if only as a small minority. By 1603, it has been estimated, the number of Catholics with access to the ministry of a priest may have been as low as 30,000–40,000 in a total population of around 4 million.[36] Many Catholics chose to avoid prosecution by attending the compulsory Sunday services of their parish church. By doing so, these 'church papists' fulfilled the minimum require-ment of the Elizabethan settlement, and so avoided the shilling fine for playing truant on Sundays and feast days. Their compromises appalled Catholic polemicists, who even tried to shame them by pointing to the stubborn Protestant heretics executed under Mary. Yet church papists made a significant contribution to the Catholic community. Moreover, as Walsham writes, 'Faced with the prospect of imprisonment and impoverishment, per-sisting in overt dissent was a course of action requiring either indomitable courage or fanaticism'.[37]

Such qualities, however, were not in short supply in the Catholic com-munity, and a considerable number did persist in overt dissent. The new legislation suggested that in the long run uncompromising recusants were faced with three unpalatable options: martyrdom, lifelong imprisonment, or exile. Yet in practice, the situation was less drastic. The courts were 'agonis-ingly slow' and the enforcement of the laws varied greatly from region to region. In Lancashire, where Catholics constituted a substantial section of the population, the government depended on the co-operation of recusants and church papists. Elsewhere, local churchwardens and JPs were often less than enthusiastic about prosecuting recusants.[38] Indeed, Wallace MacCaffrey has argued that 'large segments of the ruling classes were more or less indifferent to the internal Catholic menace. They simply failed to per-ceive their recusant neighbours as anything more than eccentrics, harmless eccentrics for the most part.'[39] Of the 1939 recusants from 22 counties listed by the Council in December 1582, a mere 55 appear to have paid fines in the five years after 1581. After new legislation in 1586, the returns increased substantially, but once again only a small minority of recusants were forced to pay very heavy fines. Of the £36,000 collected between

1587 and 1592, over £26,000 was collected from just sixteen wealthy Catholics. Along with some poor recusants who had two-thirds of their land sequestrated, these laymen were made scapegoats for the whole community. The government was content to make an example of a few, and leave the majority of recusants at peace so long as they did not create trouble.[40]

Yet for missionary priests and those who sheltered them, the outlook was grim. The likelihood of the priests being caught and imprisoned was very high. In order to avoid detection, priests moved frequently from place to place keeping one step ahead of pursuivants, and sometimes hiding in 'priest holes' built into the houses where they stayed. Of 471 seminary priests who came to England after 1574, more than half (285) were captured and imprisoned. At least seventeen of these died in prison. Over 30 priests were imprisoned for more than ten years. Lay Catholics were also put in prison. Francis Tregian was imprisoned for 24 years for sheltering the seminary priest Cuthbert Mayne. Others were imprisoned for refusing to go to church or have their child baptised, for hearing mass or possessing popish books or for worshipping at a crucifix. In all, it has been calculated that at least 98 Catholic laypeople died in Elizabethan prisons, some after many years in captivity.[41]

Conditions in Tudor prisons varied enormously. At times, prison afforded a relatively comfortable lifestyle and greater opportunities to practise the faith. Because so many Catholics were imprisoned, it was often possible for them to take mass together. At York prison, Catholics had smuggled in chalices, crucifixes, relics, pictures and 'a great store of books'. Visits from relatives and friends were possible, and like other prisoners, Catholics were often allowed out of gaol for short visits home. Some prisoners enjoyed well-furnished rooms, a good supply of food and feather beds. Because prison wardens were poorly paid, they were easily bribed, and no less than 50 Catholics escaped from prison. The Jesuit John Gerard even broke free from the Tower, and William Watson escaped on no less than three occasions (though one woman who assisted him was executed).

On the other hand, prison could be brutal. Catholic prisoners sometimes had to contend with fetters, hunger, bitter cold, solitary confinement, attacks from other prisoners, and filthy conditions. Roger Wakeman was said to have died in Newgate in 1583 because of the stench of the slops and the burned quarters of executed prisoners. Beyond all this lay the potential horrors of torture. Torture was used to extract information rather than as punishment, but its use was regular. On various occasions, priests were stretched on the rack, compressed in an iron ring known as 'The Scavenger's Daughter', forced to wear iron fetters on their feet, and tormented by sharp spikes driven under their fingernails. In his autobiography, John Gerard recorded his own torture in graphic detail:

> We went to the torture-room in a kind of solemn procession, the
> attendants walking ahead with lighted candles. The chamber was
> underground and dark, particularly near the entrance. It was a vast place
> and every device and instrument of human torture was there. They
> pointed out some of them to me and said that I would try them all.

Hung up by his arms, Gerard was left dangling for hours. 'All the blood in
my body seemed to rush into my arms and hands', he wrote, 'and I thought
that blood was oozing out of the ends of my fingers and the pores of my
skin. But it was only a sensation caused by my flesh swelling above the irons
holding them. The pain was so intense that I thought I could not possibly
endure.' But despite fainting, Gerard did endure.[42]

Torture was often a mere precursor to execution. The first missionary
priest to be executed was Cuthbert Mayne, put to death in 1577. Between
this date and 1603, between 120 and 130 other priests were executed, along
with around 60 lay recusants.[43] The peak in executions in the 1580s coincided with the greatest threat to England's security. In 1581, four Catholics were executed, in 1583 eleven, and in 1588, the year of the Spanish
Armada, thirty. Many of those executed were simply hanged until they
had died, but in other cases the rope was cut before the victim had been
strangled, and he was disembowelled while still alive, then beheaded and
quartered. This was the fate of Father Robert Sutton, who while he was
being disembowelled cried, 'O! thou bloody butcher! God forgive thee'; he
died calling upon Jesus and Mary. In 1600, the Lancashire layman John
Rigby was hanged, cut down while still alive, and thrown to the floor,
where one man stamped on his throat to prevent him speaking. According to the martyrologist Thomas Worthington:

> Others held his arms and legs whiles the executioner dismembered and
> unbowelled him. And when he felt them pulling out his heart, he was yet
> so strong that he thrust the men from him which held his arms. Finally,
> they cut off his head and divided his quarters, disposing of them in several
> places in Southwark, as is accustomed. The people going away muttering
> much at the cruelty used in the execution. And generally all sorts bewailed
> his death.[44]

Yet if these executions sometimes aroused revulsion, they also relied on the
humdrum compliance of ordinary people. The corporation accounts for
Newcastle describe the costs involved in staging the execution of Father
Joseph Lambton in 1592, and contain a chilling juxtaposition of bureau-
cratic detail and butchered human flesh:

> Paid to a Frenchman which did take forth the seminary priests bowels after
> he was hanged, 20s ... and for a wright's axe, which headed the seminary,

Table 4.1 English Catholic martyrs, 1535–1680[45]

1535–44	50
1570–1603	189
1604–18	25
1641–6	24
1651–4	2
1678–80	24
Total	314

4s 6d–5s; for a hand axe and a cutting knife, which did rip and quarter the seminary priest, 14d, and for a horse which trailed him from the sledge to the gallows, 12d–2s, 2d . . . for carrying the four quarters of the seminary priest from gate to gate, and other charges, 2s.[46]

Altogether around 189 Catholic martyrs were executed in Elizabethan England. By contrast, the number of Catholic martyrs in the seventeenth century was just 75 (see Table 4.1).

The Catholic martyrs of Elizabethan England were to be celebrated by their own tradition as passionately as Protestants celebrated the Marian martyrs. Yet Protestants insisted that the two cases were quite different. In *The Execution of Justice in England* (1584), William Cecil vigorously defended the government's position. He complained that Catholics loudly lamented the number of their martyrs, which did not exceed 60 in a quarter of a century, whilst conveniently forgetting that in a fifth of that time Mary's government had burned hundreds of Protestants at the stake. Cecil insisted that the Elizabethan regime had only executed Catholics who were 'manifest traitors in maintaining and adhering to the capital enemy of Her Majesty and her Crown'. The executed Catholics were martyrs for the pope, not for the Catholic faith; they had been put to death for refusing to deny the pope's authority to depose monarchs. Those who were 'unarmed scholars and priests' were still acting as spies for 'a foreign potentate and open enemy' (the pope), and they were closely associated with men who were plotting the overthrow of the queen's government. If the political plots ceased, so would the prosecution.[47]

A short document appended to *The Execution of Justice* defended 'Her Majesty's most mild and gracious government' against accusations of 'heathenish and unnatural tyranny and cruel tortures'. Torture, it stated, had only been used as a last resort to extract information about plots from those who had already been proven guilty but refused to divulge details. The torture was not as bad as Catholic propagandists had claimed. Alexander Briant, the Jesuit who had gone without food and been forced to 'eat clay out of the walls', had only himself to blame, for the government had offered to give him food if only he would write something so that his handwriting could be compared to that on a manuscript of 'traitorous writings'. It was true that Campion had been racked, but 'he was charitably used' and was able to walk again after his ordeal.[48]

Such arguments, of course, would cut little ice with Amnesty International. Modern human rights investigators would no doubt produce a scathing report on a regime that tortured and executed 'prisoners of conscience' on the assumption that they were a threat to the state, but without any really firm evidence that they had actively plotted against it. Yet this just serves to remind us of the great gulf between sixteenth-century values and those of modern political liberalism. Few people in sixteenth-century Europe opposed capital punishment and torture *per se*, despite the fact that early church Fathers had been hostile to both practices.[49] In the 1570s and 1580s, France was being ravaged by religious wars, and England was threatened by foreign invasion; the Elizabethan regime was determined to avoid these calamities even at great cost to the Catholic community. Within the context of contemporary attitudes, Cecil had made a strong case for his government's policy.

In his response to Cecil, William Allen insisted that the English mission was purely pastoral, not political. He defended the pope's authority to depose monarchs, but argued that this ought not to worry the queen. The papal bull had been suspended and English Catholics were loyal to Elizabeth's government. However, Allen failed to point out that the papal bull had never been cancelled, and he himself worked tirelessly throughout his career to secure the overthrow of Elizabeth and her heretical regime. He plotted with Spain, the Vatican and the Guises to place Mary Stuart on the throne of England, and after Mary's execution in 1587 he gave his full support to the Spanish Armada. As Kenneth Campbell has argued, 'Allen was obviously hypocritical; he maintained the purely religious nature of the English mission and even feigned loyalty to Elizabeth, while he vigorously worked for the downfall of Elizabeth's government'.[50] Indeed, along with Pius V and Philip II, Allen and other Catholic exiles must shoulder a good deal of responsibility for the persecution of their fellow Catholics back home. Missionary priests who themselves were innocent of plotting were executed because their superiors were guilty of it.

However, political sedition was not restricted to Catholics overseas. Michael Questier has recently argued that 'practical antipapistry' in the north of England was motivated by genuine (and sometimes well-substantiated) fears of Catholic subversion. 'The simple fact of northern Catholicism', he writes, 'was that in late 1569 Catholic resistance to the established church's Protestant identity had been used to justify a quasi-feudal revolt.' Even after the revolt was crushed, the exiled Charles Neville, the attainted Earl of Westmorland, continued to plot against the government with the help of associates among the northern Catholics. 'There was a very dangerous fusion of Catholic religious dissent with the political threat from Scotland and Spain, helped along by opinions about the papal deposing power.' The prosecution of papists was 'not just an irrational excess', it seemed to make good practical sense.[51]

Geoffrey Elton once wrote that 'the persecution [of Elizabethan Catholics] cannot be described as religious in the real sense. The queen did not want to save souls or make converts; she wanted to protect the safety of her realm.'[52] We have seen that there is much to be said for his claim. But this restatement of Burghley's case ignores the fact that the queen's realm had been defined in explicitly religious terms. Elizabethan England was not a modern secular state threatened by religious militants, it was an exclusive Protestant state; for this reason, it was simply unable to differentiate between religious dissent and political subversion. In the great majority of cases, Catholic priests were imprisoned and tortured and executed not because there was any evidence of political plotting on their part, but merely because they were exercising their ministry in England as ordained Catholic priests and thus committing a treasonable offence under the 1585 Act against Jesuits and Seminary Priests.[53] If Elizabeth may not have persecuted to save souls or make converts, she did persecute to defend the Protestant state.

Elton's point makes more sense when we contrast the Elizabethan with the Marian persecutions. Under Mary, Protestants were burned at the stake for heresy; under Elizabeth, Catholics were executed on the gallows for treason. Mary was motivated by her zeal to purge heresy from the land, whereas Elizabeth acted out of fear for the security of her realm. The Marian persecution was aggressive, the Elizabethan defensive. Whereas the Marian regime instigated the burnings shortly after coming to power, the Elizabethan regime only began to execute Catholics after considerable provocation from the Catholic powers and popish plotters. From a modern point of view, it is much easier to understand the fears that motivated the Elizabethan persecution; a government that talks of national security still makes sense, a government that talks of purging heresy does not. From the point of view of the victims, however, this distinction was little comfort. If the persecutors differed sharply in their motivations, the victims for the most part had this in common: innocent of anti-government plots, they could only conclude that they were being executed for their religion. Tudor historians have usually written about the Elizabethan persecution from the government's point of view; from the side of the victims things looked very different.

The Puritan movement

No other religious group in Elizabethan England suffered as much as the Catholic priests, but other groups did undergo persecution, including Puritans. Puritans were zealous Protestants. In contrast to most of their neighbours, they embraced the new faith with great enthusiasm, throwing themselves into a life of Bible study, prayer, fasting, sermon consumption, and strict sabbatarianism.[54] One contemporary referred to them as 'the hotter sort of Protestants', and Puritans thought of themselves as 'the godly'.[55] The vast majority of Puritans were committed members of the Church of England, but the government did not always appreciate their zeal for the Protestant faith. The problem was that whilst Puritans accepted the Church of England as a true church, they also felt that it was 'but halfly reformed'. Throughout Elizabeth's reign, their passion for 'further reformation' was to land them in trouble with the church authorities.[56]

The first rumblings of discontent began to be heard in the early 1560s. The government had insisted that the clergy should wear the surplice and cope traditionally worn by Catholic priests. To zealous Protestants, determined to eschew all 'remnants of popery', this was too much to swallow. Led by Laurence Humfrey and Thomas Sampson, both heads of Oxford colleges, Puritans organised a campaign of protest against the regulations. The queen was appalled by their insolence. She wrote to Archbishop Parker, complaining of the 'diversity, variety, contention and vain love of singularity' within the church, and urging him to establish 'uniformity of order'. In 1566, 37 London ministers were suspended from office and threatened with deprivation if they failed to conform within three months. Militant Puritan women organised protests against the bishops, and one was placed on a cucking-stool for heckling Grindal in church with cries of 'horns' (probably an allusion to the Beast of Revelation).[57] Although some bishops, like Edmund Grindal, wished to allow a latitude of opinion and practice within the church, the queen and Archbishop Parker were firmly opposed to such a policy.

The conformist argument was that certain things in the church – clerical dress, the mode of receiving communion, the exact form of church organisation, for example – were *adiaphora* ('things indifferent' or not determined by Scripture), and that God had left such things for human authorities to decide. Puritans, however, claimed that many of these issues *had* been determined by Scripture, and that those things which were *adiaphora* should be left to the individual conscience. Both sides in the debate were hostile to the idea of a broad church that would tolerate a wide range of practices and customs. Conformists stressed the authority of the magistrate to determine how people should worship, whilst Puritans often claimed that the Bible dictated the precise way in which one should organise the worship and government of the church. The debate over *adiaphora* was still raging during the Restoration period a century later, for it was central to the question of ecclesiastical tolerance, of how much one would tolerate within a church.

In the mid-1560s, the nonconformist clergy were shocked at the way they had been treated by the bishops. They wrote to the Swiss Reformer Bullinger, asking, 'Why do they cast us into prison? Why do they persecute us on account of the habits?' Yet the ecclesiastical intolerance of Parker eventually proved effective; very few clergy were deprived of their livings, because most decided to compromise. Those who refused to conform were still treated leniently; Sampson, for example, was given the mastership of a hospital, where he could carry on preaching without having to wear a surplice.

However, the intolerance of the bishops during the Vestiarian Controversy convinced some Puritans that the government of the church required a fundamental overhaul. In 1570 a Cambridge divinity professor, Thomas Cartwright, gave a series of lectures in which he argued that the roles of bishops and archdeacons should undergo major reform to bring them into line with biblical teaching on the parity of ministers. Cartwright was removed from his professorial chair and left England for Geneva. In 1572, however, John Field and Thomas Wilcox published *An Admonition to Parliament*, which went beyond Cartwright by calling for the outright abolition of episcopacy. Field and Wilcox were sent to Newgate prison for a year, but the Admonition Controversy was to continue for the next two decades.

During this period, many ministers with Presbyterian sympathies were suspended or deprived of their livings. In London in 1573, a number of Puritan clergy were put in prison, and one of them, Robert Johnson, wrote to Bishop Sandys, to complain of 'filthy and unclean places, more unwholesome than dunghills, more stinking than swine sties'. Before long, Johnson became the fourth Puritan to die in London's prisons.[58] Once again, Puritans complained of their 'bloody persecutors', but once more, the persecution was quite effective. It exposed the divisions within the Puritan movement and isolated the Presbyterian minority, removing several of their key leaders.

In 1576, the Puritan movement experienced another crisis. Archbishop Grindal, who had been highly sympathetic towards the godly, was suspended from his office because he refused to suppress the 'prophesyings', preaching conferences held in various parts of the country by the Puritan clergy. Infuriated by Grindal's courageous stand, the queen ensured that the new generation of bishops appointed in the later 1570s – men like Edmund Freke, John Aylmer and John Whitgift – were zealous proponents of conformity. When he took office, Aylmer was told 'to cut off (even as her Majesty termed it) and to correct offenders on both sides which swerve from the right path of obedience'.[59] The new bishops were vigorous in their campaign to stamp out nonconformity within the church; many more ministers were suspended, and a few deprived of their livings. Puritans, however, were often able to call on the support and protection of influential lay patrons among the local gentry or in government. John Field, for example, was made a parish lecturer through the intervention of Leicester and Sir Francis Knollys, whilst Walter Travers was appointed a reader at the Temple Church thanks to the patronage of Burghley.

Thus the Presbyterian movement survived, and in the 1580s Puritan ministers began to meet in regional classes or synods, a development that Field hoped would prepare the way for a Presbyterian church. When Whitgift became archbishop of Canterbury in 1583, however, he compared Puritans to 'Papists, Anabaptists and Rebels' and announced a new drive for conformity. The queen was wholeheartedly behind this programme of ecclesiastical intolerance, and even the Puritans' most powerful patrons could not stop the archbishop. Burghley had remarked that Whitgift was proceeding in 'Romish style' like 'the inquisitors of Spain',[60] but although the Lord Treasurer secured Cartwright's release from a short spell in prison, he could not prevent another Puritan divine, George Gifford, being deprived of his living. In 1586, Whitgift secured the Star Chamber decree on printing which allowed him to censor objectionable material and destroy Puritan presses. The net was closing in on those who refused to conform.

By the late 1580s, things were getting desperate for the Presbyterians. In 1588 and 1589, radical Puritans published a series of satirical writings by one 'Martin Marprelate'. The Marprelate Tracts combined lampoon with vitriolic denunciation and they intensified the level of polemical bitterness, preparing the way for the 1590s, 'a rather ugly decade, when the going got tough and unpleasant for all parties'.[61] Marprelate declared that Whitgift was 'Belsebub of Canterbury. The Canterburie Caiaphas. Esau. A monstrous Antichristian Pope: a most bloudie oppressor of Gods saintes: a very AntiChristian beast: a most vile cursed tyrant'.[62] The new bishop of London, Richard Bancroft, responded bitterly from the pulpit and in print. He insisted that Puritans were not innocent lambs led to slaughter, but dangerous subversives who 'seditiously endevour to disturbe the land'.[63]

Bancroft and Whitgift devoted the years from 1589 to 1593 to hunting down and destroying the Presbyterian movement. Pursuivants were employed to gather information and detect the ringleaders, and scores of ministers were interrogated. Government agents even loitered around the bookstalls in St Paul's churchyard, engaging clergy in conversation and pretending to be sympathetic to the Presbyterian cause. Once again, Puritan ministers were suspended or deprived of their livings. The propagandist John Udall was sentenced to death for felony for writing the Demonstration of Discipline, though after an intervention from the Scottish king, James VI, the sentence was commuted to exile. Nine Puritan ministers, including Cartwright, were imprisoned and brought before the High Commission, before being sent to Star Chamber for trial. The prisoners were allowed to meet with friends and even leave their prisons for short periods, but the health of four or five of them deteriorated badly. One, who had a 'poor lame wife and seven small children' to look after, 'continually voided blood by urine' for several months. Yet although there was talk of 'some exemplary corporal punishment', the prisoners got off more lightly. Their names were not fully cleared, but they were eventually released from prison.

Yet the campaign of repression had had its desired effect. Presbyterianism had been crushed, and it was not to become a significant force again until the 1640s. Puritans turned away from campaigns to overhaul the church's polity and liturgy, and concentrated instead on promoting Protestant piety in parishes and households across the land. By making their peace with the half-reformed Church of England, they stepped out of the line of fire. Yet in comparison with Catholics, Puritans had experienced little suffering. At worst they were imprisoned or forced into exile, but none were executed. Even the Presbyterian clergy continued to serve the church in some capacity, and usually carried on preaching. Moderate Puritans, who greatly outnumbered Presbyterians, were largely untroubled.

Separatists

Puritans who decided to abandon the national church, however, faced greater penalties. Although Separatists were very few in number during this period, they were still treated as a major threat. Imitating the underground Protestant church of Mary's reign, they arranged clandestine meetings in houses and halls, mainly in London and East Anglia. In 1567, the authorities discovered 100 people meeting in Plumbers' Hall in London; this group seems to have been more presbyterian than congregational in ethos, but they had separated from their parish churches and taken communion together. Although seventeen or eighteen were arrested, imprisoned and questioned by the Lord Mayor and Bishop Grindal, their treatment was mild. In March 1568, another illegal gathering was uncovered in London, and 77 arrests were made; at least eight of those arrested were imprisoned and only released in April 1569. The release was 'without condition . . . saving only an earnest admonition to live in good order hereafter'.[64]

Unfortunately for the authorities, the Separatists did not respond to this leniency. They continued to organise conventicles, and in 1570 a new wave of arrests followed. In a 1571 petition, a group of poor Separatists complained that their pastor, Richard Fitz, and three other members of their conventicle had died of 'long imprisonment'. The government was unmoved; other members of Fitz's congregation died in prison, and the Separatists arrested in 1570 were still in gaol a decade later. Under the pressure of persecution, some buckled and rejoined the established church. One man who recanted, John Bolton, was excommunicated by his Separatist congregation and later hanged himself.

Despite their sufferings, Separatists were not advocates of toleration. The 1571 petitioners had called on the queen to 'cast down all high places of idolatry within her land'; her intolerance should be directed at popery, not at godly Protestants. Most Elizabethan Separatists wanted to see the Church of England purified and all vestiges of popery destroyed; they simply believed that in its present state the national church was intolerable to the godly. Reformation had to begin outside the parish churches, in congregations of true believers.

In 1583, a royal proclamation condemned the 'seditious, schismatical, and erroneous printed books' of Separatist writers Robert Browne and Robert Harrison. Separatists were described as 'lewd and evil disposed persons . . . ready to violate and break the peace of the church, the realm, and the quietness of the people'.[65] Because church and nation were so intertwined, schism was automatically identified with sedition. To challenge the established church was to question the state as well. In a state that defined itself in exclusive religious terms, religious dissent could never be a purely private matter; it was seen as profoundly political.

In June 1583, John Copping and Elias Thacker were hanged at Bury St Edmunds for circulating Separatist writings in East Anglia, and it is possible that two more unnamed Separatists were executed at Bury in July 1584.[66] Another Separatist, William Dennis of Norfolk, was hanged at Thetford, though the date of his death is uncertain.[67] Others were imprisoned. Thomas Wolsey was sent to Thetford gaol in 1584 and appears to have spent the last 30 years of his life in prison, though in a typically sixteenth-century arrangement, he was given a key and allowed to go in and out 'as he pleased'. Robert Browne himself was arrested in 1585, but he happened to be a kinsman of Lord Burghley, who stepped in to save him from death. Shortly afterwards, Browne turned his back on Separatism and returned to the Church of England. Most Separatists, however, refused to compromise and paid the penalty. In October 1587, John Greenwood was arrested along with twenty others meeting in a conventicle near St Paul's. When Greenwood was visited in prison by the young Henry Barrow, he too was arrested on Whitgift's orders. Barrow described the archbishop as 'a monster, a miserable compound . . . neither ecclesiastical nor civil, even that second beast spoken of in the Revelation'.[68]

In 1593 Barrow and Greenwood were still in prison, along with 'three-score and twelve persons, men and women, young and old, lying in cold, hunger, dungeons, and irons', without meat, fire or drink. Deprived of fresh air and exercise, Barrow complained of 'most miserable and strait imprisonment'. The future bishop Lancelot Andrewes had little time for such moans. 'For close imprisonment you are most happie', he told Barrow. 'The solitarie and contemplative life I hold the most blessed life. It is the life I would chuse.' This crassly romantic picture of the 'solitarie and contemplative life' in London's gaols hardly squared with the fact that seventeen or eighteen Separatists had died in prison in the previous six years. One wonders how Andrewes would have enjoyed the odour of the open sewer that ran under the walls of the Fleet prison. Yet the unfortunate Separatists were able to purchase reasonable food and accommodation with money from friends. Barrow and Greenwood also conducted marriages in the prison, wrote Separatist literature and on one occasion even arranged a full-scale disputation with a Puritan minister.[69]

1593, however, was to prove a 'vindictive year'.[70] In March, Barrow and Greenwood were convicted of devising 'seditious books'. On 24 March, they were taken to the gallows and then pardoned; a week later, they even had the nooses around their necks, but once again they were reprieved. Finally, on 6 April, they were hanged at Tyburn. Six weeks later a young Welshman, John Penry, who had participated in writing the Marprelate tracts, was also hanged. The executions of these men were of questionable legality, and seem to have provoked much uneasiness. But the government was determined to drive home its point. In the same month as Penry's execution, Parliament passed An Act for Retaining the Queen's Subjects in their due Obedience. This declared that all adults who refused to attend church or who belonged to illegal conventicles would be automatically imprisoned. If they failed to conform within three months, they would face the choice of exile or death. From this point on, many Separatists decided that emigration to the Netherlands was the only realistic option. For Protestants who chose to establish illegal congregations, England was simply too perilous.

Table 4.2 Heresy executions in England, 1401–1612[71]

1401–1534	*c.*50
1534–47	*c.*50
Edward VI (1547–53)	2
Mary I (1553–8)	*c.*290
Elizabeth I (1558–1603)	6
James I (1603–25)	2

Anabaptists and Arians

Most of the religious dissenters who were executed in Elizabethan England were executed for treason and sedition, not for heresy. Catholics and radical Puritans were, after all, orthodox Trinitarians. Anti-Trinitarians, however, were in a very different position. As we saw in chapter 2, leading Elizabethan churchmen like John Jewel strongly supported the application of the death penalty to obstinate heretics, and in the course of Elizabeth's reign we know of six men who were burned for their heretical beliefs.

This statistic is small indeed when compared to the overall number of heresy executions in England since the fifteenth century. Although it is impossible to give definitive statistics, approximately 50 people seem to have been burned as heretics between 1401 and the passing of the Act of Supremacy in 1534, and around the same number of heretics were burned in the remainder of Henry VIII's reign.[72] Under the Protestant monarchs, by contrast, heresy burnings were few and far between (see Table 4.2).

The stark contrast between the figures for Catholic and Protestant periods is easily explained. Generally speaking, sixteenth-century magistrates only executed as heretics people who were less theologically conservative than themselves. Catholic magistrates, in other words, burned a whole range of heretics to their 'left', including Lollards, Lutherans, Calvinists, and Anabaptists, but we know of only one case in the sixteenth century when an orthodox Catholic was burned for heresy rather than being beheaded for treason; predictably, this anomaly occurred under Henry VIII, in 1538, when Friar John Forrest was burned as a heretic for affirming papal supremacy.[73] In contrast to Catholics, Lutherans only employed the death penalty against 'sacramentarians' (Zwinglians and Calvinists) and Anabaptists, whilst Calvinists only felt justified in executing Anabaptists or anti-Trinitarians. It is significant that in his 'Lutheran' phase, Thomas

Cranmer supported the burning of sacramentarian heretics whose views he would later come to share. Once he had adopted a more radical position on the sacrament, only Anabaptists and anti-Trinitarians remained to his left, and like Calvin, he had few qualms about condemning their stubborn leaders to death.[74]

Under Elizabeth too, only Anabaptists and anti-Trinitarians were in danger of being burned as heretics. The first (and best-known) case took place in 1575. In 1568 and 1574, searches within the Dutch immigrant community had uncovered the presence of Anabaptists, who were then banished from the country. On Easter Sunday 1575, the government discovered another Anabaptist meeting in a private home, and arrested 25 people. Five recanted, and fourteen women and a young boy were banished (though the boy was also flogged). The five remaining men were sentenced to be burned for heresy. They were accused of propounding typical Anabaptist beliefs: that Christ did not take flesh of the Virgin Mary, that infants should not be baptised, and that Christians should not serve as magistrates, bear arms or take oaths.

John Foxe was appalled at the prospect of the fires of Smithfield being rekindled, and although he thoroughly disapproved of the Anabaptists' teaching, he campaigned vigorously against the sentence of death. In two Latin letters, one addressed to the queen, the other to the Privy Council, Foxe argued that burning heretics was a popish practice incompatible with Protestant clemency, and that it was of dubious legality. The medieval statutes that sanctioned the burning of heretics had been repealed by Elizabeth's first Parliament, and the famous statute of Henry IV, *de haeretico comburendo*, had never been promulgated by an act of Parliament. Whether this made the statute invalid was open to debate, but Foxe was convinced that burning these men was wrong. If the government insisted on punishment, they could be branded or imprisoned, or perhaps sent to the gallows.[75]

Eventually, Foxe secured a reprieve of a month or so, but his energetic attempts to persuade the Anabaptists of their error met with no success. One of the men, Christiaen Temels, died in gaol, and two more were released. But the two that remained, Jan Pieters and Hendrick Terwoort, were burned at Smithfield on 22 July. Elizabeth declared that since she had already executed men for treason, for 'now sparing these blasphemers, the world would condemn her, as being more in earnest in asserting her own safety than God's honour'. Yet these 'blasphemers' were reverent and devout, and at their executions they seem to have expressed firmly Trinitarian beliefs.[76]

It is often assumed that Pieterss and Terwoort were the only two men to be executed for heresy in Elizabethan England. However, four others were burned to death in Norwich between 1579 and 1589. In the Tudor period,

Norwich was the second largest city in England, with a population of around 12,000. It was also home to a substantial Dutch community and various continental heresies were in circulation. Although Norwich has been described as a rather tolerant city by sixteenth-century standards, the execution of four heretics in a decade casts doubt on this reputation.[77]

The first man to be burned was Matthew Hamont, a layman of Dutch origins.[78] Hamont first got into trouble for seditious and slanderous words against the queen, and was then questioned about his religious beliefs by the bishop of Norwich, Edmund Freke, an aggressive hunter of dissent. It seems that Hamont was a kind of Arian, for he denied the deity, atonement and resurrection of Christ, and declared that Christ had been turned into an idol. He was also said to have repudiated baptism and the Lord's Supper and condemned the New Testament as a mere fable. The bishop found him guilty of heresy and he was turned over to the city authorities, which cut off his ears for insulting the queen, and then burned him at the stake in a ditch for his heresy. According to contemporary reports, two later heretics who shared many of Hamont's ideas were also burned in the same ditch. In 1583, John Lewes was executed there, and Peter Cole followed in 1587. One contemporary minister, William Burton, described their executions as follows:

> I have known some Arian heretiques, whose life hath beene most strict amongst men, whose tongues have been tyred with scripture upon scripture, their knees even hardened in prayer, and their faces wedded to saddnesse and their mouthes full of praires to God, while in the meantime, they have stowtly denied the divinity of the Sonne of God . . . such were Hamont, Lewes and Cole heretikes of wretched memorie lately executed and cut off in Norwich.[79]

The fourth person to be executed for heresy in Norwich was a native Englishman who had been a fellow at Corpus Christi College, Cambridge. Francis Kett was a deeply devout man, who was constantly praying and reading the Scriptures.[80] He also propounded a strange mixture of beliefs, combining Arianism with his own idiosyncratic apocalyptic ideas. He was accused of teaching that Christ had returned to Jerusalem and was gathering the true church, and that in order to be saved men had to be baptised as adults and visit the Holy City before they died. It is difficult to know whether this is a caricature of Kett's convictions, but Edmund Scambler, the new bishop of Norwich, was convinced that Kett was promoting 'blasphemous opinions', and he was burned alive in the castle ditch at Norwich in January 1589. William Burton provided a vivid eyewitness report of Kett's final agony and ecstasy:

when he went to the fire he was clothed in sackcloth, he went leaping and dancing: being in the fire, above twenty times together, clapping his hands, he cried nothing but blessed be God . . . and so continued untill the fire had consumed all his neather partes, and untill he was stifled with smoke.[81]

A persecuting state

The burnings of Hamont and Cole, Lewes and Kett, are little known, even among historians of Elizabethan England.[82] By contrast, the execution of Servetus in Calvin's Geneva is notorious, and helped to form the image of Calvin as the city's ruthless dictator. In the United States, nineteenth-century history textbooks presented a Calvin guilty of un-American activities, an authoritarian theocrat devoid of warmth or intelligence.[83] Elizabethan England, however, has usually enjoyed an excellent (Protestant) press. This was the colourful Age of Shakespeare, when England flourished under her Virgin Queen.

But these pictures of Calvin's Geneva and Elizabeth's England are caricatures. In reality, the gulf between the two societies was nowhere near as great as popular myth suggests. Calvin's authority in Geneva was much more fragile than is often supposed, and he was no enthusiast for burning heretics; Servetus was the only person to suffer such a fate under Calvin, and even then the Reformer disagreed with the decision to burn him alive.[84] Moreover, Elizabeth and James I were willing participants in the trial and execution of heretics, though their reputations did not suffer as a result. Ironically, this may count as evidence of the greater intolerance of England: the case of Servetus became notorious because radical Protestants in Basle like Castellio condemned it in angry and eloquent pamphlets.[85] In England, by contrast, the burning of heretics was followed by a deafening silence. No Marprelate satirised the persecutors, no Castellio orchestrated a campaign of protest.

The truth is that the Elizabethan regime was not as mild as its defenders have claimed. W. K. Jordan consistently exaggerated Elizabethan tolerance and always strove to paint government policy in the best light. But this was a regime that executed almost 200 Catholics, hanged six Separatists, and burned the same number of heretics. Many others were deported or imprisoned, and not a few died in gaol. The vast majority of these victims had never been involved in plotting the overthrow of the regime. Catholics and Separatists were punished because their religious deviance was seen as *ipso facto* seditious. In a nation where the queen was supreme governor of the church as well as head of state, dissent from the church could not be a private, apolitical affair. Heretics were burned because the Elizabethan establishment wholeheartedly accepted the traditional belief that the Christian magistrate had a solemn duty to cut out the gangrene of heresy.

If we compare England with other European states, the picture becomes clearer. Conrad Russell has said that 'With the exception of Spain, Italy and possibly Scotland, the English government was more successful and persistent in its attempts to enforce unity of religion than its counterparts'.[86] The Jesuit scholar Joseph Lecler went even further, and claimed that 'among all the countries that were divided by the Reformation . . . England comes last so far as tolerance is concerned'.[87] This seems harsh, since England never experienced anything as terrible as the St Bartholomew's Day massacres; in France, thousands of Protestants were slaughtered in the streets by Catholic mobs, but it is hard to recall a single Catholic in Elizabethan England who was attacked and killed by a crowd because of his religion. Indeed, Elizabeth and her ministers insisted that their policy of uniformity forestalled the possibility of anything as bloody as the French Wars of Religion. Yet Lecler's claim about English intolerance cannot be so easily dismissed. No other Protestant state was quite so crude in lumping together profession of Catholic faith and high treason, and none displayed the same commitment to executing priests. In Scotland, Catholic priests were sometimes subjected to humiliating rituals of public mockery, but very few were put to death in the decades following the Reformation of 1560.[88] In the Dutch republic, Catholics constituted over a third of the population and enjoyed some security in numbers. There had been Catholic martyrs during the Dutch revolt, and Catholics continued to endure many hardships, but their situation was better than that of the English Catholic community, which despite being a smaller minority aroused greater fears.[89] All in all, the Elizabethan repression of Catholics seems to be unparalleled in other Protestant countries.

The harshness of the government's crackdown on Protestant dissent also seems excessive. Elizabeth's hostility to ecclesiastical tolerance cut off the possibility of a broad church that could have accommodated strict Puritans with scruples about vestments. The harsh repression of Separatists in the 1580s and 1590s was also out of all proportion to their threat. Champlin Burrage once wrote that 'at no time before 1630, and possibly even before 1640, can there have been more than five or six hundred genuine Brownists or Barrowists in England'.[90] The Elizabethan regime treated this tiny minority like a virulent plague that would rage through the nation unless it was ruthlessly contained. Separatist congregations were hunted down and incarcerated, their ringleaders put to death. The contrast with the Dutch republic, where Lutherans and Mennonites were tolerated minorities, was startling. By the late sixteenth century, there were roughly 100,000 Mennonites in the United Netherlands, meeting in hundreds of congregations and comprising around 5 per cent of the population. In Haarlem, 15 per cent of the population was Anabaptist, and in some parts of the country they even outnumbered the members of the Reformed church.[91] Hardline Calvinists campaigned vociferously to suppress Mennonite and Lutheran worship, but their success was very limited.[92] Elizabethan and early Stuart Separatists knew that in the Dutch republic they would find a safe haven, and in the half-century leading up to 1640, substantial numbers emigrated to escape persecution in England. The Netherlands was living proof that Elizabeth and Burghley were mistaken: religious dissent did not have to be read as political dissent, and pluralism did not have to mean anarchy.

Yet we should remember that even in the Netherlands religious pluralism was seen as inherently destabilising. The philosopher Hugo Grotius, so often regarded as a model tolerationist, actually envied the order and stability of England, and believed that unrestrained pluralism would damage the Dutch republic.[93] If we moderns see religious uniformity as something to avoid, most early moderns saw it as something to be prized.

Notes

1   See W. Monter, *Judging the French Reformation: Heresy Trial by Sixteenth-Century Parlements* (Cambridge, MA, 1999), pp. 46–8.

2   See J. A. Thomson, *The Later Lollards, 1414–1520* (Oxford, 1965), pp. 237–8; A. G. Dickens, *The English Reformation*, 2nd edn (London, 1989), pp. 49–56.

3   Monter, *Judging the French Reformation*, p. 47.

4   See B. Gregory, *Salvation at Stake: Christian Martyrdom in Early Modern Europe* (Cambridge, MA, 1999), p. 274.

5   D. MacCulloch, 'Archbishop Cranmer: concord and tolerance in a changing Church', in O. P. Grell and R. Scribner, eds, *Tolerance and Intolerance in the European Reformation* (Cambridge, 1995), pp. 199–215, quotation at p. 204.

6   Quoted in D. MacCulloch, *Thomas Cranmer: A Life* (New Haven, CN, 1996), p. 349. See also pp. 364–5.

7   See ibid., pp. 369, 442–3, 449, 484, 492 (for Gardiner, Bonner, and other conservatives), 482 (for Hooper), and 474–7 (for Bocher and van Parris).

8   E. Peters, *Inquisition* (Berkeley, CA, 1988), p. 158.

9   Reprinted in G. R. Elton, ed., *The Tudor Constitution*, 2nd edn (Cambridge, 1982), p. 410.

10   P. Jenkins, 'From gallows to prison? The execution rate in early modern England', *Criminal Justice History* 7 (1986), 51–71.

11   R. Tittler, *The Reign of Mary I* (Harlow, 1991), p. 33.

12   *The Acts and Monuments of John Foxe*, ed. G. Townsend and S. R. Cattley, 8 vols (1837–41), VII, p. 631.

13   G. Elton, *Reform and Reformation: England, 1509–1558* (London, 1977), p. 387 n. 9.

14   Elton, *The Tudor Constitution*, p. 373.

15   Patrick Collinson, 'Windows in a woman's soul: questions about the religion of Queen Elizabeth I', in his *Elizabethan Essays* (London, 1994), ch. 4, quotation at p. 114.

16   See C. Russell, *The Crisis of Parliaments, 1509–1660* (Oxford, 1971), p. 149.

17   W. K. Jordan, *The Development of Religious Toleration in England*, 4 vols (London, 1932–40), I, p. 96.

18   J. Hurstfield, 'Church and state, 1558–1612: The task of the Cecils', in G. J. Cuming, ed., *Studies in Church History*, 2 (1965), pp. 119–40, quotation at p. 123.

19   H. Hillerbrand, 'Persecution', in Hillerbrand, ed., *Encyclopedia of the Reformation*, 4 vols (Oxford, 1996), III, p. 247.

20   Elton, *The Tudor Constitution*, pp. 410–13.

21   J. F. Larkin and P. L. Hughes, eds, *Tudor Royal Proclamations*, vol. II, *The Later Tudors 1558–87* (New Haven, CN, 1969), pp. 117–19, 123, 126.

22   M. Aston, *Faith and Fire: Popular and Unpopular Religion, 1350–1600* (London, 1993), p. 305.

23   M. Aston, *England's Iconoclasts* (Oxford, 1988), pp. 294–342.

24   A. Walsham, *Church Papists: Catholicism, Conformity and Confessional Polemic in Early Modern England* (Woodbridge, 1993), p. 15.

25   See C. Haigh, *English Reformations: Religion, Politics, and Society under the Tudors* (Oxford, 1993), ch. 14; E. Duffy, *The Stripping of the Altars: Traditional Religion in England, 1400–1580* (New Haven, CN, 1992), ch. 17.

26   Jordan, *The Development of Religious Toleration*, I, pp. 99–100.

27   J. Maltby, *Prayer Book and People in Elizabethan and Early Stuart England* (Cambridge, 1998), p. 2.

28   A useful overview is provided by A. Morey, *The Catholic Subjects of Elizabeth I* (London, 1978).

29   The text of the papal bull can be found in Elton, *The Tudor Constitution*, pp. 423–8.

30   A point demonstrated by A. Pritchard, *Catholic Loyalism in Elizabethan England* (London, 1979).

31   Walsham, *Church Papists*, pp. 34–5.

32   See T. Clancy, *Papist Pamphleteers: The Allen–Persons Party and the Political Thought of the Counter-Reformation in England, 1572–1615* (Chicago, 1964); P. Holmes, *Resistance and Compromise: The Political Thought of the Elizabethan Catholics* (Cambridge, 1982), esp. part iii.

33   The most important legislation can be found in Elton, *The Tudor Constitution*, pp. 419–42.

34   A. Dures, *English Catholicism, 1558–1642* (Harlow, 1983), p. 30.

35   E. Rose, *Cases of Conscience: Alternatives open to Recusants and Puritans under Elizabeth I and James I* (Cambridge, 1975), p. 15.

36   J. Bossy, *The English Catholic Community, 1570–1850* (London, 1975), pp. 190–3.

37   See Walsham, *Church Papists*, pp. 1, 74.

38   Rose, *Cases of Conscience*, pp. 15, 26–7.

39   W. MacCaffrey, *Queen Elizabeth and the Making of Policy, 1572–1588* (Princeton, NJ, 1981), p. 153.

40   Ibid., pp. 140–4.

41   See P. McGrath and J. Rowe, 'The imprisonment of Catholics for religion under Elizabeth I', *Recusant History* 20 (1991), 415–35.

42   *John Gerard: The Autobiography of an Elizabethan*, ed. P. Caraman (London, 1951), pp. 107–11.

43   For a more or less complete list of Catholics executed in England between 1535 and 1680 see P. Caraman, 'Martyrs of England and Wales', *New Catholic Encyclopedia*, 17 vols (Washington, 1967), IX, pp. 319–32. See also P. McGrath and J. Rowe, 'The Elizabethan priests: their harbourers and helpers', *Recusant History* 19 (1989), 209–33.

44   Quoted in P. Caraman, ed., *The Other Face: Catholic Life under Elizabeth I* (London, 1960), pp. 254–5.

45   Taken from G. Nuttall, 'The English martyrs 1535–1680: a statistical review', *Journal of Ecclesiastical History* 22 (1971), 191–7. Nuttall compiles his list from the Catholic church's own 1967 list of the English martyrs. As he notes (pp. 196–7), there is an arbitrary element to the table, since some of those included died in prison rather than being executed, whilst some Catholics who were executed for treason have not been included in the list.

46   Quoted in ibid., pp. 260–1.

47   'The Execution of Justice in England' by William Cecil and 'A True, Sincere and Modest Defense of English Catholics' by William Allen, ed. R. M. Kingdon (Ithaca, NY, 1965), pp. 7, 14, 37, 39–40.

48   Ibid., pp. 45–50.

49   J. H. Burns, ed., The Cambridge History of Medieval Political Thought, c.350–c.1450 (Cambridge, 1988), p. 18.

50   K. Campbell, The Intellectual Struggle of the English Papists in the Seventeenth Century (Lewiston, NY, 1986), p. 15.

51   M. Questier, 'Practical antipapistry during the reign of Elizabeth I', Journal of British Studies 36 (1997), 371–96.

52   Elton, The Tudor Constitution, p. 423.

53   See ibid., p. 434.

54   See C. Durston and J. Eales, eds, The Culture of English Puritanism (London, 1996).

55   On the definition of Puritanism see P. Lake, 'Defining Puritanism: again?', in F. Bremer, ed., Puritanism: Trans-Atlantic Perspectives on a Seventeenth-Century Anglo-American Faith (Boston, MA, 1993), pp. 3–29.

56   The definitive study is P. Collinson, The Elizabethan Puritan Movement (London, 1967).

57   See M. M. Knappen, Tudor Puritanism (Chicago, 1939), pp. 210–11.

58   Collinson, Elizabethan Puritan Movement, p. 152.

59   Ibid., p. 201.

60   Ibid., p. 270.

61   See P. Collinson, 'Ecclesiastical vitriol: religious satire in the 1590s and the invention of Puritanism', in J. Guy, ed., The Reign of Elizabeth I: Court and Culture in the Last Decade (Cambridge, 1995), p. 153.

62   Quoted in [Richard Bancroft], Dangerous Positions and Proceedings (1593), p. 60.

63   Ibid., p. 183.

64   M. Watts, The Dissenters: From the Reformation to the French Revolution (Oxford, 1978), pp. 19–22.

65   Larkin and Hughes, eds, Tudor Royal Proclamations, II, no. 667, pp. 501–2.

66   See A. Peel, 'Congregational martyrs at Bury St Edmunds. How many?', Transactions of the Congregational History Society 15 (1945–8), 64–7.

67   See also Watts, The Dissenters, p. 33.

68   Ibid., pp. 35–6.

69   P. Collinson, 'Separation in and out of the church: the consistency of Barrow and Greenwood', *The Journal of the United Reformed Church History Society* 5 (1994), 239–58.

70   Ibid., 242.

71   Given the incompleteness of the sources, and the difficulty of differentiating between heresy and sedition in some cases, it is impossible to provide a definitive table of heresy executions, especially for the fifteenth century. I have made substantial alterations to W. H. Summers, 'List of persons burned for heresy in England', *Transactions of the Congregational Historical Society* 2 (1905–6), 362–70. Summers's list should be treated with care, since some of the fifteenth-century cases are poorly attested, and Summers included Lollards executed for their part in Oldcastle's rebellion of 1414. He was also unaware of the burning of Peter Cole in 1587. I have given round numbers for the larger totals to highlight the element of uncertainty.

72   L. Levy, *Blasphemy: Verbal Offense against the Sacred, from Moses to Salman Rushdie* (Chapel Hill, NC, 1993), pp. 80, 84.

73   See P. Marshall, 'Papist as heretic: the burning of John Forrest, 1538', *Historical Journal* 41 (1998), 351–74. Francis Edwards suggests that in 1581 some wanted to see the Jesuits burned as heretics, but he gives no evidence for this claim. See Edwards, *Robert Persons: Elizabethan Jesuit, 1546–1610* (Saint Louis, n.d.), p. 51.

74   See MacCulloch, *Thomas Cranmer*, pp. 101–2, 230–4, 474–7, and *idem*, 'Archbishop Cranmer', pp. 199–215.

75   See G. R. Elton, 'Persecution and Toleration in the English Reformation', in W. J. Sheils, ed., *Persecution and Toleration* (London, 1984), pp. 175–7.

76   The fullest account of this case was provided by the Dutch Anabaptist martyrologist Thieleman J. van Braght, *Martyrs Mirror*, tr. J. F. Sohm (Scottsdale, PA, 1977), pp. 1008–24. See also Levy, *Blasphemy*, pp. 91–2.

77   See M. McClendon, 'Religious toleration and the Reformation: Norwich magistrates in the sixteenth century', in N. Tyacke, ed., *England's Long Reformation, 1500–1800* (London, 1997), ch. 4.

78   The fullest account of these executions is in Levy, *Blasphemy*, pp. 93–5. The *Dictionary of National Biography* (*DNB*) also contains a brief article on Hamont.

79   William Burton, *David's Evidence* (1590), pp. 124–5.

80   There is a short article on Kett in the *DNB*.

81   Burton, *David's Evidence*, p. 125.

82   Collinson, *Elizabethan Essays*, p. 165, assumes that Terwoort and Pieters were the only heretics burned under Elizabeth.

83 T. J. Davis, 'Images of intolerance: John Calvin in nineteenth-century history textbooks', *Church History* 65 (1996), 234–48.

84 See F. Wendel, *Calvin* (London, 1963), pp. 93–9.

85 See J. Lecler, *Toleration and the Reformation*, 2 vols (London, 1960), I, Book iv; H. Guggisberg, 'Tolerance and intolerance in sixteenth-century Basle', in Grell and Scribner, eds, *Tolerance and Intolerance in the European Reformation*, ch. 9.

86 C. Russell, 'Arguments for religious unity in England, 1530–1650', *Journal of Ecclesiastical History* 18 (1967), 201.

87 Lecler, *Toleration and the Reformation*, II, p. 493.

88 See M. Mullett, *Catholics in Britain and Ireland, 1558–1829* (London, 1998), pp. 33–54.

89 See R. Po-Chia Hsia, *The World of Catholic Renewal* (Cambridge, 1998), pp. 84–6; J. Israel, *The Dutch Republic: Its Rise, Greatness and Fall, 1477–1806* (Oxford, 1995), pp. 377–91.

90 C. Burrage, *Early English Dissenters*, 2 vols (Cambridge, 1912), I, p. 152.

91 See J. Stayer, 'The Radical Reformation', in T. Brady, H. Oberman, and J. Tracy, eds, *Handbook of European History, 1400–1600*, 2 vols (Leiden, 1995), II, pp. 273, 275; Israel, *The Dutch Republic*, pp. 395–8.

92 See Israel, *The Dutch Republic*, pp. 372–7.

93 See ibid., pp. 430–1, 439–40, 501–2.

CHAPTER 5

The Early Stuarts, 1603–40

The accession of James VI of Scotland to the throne of England was warmly welcomed by those who had experienced persecution under Elizabeth. While Catholics hoped for toleration, Puritans eagerly anticipated a full reformation. Catholics were heartened by the knowledge that James was the son of a devout Catholic, Mary Queen of Scots, and the husband of Anne of Denmark, a Lutheran convert to Rome. Some were also aware that in correspondence with the Earl of Northumberland, James had promised: 'As for the catholics, I will neither persecute any that will be quiet and give but an outward obedience to the law, neither will I spare to advance any of them that will by good service worthily deserve it.'[1] Moreover, as Jenny Wormald has pointed out, 'James had no record of persecution',[2] at least of Catholics (though he had encouraged the Scottish witch-hunts of the 1590s). In stark contrast to England, not one Catholic priest had been executed in Scotland up to 1603; the only Scottish Catholic to be martyred was John Ogilvie, put to death in Glasgow in 1615. When the bishop of the Isles called for a campaign against the Jesuits in Argyll, James had laughed and said he would welcome anyone who could civilise the highlanders. Such tolerance had infuriated the Presbyterian clergy, and James had expended more energy combating Presbyterians than Jesuits. But the king was also a committed Calvinist, and the Scottish kirk was more thoroughly reformed than the Church of England. English Puritans hoped that he would thus be more sympathetic than Elizabeth to godly preachers prepared to work within an episcopal church.

In the long run, the hopes of both Catholics and Puritans were to be partly fulfilled. But though James had no zeal for persecution, he was far too rooted in the traditions of Christendom to introduce bold new measures of religious toleration, especially for those who refused communion with the established church. He stood self-consciously in the line of the kings of ancient Israel and the early Christian emperors, as the custodian of both tables of the Ten Commandments (*custos utriusque Tabulae*), required to punish false religion as well as crimes like murder and adultery.[3] In *The Trew Law of Free Monarchies* (1598), he noted approvingly that all Christian kings swear at their coronation 'first to maintaine the Religion presently professed within their countrie, according to their lawes, whereby it is established, and to punish all those that should presse to alter, or disturbe the profession thereof'.[4] No less than Elizabeth, James regarded religious uniformity as an ideal to be cherished and pursued.

James I and English Protestantism

Theologically, James was a Calvinist who believed in the Reformed doctrine of absolute predestination and prided himself on his theological expertise. Ecclesiastically, however, he had no time for the Presbyterianism inspired by Calvin's Geneva. In Scotland, he had had running battles with the Presbyterian clergy, and had come to view Presbyterianism as a populist form of church government which robbed the monarch of his proper ecclesiastical authority. In *Basilikon Doron* (1599), James had warned his eldest son, Prince Henry, to beware of Presbyterians and Separatists: 'such Puritanes' were 'verie pestes in the Church and Common-weale'. He especially deplored 'braine-sicke and headie preachers' like Browne and Penry, who had brought their subversive message to Scotland. Yet he was at pains to point out that he had nothing against godly 'Preachers' who had scruples about bishops or liturgy but were willing to live quietly within the national church.[5]

This distinction between radical subversives and moderate quietists was to guide James's ecclesiastical policy in England.[6] Aware of the king's statements, English Puritans in 1603 greeted their new monarch with the Millenary Petition, an essentially moderate plea for further reformation of the church which studiously avoided Presbyterianism. At the Hampton Court Conference in January 1604, James met some of the moderate Puritan demands, but he also went out of his way to stress the need for conformity within an episcopal church. He made it clear that he was willing to support the Puritan dream of a godly preaching ministry in every parish, but in exchange he wanted Puritans to conform to the liturgy and government of the Church of England. James's goal was 'unity and uniformity', and he was not prepared to tolerate the scruples of 'a few private men' enamoured with the anabaptistical principle of Christian liberty.

In July 1604, the king issued a proclamation ordering all clergy to conform fully to the Book of Common Prayer by 30 November 1604. He
believed that he had a solemn duty before God 'to put in execution all
wayes and meanes that may take from among Our people, all grounds and
occasions of Sects, Divisions, and Unquietnesse', and ensure 'an universal
conformitie'. Yet this uniformity was to be 'wrought by Clemencie, and by
weight of Reason, and not by Rigour of Law'. The bishops were to find
conformist replacements for those clergy who 'shall wilfully abandon their
Charges upon so sleight causes'.[7]

As a result of James's campaign for uniformity, around 90 clergy were
deprived of their benefices, the majority in the early months of 1605. They
included prominent Puritan preachers like Arthur Hildersham. As persecution went, of course, deprivation was one of the milder forms. It did involve
hardship, particularly for ministers with a family to support, but some managed to find employment as domestic chaplains or schoolmasters, and most
received generous support from Puritan sympathisers. Furthermore, although
James continued to insist on the need for conformity in the rest of his reign,
there was in practice a good deal of toleration for Puritan nonconformists
within the church. The king's chief minister, Robert Cecil, took over his
father's role of protecting godly clergy from prosecution; the Puritan Andrew
Willett dedicated a book to Cecil in 1605 which advocated 'tolerance and
forbearance towards friends and brethren'.[8] Many of the bishops also showed
little zeal for pursuing moderate Puritans with scruples over ceremonies,
and only flagrant nonconformists were prosecuted. In London, for example, the admittedly incomplete records speak of only two ministers deprived
for nonconformity between 1611 and 1625. Moreover, James was determined to make the Church of England a broad church. Though he himself
was a moderate Calvinist, he was prepared to promote Arminian clergy like
Richard Neile and Lancelot Andrewes. His church stretched to accommodate moderate Puritans, conformist Calvinists, the new Arminians, and
church papists.[9] Under James, moderate Puritans were an integral part of
the Church of England.[10]

Yet if James permitted a considerable degree of latitude to those who
remained within the church, he refused to tolerate radical Protestants who
turned their backs on it. A substantial number of those who were deprived
of their livings in the first decade of the century recognised that their future
in England was bleak, and emigrated to the Netherlands where Protestant
dissent outside the public church was tolerated. John Robinson, deprived of
his living in Norwich in 1604, emigrated in 1608 with a group of fellow
Separatists, including William Bradford, the future governor of Plymouth
colony. Bradford later wrote that they had been 'hunted and persecuted on
every side . . . For some were taken and clapped up in prison, others had

their houses beset and watched day and night, and hardly escaped their hands; and the most were fain to flee and leave their houses and habitations, and the means of their livelihood.'[11] John Smyth, deprived of his lectureship at Lincoln in 1603, led another Separatist church to Amsterdam in 1608. William Ames, who was driven from his fellowship at Christ's College, Cambridge, in 1610, also fled to the Netherlands where he developed a European reputation as a leading Reformed theologian.

Smyth, Robinson and Ames adopted different positions vis-à-vis the Church of England. The followers of Ames and Henry Jacob met in gathered congregations of the godly, but they continued to associate with the established church, refusing to separate from it entirely. Smyth and Robinson, by contrast, were uncompromising Separatists, but Smyth scandalised other Separatists by rebaptising himself, repudiating infant baptism, and eventually joining a branch of the Dutch Mennonites.[12] Part of his congregation disagreed with his union with the Mennonites, and formed a breakaway group; led by Thomas Helwys, they returned to England in 1611 to establish the nation's first Baptist church in London. They were fully aware of the dangers. Helwys wrote that they were willing to 'lay down their lives in their own country for Christ' rather than flee persecution. Drawing on the book of Revelation, Helwys identified persecution as the policy of Antichrist, and denounced the Church of England as the second Beast. True Christians, he argued, must repudiate the beastly principle of persecution and advocate the toleration of heretics, Jews and Muslims, 'for men's religion . . . is betwixt God and themselves'.[13] Unfortunately, the authorities did not agree, and a number of the Baptists were arrested and imprisoned in 1613. In 1620, the Baptist leader John Murton smuggled a tract out of Newgate prison written in milk to make the text invisible until scorched by a flame. The tract complained that Baptists had been subjected to 'long and lingering imprisonments for many years in divers counties of England, in which many have died and left behind them widows and small children'.[14] The outlawed General Baptists remained a tiny sect in Jacobean England, but they did expand. By 1626, the London congregation was said to number 150, and churches had been established in Coventry, Lincoln, Salisbury and Tiverton.

Unlike the General Baptists, Robinson's group did not return to England. In the relative freedom of the Netherlands they flourished and attracted new English immigrants; by the early 1610s their congregation had some 300 communicants. In 1620, William Brewster led a section of the church to the New World, sailing from Leyden to Southampton, and then from Plymouth to North America. This group was to be immortalised as the 'Pilgrim Fathers', but contrary to popular belief, they were not fleeing persecution. They had already done this when they emigrated to the

Netherlands, and there they had enjoyed real freedom of worship. But they still felt like strangers in a strange land, excluded as they were from guilds and full participation in Dutch life. By sailing to the New World, they hoped to create a godly English society in which they could feel at home. In contrast to the General Baptists, these Separatists still adhered to the magisterial Reformation ideal of a Christian magistrate who would suppress heresy and idolatry and promote true religion. Far from wanting to break free from the stifling constraints of the Old World and build a free America, the Pilgrims were appalled by the hedonism and Sabbath-breaking of the Dutch, and feared that their children would be corrupted by 'the great licentiousness of youth in that country and the manifold temptations of the place'. They dreamt of leaving behind the moral and religious laxity of the Dutch republic and fashioning a more disciplined and godly society across the ocean.[15]

Separatists and Baptists faced considerable difficulties and hardships because of persecution, but as in the reign of Elizabeth, the fiercest persecution was directed against anti-Trinitarians. In 1612, Bartholomew Legate and Edward Wightman were burned for heresy.[16] Legate was one of three brothers who believed that they were God's latter-day apostles; their mission was to purge Christianity of a thousand years of popish corruption and to re-establish the true church. One of the brothers had died in Newgate prison, and in 1612 Bartholomew was brought before the king himself to explain his mixture of Anabaptist and anti-Trinitarian teachings. James revelled in theological debate, but he was furious when Legate declared that he had not prayed to Christ for seven years, ever since he recognised that Jesus was 'a meere man'. The heretic was handed over to the bishops, whose own attempts to reason him out of his heresy also came to nothing. Archbishop Abbot wished to try Legate under *de haeretico comburendo*, despite the claims of Sir Edward Coke that the statute was no longer legally valid. The king weighed in on Abbot's side, and after a formal trial establishing Legate's guilt, the Lord Chancellor issued a writ of execution. Legate was condemned for 'very many wicked errors, false opinions, heresies, and cursed blasphemies', and burned at Smithfield before a huge crowd.

Like Legate, Edward Wightman espoused Anabaptist and anti-Trinitarian beliefs and regarded himself as a divinely anointed prophet. In 1611 he sent a manuscript containing his ideas to the king, who responded by ordering his imprisonment. For six months, the bishop of Lichfield, Richard Neile, his young chaplain, William Laud, and other theologians debated with Wightman in an effort to change his mind. Failing, they held a trial at Lichfield Cathedral in November and December. Wightman was condemned as a 'blasphemous heretique', and sentenced to be burned. As the flames began to singe his body, Wightman recanted, and onlookers rushed to his rescue. Several weeks later, however, he withdrew his recantation. On

11 April 1612, he 'died blaspheming' at the stake. According to Thomas Fuller, who wrote in 1655, 'Such burning of heretics much startled common people, pitying all in pain, and prone to asperse justice itself with cruelty, because of the novelty and hideousness of the punishment'. Fuller claimed that James himself was so disturbed by the burnings and the reaction to them that he determined to imprison heretics in future, rather than execute them. A Spanish Arian who had been sentenced to death around this time was simply allowed to live out his days in prison.

Wightman was the last person burned for heresy in English history. Yet the notion of executing heretics and blasphemers was not extinguished by his death. In December 1612, Archbishop Abbot wrote to John Jegon, bishop of Norwich, about the case of William Sayer, a stubborn Separatist with Anabaptist tendencies, who also seemed to deny the deity of Christ and the Holy Spirit. Abbot declared to Jegon that Sayer would never 'burne as a Hereticque, vnlesse hee denie something expressly conteyned in the three Creeds or in the foure first Generall-Counsells'. However, if he did 'persist obstinately' in denying the Trinity, 'the Lawe will holde of him, as it did this last yeare vpon Legate, and Wightman, to frie him at a Stake'.[17] We know no more of what happened to Sayer, but he clearly avoiding being fried at the stake.

The horrors of persecution in Elizabethan and Jacobean England tempt us into exaggerating the degree of uniformity and religious coercion in the period. Persecution, by its very nature, attracts attention. The burning of a single heretic overshadows a thousand unspectacular acts of tolerance. And there is a real danger that in focusing on persecution, we forget the reality of diversity and coexistence. The religious situation in Elizabethan and Jacobean England was anything but monolithic. We have already mentioned the range of groups that did not fully conform to the Church of England: recusants, church papists, 'Stranger Churches', Separatists, Anabaptists and Arians. These represented only a small proportion of the population, but they remind us that the theory of uniformity was an ideal that did not always reflect the situation on the ground.

Alongside the official Protestant Christianity, moreover, there flourished a bewildering plethora of folk beliefs and magical practices. As Keith Thomas demonstrated in his classic work *Religion and the Decline of Magic* (1971), popular culture in the sixteenth and seventeenth centuries was riddled with the weird and the wonderful. Conformist members of the national church often maintained a lively interest in astrology, alchemy, divination, magical healing, Neo-Platonism, lucky charms, omens, ancient prophecies, ghosts and fairies. Thomas may have exaggerated the importance of these phenomena, and more recent studies have suggested that religious indifference, anticlericalism and magic were less common than he suggested; the religion of the majority was one of 'stolid conformity' and 'unspectacular ortho-doxy'.[18] But no one would deny that a complex array of spiritual beliefs and practices existed in a nation that was theoretically orthodox and Protestant.

Furthermore, as Nabil Matar has demonstrated in two strikingly original works, Elizabethan and Jacobean England was not entirely sealed off from non-Christian religions. The world of Islam made a particularly significant impression. Turks and Moors traded in English ports, and their ambassa-dors proudly displayed their food and horses to London audiences. Thou-sands of English people were captured by Muslim pirates, and many of these converted to Islam. Islam loomed surprisingly large in the English imagination: 'In drama and theology, in domestic and in foreign state records, among home-bound preachers and expatriated renegades, in churches and in coffee-houses, among merchants and weavers, sailors and soldiers, the Islam of the Ottoman Empire and the North African regencies was en-gaged, attacked, discussed and described.'[19] Although attitudes to Islam were often hostile, it could not be ignored, and this fact alone should com-plicate our picture of the English religious mentality.

Christopher Marsh has suggested that the story of intolerance in this period needs to be complemented with 'a more attractive tale'. The claims of conformity and orthodoxy were often counterbalanced by the claims of neighbourliness.[20] Catholics were often well integrated into the local com-munity through marriage, economic relations and even office-holding, and they could be sheltered by sympathetic neighbours from the full blast of persecution. Marsh's own research into the heretical Family of Love demon-strates that they too enjoyed the considerable tolerance of their neigh-bours. In the Cambridgeshire village of Balsham and elsewhere, Familists 'held secular offices, witnessed the wills of co-parishioners, made generous gifts to the local poor and played a very full part in the lives of their communities'.[21] Social tolerance was clearly a living reality in many towns and villages.

The Family of Love, however, was an unusually quietist and non-confrontational sect. The fact that they held office in their local commun-ities tells us as much about the demand for willing public servants as it does about the extent of religious tolerance. More militant religious movements were rarely treated with the same equanimity. The word 'Puritan' is itself evidence of social intolerance, for 'Puritan' was a term of abuse hurled at zealous Protestants who liked to think of themselves as 'the godly'. For many contemporaries, the rigorous religiosity of the 'hotter sort of Prot-estants' was too much to bear, and the relationship between the godly and their neighbours was often fraught. Puritans themselves could be 'exclus-ivist and aggressively self-righteous', and this often created real tension within local communities.[22] As Patrick Collinson has emphasised, Puritan campaigns to abolish Sunday sports, maypole dancing and church ales often provoked popular protest and abuse. In the famous words of Richard Baxter, 'The war was begun in our streets before the King and the Parliament had any armies'.[23]

James I and English Catholicism

In 1603, English Catholicism was deeply divided. Most Catholics supported James's accession to the throne and simply hoped for toleration. In Elizabeth's final years, secular priests like William Watson had entered into negotiations with the English government, pledged their allegiance to the crown, and repudiated the Allen–Persons tradition of hostility to the current Protestant regime. Not all the seculars were entirely quietist. In 1603, Watson had conspired to seize James; but the aim of this failed Bye Plot was not to depose the king, but to force him to grant toleration. Other Catholics, however, particularly those associated with the Jesuits, continued to look to Spain for deliverance from Protestant tyranny. In 1598, the Jesuit Joseph Cresswell had started to lobby the Spanish government to send a rapid invasion force to prevent the accession of the 'heretic', James VI. Not content with being a tolerated minority like the French Huguenots, the ultimate aim of these Catholics was to seize power from the Protestant regime.[24]

At the outset of the reign, the prospects for toleration looked good. James remitted the fines of many recusants for a year, causing the receipts from recusancy fines to drop dramatically from over £7000 in 1603 to less than £1500 in 1604. Yet it soon became clear that James was not going to break decisively with the policies of Elizabeth. To do so would have been politically inexpedient; James needed to reinforce his Protestant credentials at a time when he was making peace with Spain and ousting Puritan preachers from their livings. In February 1604, a royal proclamation commanded all Jesuits and seminary priests to leave the realm. It explained that the king had a 'Royall duetie . . . to use all good meanes to keepe our Subjects from being infected with superstitious opinions in matters of Religion, which are not only pernitious to their owne soules, but the ready way and meanes to corrupt their duetie and allegiance'.[25] In July, a priest and a layman were executed at Warwick, and another layman was put to death at Lancaster in September. In November, James underlined his commitment to an anti-Catholic policy by ordering the reimposition of recusancy fines.

It has often been suggested that this renewal of persecution was the major factor behind the infamous Gunpowder Plot of 1605.[26] Yet according to John Bossy, 'the condition of lay Catholics in 1604–5 was very tolerable. Most of the plotters and their friends were very well off and had constant access to priests and their ministrations.'[27] Catesby and his associates seem to have been conspiring before the setbacks of 1604, and the motivation for their daring and reckless plot lay less in frustration at the king's failure to grant toleration than in their anger at the accession of another Protestant to the throne. As Wormald argues, 'Their hope was for a Catholic England, not an England containing tolerated Catholics'.[28] Men like Thomas Wintour and Robert Catesby had longed for the day when Spain would lead a successful Catholic crusade against England's heretical government. By destroying Parliament and the king they aimed to stir the Catholic powers into action and effect the spectacular reconversion of England.

The fanatical extremism of these religious terrorists was at odds with the caution and loyalism of most English Catholics. But the discovery of the 'Powder Treason' inevitably damaged the entire Catholic community. The plot terrified James, and though he had no wish to destroy innocent Catholics along with politically subversive ones, he did sanction tough new measures. Henry Garnet and Edward Oldcorne, two Jesuits who had been in contact with the plotters, were tortured at the rack and then executed, despite their insistence that they detested such treasonable practices. Oldcorne's servant, Ralph Ashley, was also put to death. In 1606, no fewer than 47 priests were removed from prison and permanently banished from England. In the same year, recusancy fines rose sharply to a total of £10,000, and they were to be strictly enforced until the Spanish marriage negotiations brought them to a temporary halt in 1623.

The new penal legislation of 1606 required Catholics to swear an Oath of Allegiance, declaring 'That I do from my heart abhor, detest, and abjure, as impious and heretical, this damnable doctrine and position, that princes which be excommunicated or deprived by the Pope may be deposed or murdered by their subjects or any other whosoever'.[29] The Oath has often been portrayed as an essentially moderate measure intended to divide loyalists from militants. However, it caused chaos among English Catholics. Although some found it acceptable, others were profoundly uneasy at the way it blurred the boundaries between papal excommunication, deposing power, deposition, and tyrannicide. They felt that the Oath was drawing Catholics towards a flat rejection of papal primacy. Rather than distinguishing between peaceful 'religious' Catholics and dangerous 'political' Catholics, it suggested that one could not owe allegiance to both London and Rome. Moreover, the Oath was widely enforced.[30] By 1613, London's prisons alone contained 40 recusants and 11 priests who had been gaoled for refusing to take the Oath. In his reports to Philip III, the Spanish ambassador, Gondomar, emphasised that the persecution of Catholics was still severe because of the Oath, and warned his king not to be deceived by James's carefully projected image of clemency.[31] Certainly, the peculiarly English habit of executing Catholic priests and laity for sedition did not die out under James; altogether 25 Catholics were martyred during the reign, though this was considerably less than the 189 martyrs under Elizabeth.

Yet for all their sufferings, the condition of the Catholics was improving. In many places, Catholics were seen as good neighbours rather than as dangerous papists, particularly after the panic engendered by the Gunpowder Plot had died down. In the small village of Egton, near Whitby, the recusant population grew from around 20 in 1580, to 61 in 1607, and by 1610 there were probably recusants in a third of all households. Yet this did not result in a polarisation of the local community. Instead of friction between Catholics and Protestants, there is evidence of friendly relations, and accommodation rather than separation was the norm for the recusant minority. This was partly due to the absence of any militant Protestant evangelism in Egton, but it reminds us once again that social tolerance was a reality in many communities.[32]

Even at an official level, the government avoided punishing recusants very heavily. The director of Jacobean recusant finance, Sir Henry Spiller, was actually married to a Catholic and tried to arrange Catholic marriages for his children. Understandably, he was accused of protecting recusants and failing to prosecute them as the laws demanded. Spiller's goal was to ensure a constant flow of revenue to the Exchequer from wealthy recusants, and he was against sequestration of lands and goods and repeated prosecutions because this forced recusants to conform and led to loss of revenue. Between 1605 and 1613 the revenue received from recusancy fines fluctuated between £7000 and £13,000, and although this was well below the theoretical maximum, it was a respectable sum. Spiller's opponents, however, were not content with this tax on a few wealthy Catholics; they wished to use recusancy fines to put intolerable pressure on the recusant community as a whole. Yet the Jacobean government clearly favoured Spiller's approach. Instead of crushing Catholicism as the Elizabethan statutes had suggested, the government was now content to tax and tolerate.[33]

Under this more lenient regime, Catholicism flourished. The number of Jesuits in England had risen from only 9 in 1593 to 106 in 1620, and was to reach 180 by 1641. James 'positively welcomed known Catholics to his court and service', and church papists attained high office, marking the emergence of 'court Catholicism' in Protestant England. The Earl of Sunderland became President of the Council of the North, Inigo Jones was made Master of the King's Works and became the nation's greatest architect, and William Byrd was the leading composer in the Chapel Royal until his death in 1622. In 1603 there were eight or nine Catholic peers, but by

1625 the number had risen to eighteen. The English aristocracy became avid consumers of the fashionable culture of Catholic France and Italy, and there was 'an influx of converts, mostly intellectuals and aristocrats'.[34]

'On the whole', claims Hugh Aveling, 'between 1603 and 1642, the English government and society were astonishingly tolerant, if not kindly, and increasingly so.'[35] James himself had a far more irenic attitude towards the Roman church than most Calvinists. Although he sometimes used the rhetoric of Antichrist and insisted on the serious errors of Rome, he also regarded it as a true church. Unlike Calvinist episcopalians like Archbishop Abbot, he did not always view Puritans as useful allies against Rome; instead, like the rising 'Arminian' party, he was more likely to see Puritans and Catholics as almost equivalent threats to the church. This was particularly true after 1618, when despite great pressure from Puritans and conformist Calvinists, he refused to intervene in the Thirty Years War and play the role of Protestant Crusader. At a time when Protestant–Catholic tension on the continent was intensifying, James worked hard to reduce it. While Archbishop Abbot saw the war as an apocalyptic conflict between Protestants and the Beast of Rome, James wrote to the pope as 'his holy father', asking him to lend his weight to the restoration of European peace.[36] After the execution of William Southerne in 1618, there were no more Catholic martyrs in the rest of his reign. But milder forms of persecution did continue, and the Parliament of 1621 called for strict enforcement of the penal laws. James responded by harassing Catholics in the capital. In March 1621, the Venetian ambassador reported that the king had ordered all Catholics to leave London for the duration of the Parliament. By 1622, however, James was negotiating a Spanish marriage for his son; determined to impress Spain, he ordered the release of recusants from prison. In September 1623 he went even further, drawing up a royal pardon for Catholics. Puritans were furious and accused the king of assisting 'the whore of Babylon'.[37]

Anti-popery was not restricted to Puritans, but had a powerful appeal among the populace too. On Sunday, 26 October 1623, a congregation of 300 had gathered next to the French ambassador's residence in Blackfriars to listen to a sermon by the Jesuit Robert Drury. When the platform on which they were seated collapsed, over 90 hearers were killed, including Drury himself and another priest. The disaster attracted a crowd, who hurled abuse at the victims, threw mud and stones, and attacked the carriages of Catholic gentlewomen. In the words of Alexandra Walsham, these were 'street wars of religion', uncannily similar to certain events in sixteenth-century France. In subsequent sermons, prints and pamphlets, Protestants asserted that far from being a tragic accident, the catastrophe was God's righteous judgement on the papists. In contrast to the lukewarm leniency of the court, the Lord had displayed his fierce intolerance of popery.[38]

By the 1620s, however, the king himself no longer shared this anti-popish mentality. Although the Spanish marriage negotiations eventually broke down, James showed little inclination to renew persecution against the Catholics. Instead of trying to find a good Protestant bride for his son, he turned his attentions to France. In November 1624, just a few months before his own death, James reached agreement with the French that Charles would marry Princess Henrietta Maria and that the recusancy laws would be suspended.

Charles I and the Popish Plot

Charles's marriage to Henrietta Maria was to have fateful consequences, for it fed the suspicion of hardline Protestants that Charles was leading the country back to Rome. Yet although Catholics were to enjoy unprecedented tolerance at court, this was not matched in the rest of the nation.

In May 1625, and in keeping with his marriage treaty, Charles instructed the Lord Keeper to suspend all proceedings against recusants. The move angered Parliament and the Privy Council, and by August Charles had backed down, issuing a proclamation calling for the enforcement of the penal laws. As in the reigns of Elizabeth and James, the penal code was rarely enforced to the letter, and only a minority of recusants were fined the full penalties prescribed. However, Charles did introduce a new require-ment that Catholics pay a double charge on subsidies. In addition, a new and more efficient system of recusancy fining was adopted in 1626-7, though the motive was as much economic as religious. As a Catholic agent reported to Rome in 1636, 'This is the only generall molestacon of Catholiques for recusancy, and these paimts are comonly racked very high by the diligence of the Commissioners, partly out of aversion in some of them from religion, but principally out of a desire in all of them to advance the Kings profitt'.[39]

During the Civil War, Puritans claimed that the king and the royalists had been soft on Catholics in the 1630s. In reality, however, it seems clear that the financial burdens on recusants increased between 1625 and 1640. As head of the Recusancy Commission and President of the Council of the North from 1628, Wentworth set rates of composition for recusants that were higher than anywhere else in the country. At his trial he boasted that he had raised income from recusants from £2300 to £11,000 per annum over just four years. Commenting on Charles's reign, Clarendon declared that 'The penal laws (those only being excepted which were sanguinary, and even those sometimes let loose) were never more rigidly executed, nor had the crown ever so great revenue from them, as in his time; nor did they ever pay so dear for the favours and indulgences of his office towards them'. Lindley concludes that 'Roman Catholics in the reign of Charles I did not experience a period of exceptional leniency and general calm; on the contrary, the reign was a period of great trial for English Catholicism. They faced mounting financial pressure from a needy monarch who showed little real interest in their general welfare.'[40] After 1625, there were no further attempts to introduce a formal toleration, and the government failed to produce an Oath of Allegiance that was more acceptable to Catholics.

The Catholic minority also continued to face discrimination in many forms. Baptisms, weddings and burials according to Catholic rites were outlawed, so most Catholics were forced to compromise with the established church in order to secure legal recognition of their age and legitimacy. Some followed Catholic rites, but then persuaded the church courts or local parsons to register the ceremonies as valid. Some had two ceremonies, one Catholic, one Protestant, and others simply accepted the Protestant rites.[41] All in all, England's Catholic minority fared far worse in the early seventeenth century than the Protestant minority in France. As a result of the Edict of Nantes (1598), French Protestants were allowed to build their own churches and enjoy complete freedom of worship in many towns and in the private homes of Protestant nobles. They were also accorded full civil rights and allowed to hold public and royal offices, including posts in the Parlements.[42] By contrast, English Catholics enjoyed no official freedom of worship at all, and had to conform to the established church in order to hold public office.

Yet for all its problems, the Catholic community in England had survived, and by the 1630s it could take pride in having weathered the worst storms of persecution. Two Catholics were executed in Lancaster in August 1628, but during the Personal Rule of Charles I (1629–40) no Catholic suffered the ultimate penalty for their faith, a striking statistic in the light of the number of executions in earlier reigns. Perhaps as many as a fifth of the English peerage and up to a tenth of the gentry were papists, even if many continued to conform to the Church of England. Prominent Catholic gentry often found themselves in the paradoxical position of being lay rectors of a parish church, with the responsibility to appoint the vicar, collect the profits from the church's lands, pay the minister's stipend, and care for the fabric of the church. In counties like Lancashire and Monmouthshire, Catholics constituted a substantial minority of the population, but even in Suffolk, a stronghold of Puritanism, they maintained a significant presence. In the country as a whole, according to John Bossy, the Catholic community had increased by around 50 per cent between 1603 and 1641, to approximately

60,000.[43] The number of priests had also risen dramatically since 1603, with several hundred scattered throughout the country, and another 70 or so in the capital.[44] London Catholics worked in a host of occupations. There were Catholic doctors, schoolmasters, weavers, royal servants, innkeepers, and even a Catholic printer in Clerkenwell. Despite attempts to stop English Catholics attending mass at foreign embassy chapels, the practice continued throughout the 1630s.

Keith Lindley has identified six reasons for the survival of the community: geographical factors, such as distance from London and the arm of government; the committed support for Catholicism given by leading noblemen; the steadfast recusancy of Catholic gentry who helped to sustain the faith in their neighbourhood; the activities of Catholic priests; the organisation of Catholic education at home and abroad, to pass on the faith to a new generation and train missionary priests; and the ingenuity with which recusants escaped conviction.[45] We should add that the Catholic community survived because many Protestant magistrates were not prepared to engage in ruthless persecution of their neighbours. Prominent lay Catholics were often respected figures in local society, and enjoyed good relations with their Protestant neighbours. In Warwickshire, for instance, Ann Hughes suggests that 'In quiescent periods the indications are that the Catholic gentry were tolerated amicably enough by most of their Protestant counterparts'.[46] Although the Catholic gentry could be subjected to recusancy fines, they also experienced a good deal of social tolerance.

At court, Catholicism did not merely survive – it seemed to thrive. Initially, this did not seem likely, for Charles and Henrietta Maria took time to warm to each other. The queen was angered by Charles's unwillingness to grant toleration to Catholics and by the expulsion of the French priests from her court in 1626. She made her disapproval of Protestant persecution clear by visiting Tyburn and kneeling in prayer before the gallows in commemoration of the Catholic martyrs who had died there. Yet although England went to war with France in 1627–8, the royal couple suddenly grew much closer, particularly after the assassination of Buckingham, the king's closest friend and confidant. Peace with France was concluded in 1629, and Henrietta Maria was allowed to invite Capuchin monks over from France. 1632 saw the opening of her new chapel, and the event was celebrated by 2000 people and by bonfires in the Catholic embassies.

1632 was also the year in which Charles I granted a patent to the Catholic courtier George Calvert, Lord Baltimore, to establish a colony in America. Calvert died in the same year, but his son oversaw the settling of Maryland in 1634. Although the proprietor and some of the colonists were Catholics, they were outnumbered by a Protestant majority, and a unique policy of mutual toleration was practised from the outset. In 1649 the colony was to pass an act granting toleration to all Trinitarian Christians. By including Catholics, this Toleration Act went further than the English Act of 1689. To prevent confessional strife, it threatened fines, whippings and imprisonment for anyone who uttered 'reproachfull words or Speeches concerning the blessed Virgin Mary', or called their neighbour 'an heritick, Scismatick, Idolator, puritan, Independant, Presbiterian, popish prest, Jesuite, Jesuited papist, Lutheran, Calvenist, Anabaptist, Brownist, Antinomian, Barrowist, Roundhead, Sepatist' or any other term of contemporary religious abuse. Although Maryland's toleration was born out of practical necessity rather than theological principle, it was a remarkable experiment in religious pluralism, civil equality and Catholic–Protestant co-operation.[47]

The success of Baltimore in establishing Maryland reflected the growing influence of Catholics in high places. In 1634, Charles welcomed the papal agent Gregorio Panzani to court, and two years later he was succeeded by George Conn, who enjoyed a friendly relationship with the king and was involved in the conversion of a number of prominent courtiers to Catholicism. Sir Kenelm Digby converted in 1636, and Countess Newport in 1637. Lord Treasurer Portland died a Catholic in 1634, and in 1636 another Privy Councillor, Cottington, pronounced himself a Catholic during an illness. When a royal proclamation forbade English Catholics from attending the chapels of the queen or foreign embassies in 1638, Henrietta Maria retorted by attending Christmas mass in the company of a group of recent converts. According to Caroline Hibbard, 'The court was swarming with Catholics, and some of the king's chief ministers were justly suspected of Catholic sympathies'.[48]

The tangible evidence of Catholicism at court engendered panic in Protestant minds. For most early modern Protestants, Catholicism was not another Christian denomination, it was fundamentally 'anti-Christian'. The Catholic church was corrupt, apostate, and idolatrous. According to most English theologians, the Roman papacy was the Beast, the Antichrist of Revelation 13. Although practising Catholics comprised only a small percentage of the population, and although the power of Spain was in decline, the fear of popery remained strong. For all their quietism, English Catholics still found it hard to bury the charge of disloyalty. Attempts to devise an Oath of Allegiance acceptable to both the crown and the papacy had failed, and even had they succeeded the Catholic minority would still have been under suspicion because of their perceived links to foreign Catholic powers like Spain. As the Puritan Oliver Cromwell later recalled, 'The papists in England – they have been accounted, ever since I was born, Spaniolised . . . Spain was their patron'. In the years between the Gunpowder Plot and the end of the Personal Rule, there were periodic rumours of bloody Catholic risings. These scares were localised and short-lived, and did not compare to the national panics of the 1580s, 1605, 1640–1 or 1678–9. But anti-Catholicism was still a potent force, and the king's failure to take account of this was ultimately to prove his undoing.[49]

Laudianism and the attack on Puritanism

Fears of a popish plot were exacerbated by the Caroline repression of Puritans. Recent historians have emphasised the contrast between the ecclesiastical policies of James and his son. Whereas James fostered a broad and internally tolerant church, Charles committed himself to a campaign against Puritanism which ultimately proved disastrous. However, while the contrast works over the entire course of their reigns, the situation between 1618 and 1628 was more complex. After the outbreak of the Thirty Years War, James's fear of Puritan subversion had been revived by the vociferous criticism of his foreign policy, and he had turned to Arminian clergymen like Richard Neile and Richard Montagu who strongly supported his irenic stance towards the Catholic powers. Although Charles was close to the Arminians in outlook, he also cultivated Puritans like his chaplain, John Preston, and supported a pro-Protestant and anti-Spanish foreign policy after the failure of the Spanish match.

Yet from the start of his reign, Charles promoted Arminians with greater vigour than his father had done. The policy was deeply controversial and damaging because Arminians seemed to represent a crypto-popery within the church that paralleled the open popery at court. At least some of them, like Arminius himself, had rejected Calvin's doctrine of predestination, and in their stress on free will they were seen as undermining the Reformation principle of *sola gratia*.[50] More significantly, and in contrast to the Dutch Arminians, they were determined to move Protestant worship in a High Church direction and reorient the service around the liturgy and communion rather than the sermon. In their churches, they moved the communion table to the east end of the church and railed it off as an altar. Repulsed by the austerity of Calvinist worship, they wished to introduce their parishioners to the 'beauty of holiness'.[51] Puritans regarded these innovations as nothing short of idolatrous, a deplorable reversal of the Reformation. In all the Parliaments of the late 1620s, there were anguished complaints about the rise of Arminianism and popery.[52]

Arminians, however, were in the driving seat, and they had no intention of tolerating dissent within the church. As political loyalists they had the ear of the king, who was alienated by the insubordination of Puritans and other Calvinist critics. In 1628, the Arminian William Laud was made bishop of

London, and in 1633 he became archbishop of Canterbury. Whereas the Dutch Arminians were a persecuted sect by the 1620s and had started to embrace radical tolerationism, the English Arminians never showed much interest in tolerating others. Neile and Laud, after all, had both been involved in the trial and execution of Edward Wightman. In 1639, Neile wrote to Laud reminding him that the burnings of 1612 'did a great deal of good in this church', and suggesting that 'the present times do require like exemplary punishment'.[53] Sectarian heretics could expect no mercy from the English Arminians, but even orthodox Puritans within the church came under increasing pressure.

As the Arminian campaign to transform the church gathered pace in the late 1620s, the ecclesiastical tolerance of the Jacobean church was replaced by a drive for rigid conformity. In 1633 the Feoffees for Impropriations, which had financed Puritan ministers, was disbanded. Laudians also used informers and episcopal visitations to identify nonconformist parishes, and then took action against the ministers, bringing some of them before High Commission for trial. In the heartland of radical Puritanism, East Anglia, the campaign was particularly intensive. According to the main historian of Essex Puritanism, 'the godly in Essex were subjected to a repression more severe than any they had endured since Elizabeth's accession'.[54] Many ministers felt under great pressure to conform. Unwilling to compromise, nonconformist Puritans were faced with some painful choices. Silenced ministers could still play a significant role in the voluntary meetings of the godly, particularly if they had the patronage of a wealthy lay Puritan, but they were robbed of the freedom to engage in public preaching and the administration of the sacraments which were central to their vocation. Frustrated, many ministers considered the option of emigration to the Netherlands or New England.[55] A substantial number took refuge in the Netherlands, where they could establish their own English congregations. However, the establishment of the Massachusetts Bay Company had opened up a new possibility, and in 1630 the flagship *Arbella* and six other ships set sail for the colony. In its first decade, Massachusetts was to attract more than 13,000 settlers.

There has been much debate among twentieth-century historians over the relative importance of religious and economic motivations for the 'Great Migration'. As in the case of Plymouth, not everyone who sailed to the colony could be described as a Puritan; indeed, both colonies had their fair share of 'ungodly' characters whose behaviour troubled the colonial leaders.[56] Yet it is hard to deny that Puritanism was the dominant force behind the migration. The Bay Company itself was in the hands of godly aristocrats and gentry, the leadership of the colony was also thoroughly Puritan, and many of the laity shared Puritan convictions too.[57] Perhaps it is going too far to say that the persecution gave birth to New England, but it was clearly a critical impetus for those who created and peopled the new colonies. Of the 79 clergy who emigrated, at least 52 had been in conflict with the authorities in England, and others felt threatened. Although all the emigrants cited a variety of reasons for taking the momentous step of leaving their homeland, many would hardly have considered the move in the first place had it not been for the religious crisis of the 1630s.[58] The 'Puritan diaspora' was not comparable to the Jewish expulsion from Spain after 1492, or the Huguenot migration from France after 1685; the numbers involved were smaller, and Puritans were not ordered into exile by the government, or threatened with imprisonment or death if they stayed. But in its own way, the exodus of the godly to New England and the Netherlands bore eloquent testimony to the reality of persecution.

Having said this, we should point out that Massachusetts itself did not reject the ideal of religious uniformity or deny the legitimacy of religious coercion. The Separatist Roger Williams was expelled from the colony for radical beliefs which threw into question the basic principles on which the colony was built. Williams had denied the right of the king to grant land to the colonists, rejected the taking of oaths by the unregenerate, called for complete separation from the Church of England, and maintained that the magistrate had no right to enforce the worship of God. Sentenced to be transported to England, he managed to escape and make his way through the winter snows to Rhode Island in 1636. Convinced that Protestants should try to imitate the voluntary, non-coercive church of the New Testament rather than the godly commonwealth of Old Testament Israel, he insisted on toleration for all religions. His new colony became a place of refuge for all kinds of dissenters. In 1638, it attracted Anne Hutchinson, another outcast from Massachusetts, expelled for accusing the ministers of legalism and claiming divine inspiration for herself. In later years, it was to become home to a substantial group of Quakers and even Jewish emigrants from England. Its principles were encapsulated in its charter of 1663, which guaranteed that 'noe person within the said colonye at any tyme hereafter shall bee any wise molested, punished, disquieted, or called in question for any difference in opinions in matters of religion'.[59] In the eyes of the Massachusetts Puritans, Williams was a well-meaning but thoroughly misguided maverick. They had not travelled across the Atlantic to create a chaotic pluralist society. Rather than offering a liberal alternative to Laudianism, they were establishing an alternative form of godly rule.

As well as prosecuting nonconformists within the established church, the Laudians also targeted the 'Stranger Churches'. Under James, the foreign Reformed churches had been allowed to maintain their distinctiveness. Laud, however, knew that Puritans looked on the foreign churches with admiration, and he viewed the French, Dutch and Italian congregations as 'great nurseries of inconformity'.[60] By tolerating their distinctive liturgy and relative autonomy, the English church had drawn unacceptable limits to its own authority and to religious uniformity. In 1634–5, all members of the Stranger Churches born in England were ordered to join the established church, and the churches themselves were urged to replace their own liturgies with the Book of Common Prayer. The congregations now 'lived through their darkest hour'. 'The very existence of these foreign communities, as religious and cultural entities within a centralising Church-State, appeared doomed by forced assimilation.'[61] The Stranger Churches naturally protested against the new measures, and Laud compromised a little by allowing them to keep their own liturgy. However, the French churches in York and Norwich were later forced to conform in 1638, and the Laudian campaign had its desired effect. In the decade after 1634, the membership of the foreign churches declined precipitously from 11,000 to just 4000.[62] In their attack on these communities, the Laudians had reiterated their hostility to schism and their zeal for uniformity.

The apogee of Laudian repression was seen in the prosecution of Puritan pamphleteers for sedition by the Star Chamber. In several notorious cases during the 1630s, vitriolic critics of the Laudian regime were subjected to savage punishments. In 1630, the militant Puritan Alexander Leighton was arrested and sentenced by Star Chamber for writing a bitter book against the bishops. As well as being fined, whipped, and imprisoned, he had his ears cropped, his nose slit, and his forehead branded. In 1633, the lawyer William Prynne, a vociferous critic of the Laudian regime, published an attack on the stage plays which were patronised by the court. He was fined £5000, sentenced to life imprisonment and had his ears cropped in 1634. Four years later, Prynne and two other Puritans, Henry Burton and John Bastwick, were brought before Star Chamber for writing polemical pamphlets against the Laudian bishops. On 30 June 1637, the three men were punished before a crowd of hundreds. Burton and Bastwick had their ears cut off, and the hangman sliced away what remained of Prynne's. He also had the letters S.L. ('seditious libeller') branded on his cheeks with a hot iron. It was popularly said that the letters should stand for *stigmata Laudis*, the scars of Laud. The fortitude of the three men impressed many onlookers, and the Catholic Kenelm Digby reported that 'Puritans keep the bloody sponges and handkerchiefs that did the hangman service in the cutting off of their ears'. Their physical ordeal complete, the three men were taken away to perpetual imprisonment – Prynne to the Channel Islands, Burton to Guernsey, and Bastwick to the Scilly Isles. In February 1638, a young apprentice, John Lilburne, was tried and condemned in Star Chamber for illegally importing books by Bastwick and others from the

Netherlands. His hands were tied to the back of a cart, and he was scourged along a 2-mile route from the Fleet prison to Westminster, and then made to stand for two hours in the pillory with the open wounds on his back still bleeding.

The punishment of these Puritans turned out to be a propaganda disaster for the Caroline government. The victims of 1637–8 became celebrated martyrs, and defiantly publicised their own sufferings to great effect in pamphlets written from prison. 'I am not in the least afraid of you', Lilburne declared, 'for I neither feare an Axe at Tower hill, nor a Stake in Smithfield, not a Halter at Tyburne, nor Whipping at a Carts-arse, nor a Pillory in the Pallice-yard nor Gagging, not Cutting of eares and nose, nor Burning in the forehead or cheekes, nor yet Banishment with John to Pathmos.'[63] It is possible, of course, to understand the government's point of view. The ferocious polemics of these Puritans were thought to warrant a fierce response. Unlike the Elizabethan Separatists, they had escaped with their lives, and in the context of the times punishment by mutilation was not in itself seen as morally problematic.[64] Moreover, although Lilburne went on to become a fervent tolerationist, opposing all forms of religious persecution as 'popish', Prynne was later a staunch advocate of the persecution of heretics. Yet for people reared on Foxe's *Acts and Monuments*, the mutilation of these godly men reactivated memories of the Marian persecution. By inflicting violence on such conscientious Protestants, the Caroline regime simply reinforced the growing perception that it was reversing the Reformation and returning England to popery.

However, the Personal Rule of Charles I was to collapse under the force of Scottish rather than English anti-popery. In Scotland, the Puritan tendency within the church was stronger and more militant than in England, and the king's attempt to introduce Laudian policies proved disastrous. When Charles visited Scotland for his coronation in 1633, he alienated his subjects by insisting on High Church ceremony. The Scottish nobility was outraged by the death sentence passed against Lord Balmerino for possessing a copy of a petition critical of royal ecclesiastical policy, and though the sentence was not carried out, the damage had been done. Nonconformist ministers were deprived of their charges, and some even set sail for New England only to be turned back by a storm. When the king imposed the Book of Canons in 1636, fears of a reversal of the Reformation started to reach fever pitch. In July 1637, when the new Scottish Prayer Book was introduced at St Giles Cathedral in Edinburgh, godly matrons rioted and denounced the new 'mass book'. A protest movement was organised bringing together the Presbyterian clergy and the nobility. In February 1638, the movement coalesced around the National Covenant, and in August, a General Assembly of the kirk overthrew the Scottish bishops.[65]

In the Bishops Wars of 1639 and 1640, the king failed in his attempt to suppress the Covenanters, and they forced him to call the Long Parliament in November 1640. Scotland's Covenanters had prepared the way for England's Puritans. In both countries, the Laudian campaign to suppress Puritanism and impose High Church worship had provoked a protest movement led by militant Protestants. They were angry at both persecution and toleration: the persecution of the godly and the toleration of popery and crypto-popery within the church. For these godly Protestants, the opportunity had arrived to purge the nation of popish impurities and establish the true reformed religion.

Notes

1   A. Dures, *English Catholicism, 1558–1642* (Harlow, 1983), p. 40.

2   J. Wormald, 'Gunpowder, treason and the Scots', *Journal of British Studies* 24 (1985), 145.

3   C. H. McIlwain, ed., *The Political Works of James I* (Cambridge, MA, 1918), p. 39.

4   Ibid., p. 55.

5   Ibid., pp. 23–4, 6–8.

6   See K. Fincham and P. Lake, 'The ecclesiastical policy of James I', *Journal of British Studies* 24 (1985), 169–207.

7   J. F. Larkin and P. L. Hughes, eds, *Stuart Royal Proclamations*, vol. I: *Royal Proclamations of King James I, 1603–1625* (Oxford, 1973), pp. 87–90.

8   P. Croft, 'Robert Cecil's religion', *Historical Journal* 34 (1991), 775–80.

9   Fincham and Lake, 'Ecclesiastical policy'.

10   See P. Collinson, *The Religion of Protestants* (Oxford, 1982), *passim*.

11   William Bradford, *Of Plymouth Plantation, 1620–1647*, ed. S. E. Morison (New York, 1963), p. 10.

12   See J. Coggins, *John Smyth's Congregation: English Separatism, Mennonite Influence, and the Elect Nation* (Waterloo, ONT, 1991).

13   T. Helwys, *The Mistery of Iniquity* (1612), p. 69.

14   J. Murton, *An Humble Supplication to the King's Majesty*, reprinted in E. B. Underhill, ed., *Tracts on Liberty of Conscience and Persecution, 1614–61* (London, 1846), pp. 181–231.

15 Bradford, *Of Plymouth Plantation*, p. 25.

16 What follows is drawn from W. K. Jordan, *The Development of Religious Tolera-tion in England*, 4 vols (1932–40), II, pp. 43–52; L. Levy, *Blasphemy: Verbal Offense against the Sacred from Moses to Salman Rushdie* (Chapel Hill, NC, 1993), pp. 96–9; and H. J. McLachlan, *Socinianism in Seventeenth-Century England* (Oxford, 1951), pp. 32–3.

17 C. Burrage, *Early English Dissenters*, 2 vols (Cambridge, 1912), II, pp. 169–71.

18 M. Ingram, *Church Courts, Sex and Marriage in England, 1570–1640* (Cambridge, 1987), pp. 116, 123.

19 N. Matar, *Islam in Britain, 1558–1685* (Cambridge, 1998), p. 184; idem, *Turks, Moors and Englishmen in the Age of Discovery* (New York, 1999).

20 C. Marsh, *Popular Religion in Sixteenth-Century England* (London, 1998), pp. 187–96.

21 C. Marsh, *The Family of Love in English Society, 1550–1630* (Cambridge, 1994), p. 249.

22 See P. Lake, ' "A charitable Christian hatred": the godly and their enemies in the 1630s', in C. Durston and J. Eales, eds, *The Culture of English Puritanism, 1560–1700* (London, 1996), ch. 5.

23 P. Collinson, 'Wars of religion', in his *The Birthpangs of Protestant England* (Oxford, 1988), ch. 5, quotation at p. 136.

24 Wormald, 'Gunpowder, treason and the Scots', pp. 154–5.

25 Larkin and Hughes, eds, *Stuart Royal Proclamations*, I, p. 71.

26 The plot is ably examined in three recent books: A. Fraser, *The Gunpowder Plot: Faith and Terror in 1605* (London, 1996); A. Haynes, *The Gunpowder Plot* (Stroud, 1994); and M. Nicholls, *Investigating Gunpowder Plot* (Manchester, 1991).

27 J. Bossy, 'A tall stranger in Hoxton', *London Review of Books*, 3 July 1997, p. 27.

28 Wormald, 'Gunpowder, treason and the Scots', pp. 152–3.

29 See J. R. Tanner, ed., *Constitutional Documents of the Reign of James I, 1603–25* (Cambridge, 1930), pp. 86–104, Oath at pp. 90–1.

30 M. Questier, 'Loyalty, religion and state power in early modern England: English Romanism and the Oath of Allegiance', *Historical Journal* 40 (1997), 311–29.

31 Dures, *English Catholicism*, p. 48.

32 W. J. Sheils, 'Catholics and their neighbours in a rural community: Egton Chapelry 1590–1780', *Northern History* 34 (1998), 109–33.

33 M. Questier, 'Sir Henry Spiller, recusancy and the efficiency of the Jacobean exchequer', *Historical Research* 66 (1993), 251–66.

34 H. Aveling, *The Handle and the Axe* (London, 1976), pp. 112, 124, 75.

35 Ibid., p. 112.

36 Fincham and Lake, 'The ecclesiastical policy of James I', 182–6, 198–202.

37 T. Cogswell, 'England and the Spanish match', in R. Cust and A. Hughes, eds, *Conflict in Early Stuart England* (Harlow, 1989), ch. 4.

38 A. Walsham, '"The fatall vesper": providentialism and anti-popery in late Jacobean London', *Past and Present* 144 (1994), 36–87.

39 K. Lindley, 'The lay Catholics of England in the reign of Charles I', *Journal of Ecclesiastical History* 22 (1971), 211.

40 Ibid., 220–1.

41 Aveling, *The Handle and the Axe*, p. 145.

42 See M. Holt, *The French Wars of Religion, 1562–1629* (Cambridge, 1995), pp. 164–5.

43 J. Bossy, *The English Catholic Community, 1570–1850* (London, 1975), pp. 188, 193. Some historians offer much higher estimates. M. Havran, *The Catholics in Caroline England* (London, 1962), pp. 82–3, suggests that the total number of Catholics may have exceeded 300,000. However, J. Miller, *Popery and Politics in England, 1660–1688* (Cambridge, 1973), pp. 8–12, concurs with Bossy's estimates.

44 Havran, *The Catholics in Caroline England*, pp. 79–82.

45 Lindley, 'The lay Catholics of England', pp. 206–9.

46 A. Hughes, *Politics, Society and Civil War in Warwickshire, 1620–1660* (Cambridge, 1987), p. 64.

47 See J. D. Krugler, 'Lord Baltimore, Roman Catholics and toleration: religious policy in Maryland during the early Catholic years, 1634–1649', *Catholic Historical Review* 65 (1979), 49–75. The 1649 Act is reprinted in J. F. Maclear, ed., *Church and State in the Modern Age: A Documentary History* (New York, 1995), pp. 45–7.

48 C. Hibbard, *Charles I and the Popish Plot* (Chapel Hill, NC, 1983), p. 16.

49 R. Clifton, 'Fear of popery', in C. Russell, ed., *The Origins of the English Civil War* (London, 1973), pp. 144–67.

50 See N. Tyacke, *Anti-Calvinists: The Rise of English Arminianism, c.1590–1640* (Oxford, 1987).

51 See P. Lake, 'The Laudian style: order, uniformity, and the pursuit of the beauty of holiness in the 1630s', in K. Fincham, ed., *The Early Stuart Church, 1603–1642* (London, 1993), ch. 7.

52   See C. Russell, *Parliaments and English Politics, 1621–1629* (Oxford, 1979), pp. 29–32, *passim*.

53   See C. Hill, *Milton and the English Revolution* (London, 1977), p. 288.

54   W. Hunt, *The Puritan Moment: The Coming of Revolution in an English County* (Cambridge, MA, 1983), p. 256.

55   T. Webster, *Godly Clergy in Early Stuart England: The Caroline Puritan Movement, c.1620–1643* (Cambridge, 1997), ch. 14.

56   See D. Cressy, *Coming Over: Migration and Communication between England and New England in the Seventeenth Century* (Cambridge, 1987), ch. 3.

57   See V. D. Anderson, *New England's Generation: The Great Migration and the Formation of Society and Culture in the Seventeenth Century* (New York, 1991).

58   S. H. Moore, 'Popery, purity and providence: deciphering the New England experiment', in A. Fletcher and P. Roberts, eds, *Religion, Culture and Society in Early Modern England* (Cambridge, 1994), pp. 257–89.

59   W. McLoughlin, *Rhode Island: A Bicentennial History* (New York, 1978), pp. 3–46, quote at p. 37. See also E. Gaustad, *Liberty of Conscience: Roger Williams in America* (Grand Rapids, MI, 1991), ch. 2.

60   R. Acheson, *Radical Puritans in England, 1550–1660* (London, 1990), p. 41.

61   B. Cottret, *The Huguenots in England: Immigration and Settlement, c.1550–1700* (Cambridge, 1991), p. 98.

62   C. Carlton, *Archbishop William Laud* (London, 1987), p. 88.

63   See J. R. Knott, *Discourses of Martyrdom in English Literature, 1563–1694* (Cambridge, 1993), pp. 134–50, quotation at p. 149.

64   See K. Sharpe, *The Personal Rule of Charles I* (New Haven, CN, 1992), pp. 758–65.

65   See J. Coffey, *Politics, Religion and the British Revolutions: The Mind of Samuel Rutherford* (Cambridge, 1997).

CHAPTER 6

The Puritan Revolution, 1640–60

On 18 August 1642, Hugh Green was executed on Gallows Hill in the Puritan town of Dorchester. Green was a Roman Catholic priest who had been condemned for treason, though on the scaffold he insisted that he was no traitor. The crowd who watched his execution were baying for blood. For several generations they had been taught that the pope was Antichrist, and in the past year they had heard terrible stories of how Protestant women and children had been massacred in the Irish rebellion. Fuelled by parliamentary propaganda about a popish plot, their fear and anger boiled over. As Green delivered his final speech, a local Puritan chaplain cried, 'He blasphemeth! Stop the mouth of the blasphemer!' When his speech was over, Green faced an excruciating ordeal. The town's barber-surgeon cut out his entrails while he was still alive, and he was hanged, drawn and quartered. His heart was put on a spear, shown to the crowd and thrown into the fire. The mob then carried out rituals of dehumanisation and desecration. Some got hold of Green's decapitated head and kicked it around like a football. When they had tired of their macabre sport, they jammed sticks into the eyes, ears, mouth and nose of the bloody head. Finally, the head was buried in the ground near the scaffold.[1]

The death of Hugh Green epitomises the ugly face of the Puritan Revolution. And yet, as John Morrill has written, 'Perhaps the most extraordinary development of the 1640s and 1650s is how a civil war that began as a struggle between two authoritarianisms became a revolution for religious liberty'.[2] The Revolution eventually threw up a regime which was more tolerant of religious dissent than its predecessors had been. And it saw the beginning of the great English toleration debate, a debate in which radical Puritans were to publish some of the century's most eloquent pleas for religious toleration. This chapter will attempt to explain this central paradox of the Puritan Revolution, the paradox of its bigotry and tolerance.

Godly warriors

When the Long Parliament assembled in November 1640, the great major-ity of MPs were united in opposition to the Laudian reforms of the previous decade. But their unity concealed a deeper division. Many wanted to see a return to the equilibrium of the Jacobean era, when the church had been unified around a broad Calvinist consensus, allowing considerable space for its Puritan tendency to flourish. However, Puritan MPs wanted more in 1640. They had been radicalised by their experience of persecution under Laud, and they harboured a far more drastic vision of 'further reformation'. The bitter experiences of the past twenty years had convinced them that Antichrist was taking over the Church of England. But suddenly the tide had turned, and they found themselves with the opportunity to destroy the devil's work and build Jerusalem in England's green and pleasant land. Their zealous drive was ultimately to split the Long Parliament down the middle.

The key leader of the Puritans in Parliament, and the spokesman for those critical of the policies of the 1630s, was John Pym. Pym was a devout Protestant, obsessed with the purity of true religion and the spectre of popery. In the 1630s, according to Oliver St John, 'fearing that popery might overgrow this kingdom', he had intended to make 'some plantation in foreign parts, where the profession of the Gospel might have a free course'.[3] But in 1640 Pym and his allies realised that they could now cut back the growth of popery and clear a free course for the Gospel in Eng-land itself. When the Long Parliament assembled in November, most MPs shared Pym's conviction that the Personal Rule had had many ill effects. Over the next few months, Parliament united in passing a series of constitu-tional measures which reversed the policies of the 1630s. The dreaded Court of High Commission was abolished and the Puritan 'martyrs' of 1637 – Bastwick, Burton and Prynne – were welcomed back from prison by large and enthusiastic London crowds.

Yet the profound divide between moderate Protestants and Puritans was eventually exposed. It first became apparent when radical Puritans issued the Root and Branch petition in December 1640. The petition decried both the persecution and the toleration of the Personal Rule. The root and branchers condemned the 'inquisition' of the 1630s, which had caused 'multitudes' to flee into exile in 'Holland and other parts':

The exercising of the oath *ex officio*, and other proceedings by way of inquisition, reaching even to men's thoughts, the apprehending and detaining of men by pursuivants, the frequent suspending and depriving of ministers, fining and imprisoning of all sorts of people, breaking up of men's houses and studies, taking away men's books, letters, and other writings, seizing upon their estates, removing them from their callings, separating between them and their wives against both their wills . . .

Yet the root and branchers wanted to remove one kind of intolerance only to replace it with another. They deplored the ecclesiastical and civil tolerance which Charles had extended to Arminians and Catholics during his Personal Rule. They called for the Church of England to be purged of false doctrine and Laudian ritual, and demanded the repression of 'Papists, Priests and Jesuits'.[4]

Many moderate Protestants would probably have gone along with this, but by blaming the bishops for England's corruption and calling for the wholesale destruction of episcopal government, the root and branchers divided Parliament. Their crusade against the 'popish Antichrist' went much further than moderate Protestants cared to go, for it aimed at 'reforming the Reformation', not merely conserving it. Many MPs were also alienated by the ruthless and legally dubious manner in which Pym secured the execution of Charles's leading minister, Sir Thomas Wentworth, in May 1641. Yet by the summer of that year, the situation seemed to have calmed. Charles was in Scotland, mollifying the Covenanters, and Pym's campaign seemed to be losing momentum.

Then, in early November, news reached England of a Catholic rebellion in Ireland which had resulted in terrible massacres of Protestants. Although it is difficult to get accurate statistics, it is probable that 2000 or 3000 Protestant settlers were killed in Ulster, where most of the massacres took place. In the county of Armagh, between a quarter and a third of the total Protestant population was destroyed.[5] The motivation for these massacres was, of course, complicated. The rebellion was far from being a simple case of gratuitous religious hatred. The dominance of militant Protestants in English and Scottish politics had fuelled Irish Catholic fears of persecution and the rising was also a protest against an oppressive colonial power. But the ordinary Catholics who participated in the massacres do seem to have been motivated by a desire to restore Catholicism and destroy heretics. As in the French Wars of Religion, the bodies of Protestants were desecrated; heads were taken from corpses and mutilated by mobs, just as in the case of Hugh Green at Dorchester.[6] Little wonder that a century later, Voltaire would cite the Irish uprising along with the St Bartholomew's Day massacre as two of the most horrific examples of Christian barbarity.[7]

When news of the massacre reached London, the effect was devastating. Contemporary reports suggested that 100,000 or 200,000 Irish Protestants had been slaughtered, though historians now estimate that the total Protestant population of Ulster was only around 34,000.[8] Because there were signs of royal involvement, Charles's reputation was fatally damaged in the eyes of many. Suspicions of a popish plot seemed vindicated, and fear of popery provided Pym with a potent source of support. Since May 1640, a series of panics about a popish uprising in England had swept across the country, and the Irish rebellion sparked off another wave of alarm. Many English Protestants seem to have been genuinely frightened by the thought of imminent attack from Catholics, and Pym's militant Protestantism enjoyed a wide appeal.[9] The Irish rebellion also raised the issue of who was to control the militia that would be sent to suppress the rising. Because many MPs would not trust the king to control it, the way was prepared for the creation of rival armies.

If the Irish rising hardened the resolve of the king's critics, their own belligerence and radicalism drove others into the arms of the king. Throughout 1641, Pym had fuelled the flames of Protestant zeal and anti-popery. After the Irish rebellion he had campaigned for the imprisonment of leading Catholic gentry, only to be rebuffed by the Lords.[10] He had also encouraged anti-popish demonstrations; unruly mobs had intimidated the lords and bishops on numerous occasions. Further pressure was applied through the parliamentary Fast Sermons.[11] The preachers of the sermons were celebrated Puritan divines who shared Pym's fear of a popish plot and his desire for further reformation. The first sermon, preached on 17 November 1640, set the tone for the rest. Cornelius Burgess reminded his audience of 'the horrid hellish Gun-powder-Treason' and the violence of 'Babylon' against the saints of God. He complained of 'people going to, and coming from the Masse in great multitudes, and that as ordinarily, openly, confidently as others go to and from our Churches'. The mass was 'the most abominable Idolatry that ever the Sunne beheld in the Christian world', and Parliament must 'purge out and cast away as a Menstrous Cloth all Idols and Idolatry'.[12] Over the next eighteen months, the parliamentary pulpit resounded to the same message.

The basic intolerance of the Puritan programme, which was so clearly revealed in the Fast Sermons, was also on display in the Grand Remonstrance of December 1641. The Remonstrance was a scathing 204-point indictment of the Personal Rule, 'drenched with the spirit of "no popery"'.[13] Point 88 condemned the Personal Rule on the grounds that 'The Popish party enjoyed such exemptions from penal laws as amounted to a toleration, besides many other encouragements and Court favours'.[14] Like the Root and Branch petition, the Remonstrance also deplored the fact that this tolerance of papists had been combined with the persecution of godly Protestants. Yet although the supporters of the document pledged themselves to protect the godly, they also emphatically asserted their commitment to a traditional policy of religious uniformity:

> we declare that it is far from our purpose or desire to let loose the golden reins of discipline and government in the Church, to leave private persons or particular congregations to take up what form of Divine Service they please, for we hold it requisite that there should be throughout the whole realm a conformity to that order which the laws enjoin according to the Word of God. And we desire to unburden the consciences of men of needless and superstitious ceremonies, suppress innovations, and take away the monuments of idolatry.[15]

In order to implement this programme of purging and uniformity, the Remonstrance recommended that a special synod of godly divines be established. Under its aegis and with the support of Parliament, pure religion could enjoy a monopoly in the land.

It should be obvious that Pym and his followers were not attempting to institutionalise modern religious liberty. They believed themselves to be engaged in a fight to the death with papists, whose religious principles 'tend to the destruction and extirpation of all Protestants, when they shall have opportunity to effect it'. They aimed, not at coexistence and religious pluralism, but at total victory and uniformity. Yet many MPs were worried by the extremist zeal of the Puritan programme. Although 159 voted in favour of the Grand Remonstrance, 148 voted against. The vote revealed that a sizeable party of MPs was now drifting back towards the king. Whereas in November 1640 the Long Parliament had presented a united front against the policies of the previous decade, it was now split down the middle. For the first time, civil war was becoming a real possibility.

In 1642, it was the religious militants who dragged the rest of the nation into war. Both Charles and Pym refused to compromise, and by the middle of the year their activist supporters were raising armies. The English people were forced to choose sides. For some this was perfectly straightforward; Laudians naturally sided with the king, and with very few exceptions Puritans became parliamentarians. But for religious moderates, the decision was an agonising one. Some decided that the rule of law would be safer with a restrained king than with a militant Parliament, whilst others, like John Selden, decided that Parliament had a stronger constitutional case. A multitude of factors came into play when people chose sides in 1642. Many seem to have been guided primarily by secular or constitutional considerations. Others simply followed the drift in their own county, or the lead of the local elite. The consequence was that although the core of the parliamentarian party was Puritan,[16] many of its supporters were not. The parliamentarian MP Henry Marten was described by John Aubrey as 'a great lover of pretty girles . . . as far from a Puritane as light from darkness'.[17]

Yet for many, religion was the key determinant of allegiance. In a study of MPs in the Parliaments of the 1620s, Conrad Russell has demonstrated that their attitudes to religion are the best predictor of their allegiance in 1642. On constitutional issues, future parliamentarians were often quiet, whilst future royalists were outspoken. But in debates over religious issues, the basis for the Civil War divide becomes clear. Whereas future parliamentarians led the attack on Arminianism and the campaign for further reformation and a Protestant crusade against Spain, future royalists were markedly unenthusiastic. 'The Civil War', Russell concludes, 'was not first and foremost about issues of law and government, but, by contrast, it was very largely about the desire of further reformation in religion.'[18] At a grass roots level, a number of local studies also emphasise the centrality of the religious factor in 1642.[19] Building on his research on Devon, Mark Stoyle concludes that right across England 'Civil War allegiance was based primarily on religious sentiment. The areas which came out most fervently for Parliament were those which had been exposed to advanced protestant ideas during the century which preceded the Civil War.'[20]

Thus we can safely say that without Puritan militancy there would have been no Civil War. For these zealous parliamentarian activists, this was indeed a war of religion.[21] Like members of the Catholic League in sixteenth-century France, many parliamentarians were *guerriers de Dieu*.[22] For these holy warriors, the English Civil War was a veritable crusade against the Antichrist and his forces – Irish papists, recusants, Laudians, lukewarm Anglicans. They saw themselves as ancient Israelites fighting to preserve pure worship and destroy idolatry, as the saints of Revelation waging epic battles in the final war against the Beast. In such a conflict there could be no compromise, and in the most famous and bloodthirsty sermon of the war, *Meroz Cursed*, Stephen Marshall denounced 'neuters' and called on Englishmen to fight the Lord's battle. The sermon was one that he preached on 60 occasions, causing royalists to accuse him of being the great 'incendiary' of the war. Inspired by Marshall and other preachers, the parliamentarians marched to war under banners which declared, 'Let God arise and his enemies will be scattered' and 'Antichrist must down'.[23]

Thus the power of religious intolerance was at the heart of the English Civil War. The opposition to Charles I was initially galvanised by the king's persecution of the godly; the godly's anti-popery was partly responsible for the Irish uprising and the slaughter of Ulster Protestants; and that massacre in its turn confirmed the Puritan conviction that popery must be destroyed.

Throughout, a vicious circle of intolerance was generated by fear of persecution. Laudians, Puritans and Irish Catholics were all guilty, and they were all frightened.

Later Whig historians highlighted the persecution of Puritans but then portrayed the parliamentarians as valiant champions of civil and religious liberty. In doing so they were accepting the interpretation of the Civil War propounded by advocates of the 'Good Old Cause' like Sir Henry Vane the younger. In his *Healing Question* (1656), Vane claimed that the war had been fought for popular sovereignty and freedom of religion for all, and in an earlier anonymous pamphlet, *Zeal Examined* (1652), he had argued at length that this freedom should extend to Roman Catholics. But as Richard Baxter pointed out, this was impossible to square with the official declarations of the Long Parliament in the early 1640s: 'The toleration of Popery, by too much connivance, and the increase of Popery thereby, was one of the great offences and grievances that this (and former) Parliaments complained of and Declared against.' Rather than fighting for 'Liberty for the Mass', Baxter insisted, the Parliament had complained that 'the Masse was so openly permitted at the Queens Chappell'. Its 'great Argument and Advantage against the King, [was] that he favoured the Papists, and intended them a Toleration or Connivance'. Far from calling for 'an Universal Toleration', Parliament had pledged itself to 'establishing the Protestant Cause'.[24]

Baxter was exactly right. As Conrad Russell has written, the English Civil War 'was not fought for religious liberty, but between rival groups of persecutors'.[25] In the early 1640s, the bulk of the parliamentarian leadership was determined to suppress popery within and without the Church of England. In the documents of 1640–2, 'toleration' was listed as one of the iniquitous policies of the Caroline regime. Pym and his party had committed themselves to a programme of ecclesiastical and civil intolerance. Firstly, parliamentarian leaders aimed to rid the established church of false doctrine, worship and government – of Arminianism, Laudianism and episcopacy. Secondly, they aimed to break the back of Catholicism in the three kingdoms.

Both aims were pursued with great energy. The campaign against 'scandalous' and 'malignant' clergy during the 1640s was carried out on a massive scale. During the two decades of the Puritan Revolution, approximately 2780 clergymen were ejected from their positions or seriously harassed by the authorities. Around 2120 of these were beneficed clergy who were driven out of their livings. The rest were curates, hospital wardens, prison chaplains, lecturers, preachers or incumbents who were forced to 'resign' or who managed to retain their benefices despite intense harassment. Some of these clergy were guilty of pluralism, scandalous behaviour or militant royalism, but many were conscientious, middle-of-the-road ministers who had not even supported the policies of the 1630s.[26] They were the victims of a Puritan purge of the church which tried to replace lukewarm moderates with politically correct hot gospellers. The godly agreed with the apocalyptic commentator Thomas Brightman that the Church of England had for too long been like the insipid church of Laodicea mentioned in the book of Revelation. Now was their chance to recreate the fiery church of Philadelphia.

The victims of this purge undoubtedly suffered a good deal. According to one Anglican 'martyrology', orthodox clergy had been 'sequestred, spoyled of their Goods and Estates and Houses, to the ruine of their Wives and Children also'. Some had been gaoled, or kept below deck on ships, or starved and murdered in prison. The Puritans had instigated 'new Spanish-English Inquisitions', and in their civil war had 'slain more thousands of Protestants in England, under colour for fighting for Protestant Religion, then Queen Mary condemned scores, within the like compass of years'.[27]

However, the 'persecution' of the 'Anglican' clergy in the 1640s should not be exaggerated. When Anglican martyrologists compared the ejection of the clergy to the tribulations inflicted by Nero or Mary I they were letting hyperbole run riot. In the first place none of the ejected clergy were executed, and very few were imprisoned. The use of the Book of Common Prayer was illegal throughout the Puritan Revolution, but little attempt was made to fine or imprison those who violated this law. Secondly, approximately 1180 of the sufferers continued to serve in the church. Almost 400 of the ejected clergy found new livings, nearly 200 pluralists managed to retain one of their livings, around 270 were harassed but still clung on to their positions, and 320 were not ejected until after 1649. Finally, although the sequestration rate was as high as 86 per cent in London, 'the severity of the persecution varied considerably from area to area'. In some counties, the sequestration rate was well below 25 per cent.[28] This reflects Puritan weakness rather than Puritan tolerance, but it also highlights the limits to the persecution of Anglicanism in the period.

Yet the ejections did cause considerable hardship, not least for the families of the clergy. Although sequestrators often took great care to ensure that the property of a clergyman was properly accounted for, tales abounded of brutal and dishonest sequestrators who seized food, destroyed libraries, and threw families out of their houses with nowhere else to go and no time to pack. Parliament responded to the sense of injustice by standardising compensation payments at one-fifth of the value of the living, and determined that these should be paid out to the minister's wife on her petition. However, this was hardly an adequate sum on which to support a family, and some intruded ministers refused to pay it. Anne Rogers, the wife of a rector ejected from benefices in London and Essex, complained in a petition to the Lords that she had been forced to sell bedding to buy food.

Ejected ministers explored different survival strategies: some found altern-ative livings in poorer benefices, some took shelter with relatives or were supported by parishioners, and many took up alternative occupations such as schoolteaching or farming. Yet even when ministers managed to eke out a living and support a family, ejection remained a painful experience.[29]

The persecution of Catholic clergy, however, was immeasurably harsher. The renewal of the anti-popish crusade in 1641 saw the first executions of seminary priests since 1628. In July, William Ward, a Douai priest who had spent twenty years in prison for his work, was hanged at Tyburn. In De-cember, Parliament petitioned the king to allow the execution of seven more priests, and although Charles refused to accede to their demands, two more priests were killed in January 1642 and seven more before the year was out. In the six years between 1641 and the end of the first Civil War in 1646, a total of 24 Catholic priests were executed for their religious activ-ities. As the case of Hugh Green so graphically illustrates, their sufferings were terrible.[30]

The Catholic laity also faced severe persecution, though their lives were not in direct danger. Parliament demanded that English papists be prohib-ited from attending the chapels in the Catholic embassies, and some tracts even called for all 'idolatrous' worship to be outlawed, even that which involved embassy staff. Mobs attacked worshippers at mass in the queen's chapel and the Lord Mayor of London was forced to provide guards for the Catholic embassies to protect them against mob attack. The queen's chapel was dismantled, her priests were ordered out of the realm, and all Catholics were ordered to remain within 5 miles of their legal residence.[31] In Essex and Sussex during August and September 1642, parliamentarian crowds numbering up to several thousand people attacked, plundered and de-stroyed the property of Catholics, Laudian ministers, and royalists. In his micro-history of this 'religious violence', John Walter argues that although the crowds did not kill their victims, 'there are striking parallels in par-ticular between the events of 1642 and events in the St Bartholomew's Massacre'. In both cases, the crowds drew legitimation from government statements and from the sermons of zealous clergy, and in both cases they were engaged in rites of 'confessional purging'.[32]

In royalist areas, however, the fate of Catholics was very different. Although the majority of Catholic peers and gentry remained neutral dur-ing the war, those who chose sides were far more likely to be royalist than parliamentarian. In Lancashire, 65.5 per cent of royalist gentry families were Catholic, though Catholics formed less than a third of the total gentry families in the county. In such a situation, the loyalty of Catholics ensured their security. Even in parliamentarian areas, concentration on the war deflected attention from the tiny recusant community. However, when

Cromwell's Ironsides stormed the largely Catholic garrison of Basing House in 1645, they cried 'Down with the Papists! Down with the Papists!', and showed no mercy. A hundred Cavaliers were butchered in the fighting, including women and six priests. 'You must remember what they were', explained a parliamentarian newspaper. 'They were most of them Papists. Therefore our muskets and swords did show them little compassion.'[33]

The fragmentation of Puritanism

Although the unexpected triumph of the godly after 1640 intensified the persecution of Catholics, it also created space for the sects that had been systematically persecuted under Elizabeth, James and Charles. In this sense, at least, the early stages of the Puritan Revolution did create religious freedom where it had not existed before. Before 1640, the sects formed a tiny minority. Their main centre was London, where there were around 1000 sectarians by 1640 gathered in ten congregations: one Independent, six Separatist, one Particular Baptist, and two General Baptist.[34] In the diocese of Canterbury, there was also a good deal of Separatist activity in the 1630s.[35] However, most Separatist conventicles were tiny, usually numbering less than 50 people, and there cannot have been more than a few thousand Separatists in the whole of England.

After 1640, the sects became visible and vocal. Riding on the back of the anti-Laudian backlash, they were able to attract substantial numbers of disillusioned Puritans, helped by the greater tolerance of the authorities. In January 1641, a group of over 60 people was discovered in a Separatist conventicle in Southwark. However, although they were examined and referred to the House of Lords, the Lords decided to free them with a warning that they should attend worship at the parish churches. The lenience of the Lords encouraged other Separatists, and throughout 1641 and 1642 there was a steady growth of such groups. The learned bishop Joseph Hall declared that there were 80 sectarian congregations in London alone. Although he was exaggerating, there were almost four times as many sectarian congregations in the city by 1648 as there had been in 1640.[36]

Conservative pamphleteers decried this development. They complained that Separatists were swarming over the land like locusts, and undermining the very fabric of society. Although some sections of the Parliament turned a blind eye to Protestant Separatism, the sects met with their fair share of hostility and violence. In August 1641, the Lord Mayor's men raided the congregation of Henry Jessey, beating and kicking the worshippers, including one pregnant woman who lost her baby and her life as a result. In December, the congregation pastored by Praise-God Barebones was attacked by a mob. Eventually, a constable dispersed the mob, but several conventiclers were put in prison.[37]

The outbreak of civil war in 1642, however, distracted those who would otherwise have concentrated their energies on suppressing heresy and schism. Royalists were powerless in London, which was the key area of sectarian growth, whilst parliamentarians were aware that Separatists were loyal to the cause. The abolition of Star Chamber and High Commission had removed two of the institutions which customarily dealt with religious dissent, whilst the effective breakdown of censorship allowed Separatists to propagate their ideas as never before. In 1640, only 22 pamphlets were published in England, but in 1642 the total was an astonishing 1966.[38] Indeed, between 1640 and 1660 more pamphlets were published than in the century and a half between 1485 and 1640.[39] Amidst the chaos and excitement of the 1640s and 1650s, radical Protestants had an unparalleled opportunity to spread their ideas.

The fragmentation of the Puritan movement was dramatically revealed in January 1644, when five members of the Westminster Assembly of Divines issued *An Apologeticall Narration* distancing themselves from Presbyterianism, and arguing for the right of congregations to govern themselves. By speaking out like this, these Independents were jeopardising the chances of the Assembly fulfilling its purpose – to draw up a uniform system of church government. Yet the Independents were respected figures and they had powerful supporters in the parliamentarian movement. Instead of their being crushed, every effort was made to reach an accommodation with them.[40]

In the confusion that ensued, other more radical groups were given vital breathing space. Separatists, General Baptists and Particular Baptists consolidated their position and won new converts after having eked out a precarious existence under the early Stuarts. Over the next decade a number of new movements emerged: Seekers, Muggletonians, Diggers, Quakers and Fifth Monarchists. In addition, many individuals promoted their own idiosyncratic theological concoctions. The English Presbyterian Thomas Edwards published a sensational exposé of the new heretics entitled *Gangraena* (1646) in which he enumerated 16 sects, 70 pernicious practices and no less than 176 different errors. Heresiographers like Edwards were prone to hyperbole, but their cries of alarm are still revealing. Before their very eyes, the godly were fragmenting. Having set out to erect the new Jerusalem, conservative Puritans now found themselves looking at a new Babel. What had started as a militant Calvinist revolt was becoming England's Radical Reformation.

The toleration debate

What made this Protestant pluralism particularly disturbing was the fact that some leading parliamentarians accepted it with equanimity. The prominent statesman Sir Henry Vane the younger had 'prolixly, earnestly, and passionately reasoned for a full liberty of conscience to all religions'.[41] In the parliamentary armies, too, sectarians seemed to be welcomed with open arms. Oliver Cromwell boldly defended Independents, Separatists and Baptists against those who took a dim view of schismatic Protestants. In one letter to another officer, he wrote:

> Ay, but the man is an Anabaptist. Are you sure of that? Admit he be, shall that render him incapable to serve the public . . . Sir, the State, in choosing men to serve them, takes no notice of their opinions, if they be willing faithfully to serve them, that satisfies. I advised you formerly to bear with men of different minds from yourself.[42]

As well as defending diversity among evangelical Protestants, some radical Puritans also began to argue, like Vane, for the toleration of all religions. 1644 saw the beginning of England's great toleration debate, as writers like William Walwyn and Roger Williams penned stinging attacks on persecution. In the years that followed, other radical Puritans joined in the chorus, insisting that toleration should be extended to Catholics, Jews, heretics, and even blasphemers.[43] In the Whitehall debates of December 1648, radical tolerationists argued with conservative Independents over the clause in the Second Agreement of the People (1648) prohibiting magistrates from punishing anyone for 'professing his faith, or exercise of religion according to his conscience in any house or place'. John Goodwin proposed 'That God hath not invested any power in a civil magistrate in matters of religion', a thesis sharply opposed to the magisterial Reformation position. But by 1648 this claim was widely accepted among radical Puritans, and Goodwin was ably assisted by a number of others, including the Leveller writers John Lilburne and John Wildman.[44] If the Putney debates of 1647 are often hailed as a landmark in the history of democratic thought, the Whitehall debates deserve to be recognised as a significant moment in the history of toleration. As organised public disputations about fundamental principles of popular sovereignty and religious freedom, Putney and Whitehall have few parallels in early modern European history.

Conservative Puritans were appalled at the fragmentation of Protestantism and at these calls for 'a total libertie of all Religions'.[45] Thomas Edwards castigated Goodwin, Walwyn and Williams, and expressed astonishment at the sea change of opinion that now saw some of the godly calling for the toleration of heresy and blasphemy:

> Who ever thought seven yeers ago he should have lived to have heard or seen such things preached and printed in England; all men then should have cryed out of such persons, Away with them, Away with them . . . if some of the godly ministers who were famous in their time should rise out of their graves and come now among us, as Mr Perkins, Greenham, Hildersham, Dr Preston, Dr Sibs &c they would wonder to see things come to this passe in England, and to meet with such Books for Toleration of all Religions.[46]

Ironically, the fragmentation of Puritanism and the rise of radical tolerationism owed much to the intense anti-popery of the parliamentarians. The anti-Catholicism of 1640–2 had fuelled a campaign for the extirpation of idolatry and the establishment of godly uniformity. But in 1642–6, apocalyptic anti-popery stimulated the growth of religious pluralism and calls for toleration. Radical Puritans came to believe that Antichrist had taken new and Protestant forms.[47] Persecution, they argued, was the hallmark of the Beast, and the Presbyterians, in particular, were dancing to the tune of Antichrist.[48] But radical Puritans were also confident that God was now restoring his church to its primitive purity and purging it of corruption. The godly must abandon the Babylon of the established church and build new congregations modelled on the early church. Above all, they must repudiate religious coercion.

Yet this radical tolerationism had limited appeal within the Puritan movement as a whole; the majority remained wedded to the idea of a state church and the suppression of heresy by the magistrate. As Blair Worden reminds us, 'more often than not in puritan England, toleration was a dirty word'.[49] The anti-Trinitarian pamphlets of Paul Best, in particular, aroused outrage, and MPs even called for his death. However, over 100 petitions on Best's behalf were presented to the Commons, and he escaped with just a short spell in prison. In May 1648, the Presbyterians in Parliament secured the passage of 'An Ordinance for the Punishing of Blasphemies and Heresies'. Under the section on blasphemy, the act prescribed the death penalty for atheism and anti-Trinitarianism, whilst the section on heresy threatened imprisonment for Arminians, universalists, Baptists, and antinomians. The Act met with severe criticism from the sects, but it was to become a dead letter. Pride's Purge in December 1648 cleared many Presbyterian MPs from Parliament and signalled a significant shift of political power towards the Independents. In January 1649, Charles I was executed.

For the eleven years of the Interregnum, the government of England was to be dominated by men who were hostile to the imposition of strict religious uniformity, and who were prepared to tolerate at least orthodox dissent outside the established church. Chief among them was Oliver Cromwell, who as Lord General of the Army (1650–3) and Lord Protector (1653–8) towered over his contemporaries.

The enigma of Oliver Cromwell

In many ways, Cromwell embodies the Puritan Revolution's paradoxical combination of bigotry and tolerance. In his case, the bigotry was displayed most terribly in Ireland. In 1649 he commanded the parliamentary armies in their conquest of Ireland. In two massacres, at Drogheda and Wexford, his troops slaughtered several thousand soldiers as well as priests and friars. By the brutal standards of European warfare at the time, the massacres were not unusual.[50] The garrison at Drogheda had refused terms of surrender, with the result that Cromwell's forces had suffered heavy casualties in storming the town and felt no obligation to give quarter. At Wexford, the sack occurred without Cromwell's express command. Yet in both cases, Cromwell was convinced that the English actions were fully justified. He hoped that such terrible defeats would break Irish resistance and so prevent 'much effusion of blood' in the future. But more importantly, he believed that events at Drogheda and Wexford were a terrible divine judgement on the Irish people for the massacres of 1641. Drogheda, he wrote, was 'a righteous judgement of God on these barbarous wretches, who have imbrued their hands in so much innocent blood'.[51]

The massacres at Drogheda and Wexford were not a simple case of sectarian killing. Cromwell did not approve of the slaughter because the victims were Catholic idolaters. But as a Protestant, he did associate popery with cruelty toward the saints of God, and was probably inspired by Old Testament notions of collective blood-guilt. In his mind, the Irish people as a whole had to share responsibility for the killing of tens of thousands of Protestants in 1641. Like the Pequot Indians slaughtered by New England Puritan forces in 1637, the Catholic Irish had been demonised and dehumanised as the enemies of God.[52] In 1649 Cromwell viewed himself as an avenging angel executing divine judgement on a bloody people.

In England, Cromwell displayed a kinder side to his character. Throughout his career, he championed an evangelical Protestant ecumenism, and saw himself as a protector of the people of God. He was quite prepared to tolerate differences so long as people had 'the root of the matter' in them.

By this he seems to have meant a minimalist Protestant belief in Christ's atonement and justification by grace through faith.[53] He rejoiced in the inward, spiritual unity of the godly in the New Model Army, telling Parliament that 'Presbyterians, Independents, all had here the same spirit of faith and prayer', and were not divided by the drive for external uniformity.[54] Throughout his time in power, he was firmly committed to defending the religious freedom of the various evangelical Protestant groups, including the Baptists.

Indeed, the underlying basis of Cromwell's tolerance was his concern for the people of God. On his deathbed, he was reported to have repeated one sentence to his son three times: 'Richard, mynd the people of God and be tender of them.'[55] Cromwell was no enthusiast for a multi-faith society, but he had no problem with pluralism within the evangelical Protestant community. His ultimate aim was to protect the godly and foster their unity. Yet in Cromwell this concern seems to have instilled a profound reluctance to hound conscientious people who were not orthodox Protestants. Roger Williams recorded that during a debate of the Committee for the Propagation of the Gospel in 1652, a member of the committee had attacked lukewarm indifference towards heresy. Cromwell swiftly retorted, 'That he had rather Mahumetanism were permitted amongst us, then that one of Gods Children should be persecuted'.[56] When the Socinian John Biddle was sent into exile in the Scilly Isles, Cromwell personally provided him with a weekly allowance of 10 shillings; although he agreed with Biddle's mild punishment, he was probably impressed by the piety of a man who had memorised the Bible in Hebrew and Greek and spent many hours each day in prayer. Cromwell's openness to the Jews may also have stemmed from a genuine appreciation of their biblicist spirituality, though when he anticipated 'the day to see union and right understanding between godly people (Scots, English, Jews, Gentiles, Presbyterians, Independents, Anabaptists and all)'[57] he was no doubt thinking of the latter day conversion of the Jews to Christianity.

Cromwell attempted to find a middle way between traditional Protestants who wished to enforce uniformity and sectarian Puritans who favoured religious liberty for all. On the one hand, he roundly condemned radical tolerationists like Williams for teaching that the magistrate had no authority to punish blasphemers and heretics – these godly tolerationists, he claimed, were involved in 'the patronizing of villainies'.[58] On the other hand, he chastised those who would not be satisfied 'unless they can put their finger upon their brethren's consciences, to pinch them there'. 'Every sect saith, Oh! Give me liberty', he observed. 'But give him it, and to his power he will not yield it to anybody else. Where is our ingenuity? Truly that's a thing ought to be very reciprocal.'[59] Perhaps Cromwell's own position was closest to that of his chaplain John Owen, the intellectual leader of the Calvinist Independents. Owen was no enthusiast for persecution, but wanted toleration limited to orthodox Trinitarian Protestants.[60] Yet Owen was an academic theologian who liked to draw sharp lines, whilst Cromwell was a layman who usually talked in looser terms about the 'spirit' and the 'root of the matter'. His own churchmanship is notoriously difficult to pin down, for he does not seem to have been a member of any particular congregation. The breadth of his tolerance in the 1650s owed much to his rejection of 'forms', and his profound respect for personal piety.[61]

Ranters and Socinians

Throughout the 1650s, Cromwell was consistently more tolerant than Parliament, but he had no time for the toleration of blasphemers. Along with most of his contemporaries, he fully supported the crackdown on irreligion and antinomian religion in 1650–1. So-called 'Ranters' were accused of violating traditional sexual morality on the grounds that they had been freed from the letter of the law. At the same time, self-anointed prophets and Messiahs claimed that they had come to bring in the last days.[62] In 1650, Parliament ordered the burning of Abiezer Coppe's 'blasphemous' pamphlet, *A Fiery Flying Roll*, and the authorities in Coventry imprisoned Joseph Salmon for blasphemy. After some months in prison, Salmon recanted and was released. Parliament voted in favour of a six-month punishment for a first offence, and passed a second Blasphemy Act in August 1650. This Act was far milder than that of 1648. Even John Milton found it acceptable. Most of those targeted by the earlier act – Socinians, Baptists, Arminians – were ignored in 1650. Instead the focus was on those who denied the external reality of sin or hell or God himself, or who claimed that sexual promiscuity or drunkenness could be sinless activities which expressed the divine life within.

In September 1650, Parliament passed an Act repealing Several Clauses in Statutes imposing Penalties for not coming to Church. For the first time since the Reformation, it was no longer legally compulsory to attend one's parish church on Sunday. Although people were still expected to attend some form of Christian worship, the abolition of penalties for recusancy signalled the formal repudiation of the religious uniformity established in 1559.[63] But the repression of the most outrageous heresies continued, not least in the army, where Jacob Bauthumley was punished by being bored through the tongue with a hot iron. A pamphlet published in December

1650 described 'one W. Smith', who was 'apprehended at York for denying the Deity, Arian-like, and putting in execution several illegal practises against the Parliament; for which, upon a fair tryal, he received sentence to be hanged'. According to the pamphlet, the sentence was carried out, with Smith uttering 'many blasphemous words' upon the scaffold.[64] However, we have no other account of the incident, and it is unclear whether Smith was executed for blasphemy or for his 'illegal practises against the Parliament'. The latter is most likely, because other heretical figures at this time were simply punished with a few months in prison. In August 1651, for example, Thomas Tany and Robert Norwood were sentenced to six months in Newgate gaol for blasphemy. Ariel Hessayon, who has made a meticulous study of these prophets, writes that 'Apart from some notorious exceptions, I have found few instances of regular and systematic convictions for blasphemy under the provisions of the Act of August 1650. Perhaps the authorities had difficulties in enforcing, or were reluctant to take too stringently the limits of liberty of conscience as delimited by the Act.'[65]

Yet the conviction that the magistrate should suppress heresy was still alive and well. When an English translation of the Socinians' *Racovian Catechism* was published in 1651, Parliament responded immediately by ordering the burning of the book. It also established a Committee for the Propagation of the Gospel headed by John Owen. Owen and his colleagues soon published *Humble Proposals* for regulating religion in England. Jordan claims that the proposals were 'the most tolerant recommendation seriously set forth thus far in the seventeenth century by a responsible body in England', for they guaranteed toleration to all sects who could agree to fundamental Christian doctrines.[66] In contrast with the traditional position adopted by the clergy of the Church of England, the Independents were quite willing to tolerate schism from the national church even though they themselves belonged to it. However, heresy was another matter, and the proposals were intended to put an end to tolerance of heresy. They met with a storm of protest. The campaign against them was orchestrated by Roger Williams, who was ably assisted by various petitioners and influential friends like John Milton and Henry Vane. The protesters were opposed to the idea of professional theologians like Owen determining the fundamentals of the faith, and to the requirement that Separatist congregations register with local magistrates. Their vigorous campaign against the Humble Proposals eventually resulted in both of these points being dropped when a new report was presented to Parliament in February 1653.[67]

The failure of Owen's proposals allowed further breathing space for the Socinians, and the religious clauses of the Protectorate's constitution, The Instrument of Government (1653), gave them further encouragement. The Instrument declared that 'none shall be compelled by penalties or otherwise' to accept the 'public profession' of the national church, and in clause 37 it guaranteed a broad liberty of conscience:

> That such as profess faith in God by Jesus Christ (though differing in judgement from the doctrine, worship or discipline publicly held forth) shall not be restrained from, but shall be protected in, the profession of the faith and exercise of their religion; so as they abuse not this liberty to the civil injury of others and to the actual disturbance of the public peace on their parts: provided this liberty be not extended to Popery or Prelacy, nor to such as, under the profession of Christ, hold forth and practise licentiousness.[68]

Since the groups explicitly excluded by this clause were Catholics, Anglicans, Ranters and political subversives, and since Socinians could claim to 'profess faith in God by Jesus Christ', the prospects for the future seemed good. By 1654 Socinians were reported to be holding weekly meetings in London. But Parliament was determined to deal with the Socinians, and in December 1654, Biddle was taken into custody and his books were burned. In January, Parliament declared his books heretical and blasphemous, and after a debate with a Baptist in June 1655, Biddle was gaoled under the Blasphemy Act for denying the deity of Christ. Cromwell admitted that toleration could not 'be stretched so farr as to countenance them who denie the divinity of our Saviour, or to bolster up any blasphemous opinions contrary to the fundamentall verities of religion',[69] but he had no intention of turning Biddle into another Servetus. Eventually, Biddle was quietly sent off into exile in the Scilly Isles. Although another Socinian, John Knowles, was also gaoled, others like Nathaniel Stuckley carried on publishing Biddle's books and spreading the Socinian message.[70]

The Quakers

The Socinians were always few in number. Far larger, and far more threatening to conservative opinion in the 1650s, were the Quakers. The Quakers were the runaway religious success of the Interregnum. By 1660 they had won perhaps as many as 50,000 converts across England, making them the largest sect in the country and only slightly smaller than the Catholic community. In London, they numbered almost 10,000, whilst in Bristol they comprised over 5 per cent of the population. They published over 1000 pamphlets and travelled with their message as far afield as Malta, Alexandria, Jerusalem, Constantinople and the Caribbean. Emphasising personal spiritual experience and downplaying the importance of doctrine, they were a charismatic movement with a powerful appeal to sectarians disillusioned by the disputes and disappointments of the 1640s. What made them so disturbing to contemporaries was their religious style. Unlike their respectable descendants, the early Quakers literally quaked with ecstatic fervour. They interrupted church services, delivered doomsday prophecies, refused to defer to social superiors, encouraged women to preach, and delighted in provocative symbolic gestures, such as going naked as a sign of their humility before Christ. To their critics, they threatened to undermine social order and stability.

From their earliest days, the Quakers were subjected to the social intolerance of the mob. In his famous *Journal*, George Fox recorded that 'it was the manner of the persecutors . . . for twenty or forty people to run upon one man. And they fell so upon Friends in many places, stoning, beating, and breaking their heads, so that they could hardly pass the highways.' Fox himself was the victim of such attacks, especially during the early days of his ministry in the north. In Ulverston in 1652, he was set upon by a mob after he had attempted to interrupt a minister's sermon and preach in the parish church. Incited by the local JP, the crowd dragged Fox out of the church and beat him until he was dazed. Fox recalled that his 'body and arms were yellow, black and blue with the blows and bruises I received amongst them that day'. A fortnight later, a man attempted to kill Fox with a pistol, only to find that it would not go off. On the very next day, another crowd of around 40 men attacked Fox and James Nayler with staves, clubs, stones and fishing poles. On this occasion, the assailants smeared Fox's face, hands and clothes with dirt, and left their victim so bruised that he could hardly speak. Yet Fox took care to record that the intolerance of his persecutors had aroused the intolerance of God. The JP who had encouraged the riot at Ulverston was later drowned, 'and the vengeance of God overtook Justice Thompson that he was struck with the dead palsy upon the Bench and carried away off his seat and died'.[71]

The cases recorded by Fox emphasise that anti-Quaker riots were often encouraged by the local authorities. In an age before police forces, compliant mobs could be usefully employed to enforce the community's norms against disruptive forces. Some of the largest anti-Quaker riots of the Interregnum occurred in Bristol in December 1654 and January 1655, when crowds of up to 1500 apprentices attacked Quaker meetings and the homes of Quaker shopkeepers and merchants. It is clear that on this occasion, the apprentices were being encouraged and unofficially licensed to riot by their masters, local magistrates, and Presbyterian ministers.

However, local magistrates also had the power to arrest and imprison Quakers, and according to Barry Reay 'there was little reluctance to act against' the sect.[72] During the course of the 1650s literally hundreds of Quakers were prosecuted for a wide variety of offences. At least 1000 were taken to court for refusing to pay tithes, whilst nearly 400 were prosecuted for interrupting services and sermons, either under old legislation or under A Proclamation Prohibiting the Disturbing of Ministers issued by the Cromwellian regime in 1655. Some were prosecuted under the 1650 Blasphemy Act, and many more were arrested under the Elizabethan Vagrancy Act, which was extended in 1657 so that Quakers could even be punished for wandering within their own parish!

One of the most striking aspects of the Quaker persecution was the suffering of female Friends. In her travelogue, Barbara Blaugdone recited a catalogue of persecutions of truly apostolic proportions. In town after town in the 1650s, Blaugdone was arrested and thrown into prison. On one occasion, she was stabbed in the side, only to be saved from serious injury by the thickness of her clothing. On another occasion, the servants of the Countess of Bath 'sent forth a great Wolf-Dog upon me, which came fiercely at me to devour me, and just as he came unto me, the Power of the Lord smote the Dog, so that he whined, and ran in crying, and very Lame'. In Exeter, she was imprisoned along with Gypsies, and the Beadle 'Whipt me till the Blood ran down my Back, and I never startled at a blow'. Instead she began to rejoice and sing, causing the Beadle to whip her harder, exclaiming, 'Do ye sing; I shall make ye Cry by and by.'[73]

Not everyone was hostile to the Quakers, however, and there are some notable cases of social tolerance towards a disturbing group. Neighbours sometimes warned local Quakers of approaching constables, refused to witness against them in court, and harvested their crops while they were in prison. In Leverton, Lincolnshire, in 1658, townspeople paid the amount owed by a Quaker labourer who had refused to pay tithes, so securing his release, and in 1657 a Bedfordshire community pressured a local minister into returning the goods confiscated from another Quaker who had resisted the payment of tithes. The Quakers were also protected on occasion by patrons among the gentry. In Bristol, the sect had powerful allies defending them against a hostile common council, including garrison commanders, the wife of an assize judge, and a former MP. In the north of England, magistrates like Thomas Fell (the husband of Margaret) and John Bradshaw (the regicide) ordered the release of Quakers from prison in 1655 and 1656.[74]

Yet local magistrates were more likely to oppose the Quakers than support them, and the *de facto* toleration of the Cromwellian regime was dependent on the whims of such men.[75] As the 1650s progressed, local officials became increasingly frustrated by central government's unwillingness to deal firmly with the Quaker problem. But in 1656, the movement's critics were handed the perfect pretext for suppressing it. In October of that year, James Nayler rode into Bristol on a horse, while his followers laid cloaks in his path and shouted, 'Holy, holy, holy, Hosannah, Lord God of Israel.' This re-enactment of Christ's own entrance into Jerusalem on Palm Sunday caused a sensation, and was widely publicised in the popular press. Nayler was arrested and interrogated by the Bristol authorities, and then passed on to a parliamentary committee which declared him guilty of blasphemy.[76]

The committee report provoked ten days of unprecedented debate in Parliament (between 5 and 17 December), leading the Victorian writer Thomas Carlyle to satirise this as 'the James Nayler Parliament'. Thanks to several contemporary accounts, particularly the diary of the MP Thomas Burton, we possess a remarkably detailed description of this set-piece debate, which has been described as the most important blasphemy trial since that of Servetus in Geneva in 1553.[77] It highlights the persistence of persecutory beliefs among Puritans. The radical tolerationist ideas of Williams and the Levellers had clearly made little impact on the thinking of MPs. No MP claimed outright that even if Nayler was a blasphemer, Parliament had no business in punishing him (though Major-General Packer came close to this in his eloquent attack on persecution).[78] Indeed, everyone seemed to agree that if Nayler was guilty of blasphemy, some punishment was appropriate.

Hardline MPs, many of them Presbyterian, argued vociferously for the death penalty. As magistrates, they insisted that they had a duty to suppress heresy and blasphemy, avert God's judgement and crush the threat of Quaker political subversion. Moderate MPs, by contrast, queried whether Nayler was intending to blaspheme, suggesting the more charitable explanation that he had been trying (rather crudely, they admitted) to symbolise the presence of Christ within the believer. These speakers also argued that if the Quaker was to be punished, he should not be put to death or muti-lated. However, the mutilators won the day. After helpfully suggesting an imaginative array of gory punishments, MPs decided that Nayler should be whipped through the streets of Westminster, placed in the pillory, have his tongue 'bored through with a hot iron', be branded on the forehead with the letter 'B', and then taken to Bristol where he could be whipped once more before being thrown in prison. Despite protests from petitioners like Joshua Sprigge and the radical publisher Giles Calvert, these punishments were carried out in full, and Nayler was kept in prison until 1659. A year after his release, he died.

For all its brutality, Nayler's punishment fell short of that meted out to Quakers in New England. In 1658, the Massachusetts authorities ordered that two Quakers who had returned to the colony after being whipped and banished should have an ear severed. The General Court also passed a law establishing the death penalty for anyone who returned from banishment (thus avoiding the need to execute Quakers purely for heresy). In 1659,

William Robinson and Marmaduke Stephenson were hanged. Mary Dyer, who had been on the scaffold with them, was reprieved. But when she returned yet again in 1660, she too was executed. The execution of a woman aroused serious criticism in both New England and back in England itself, and in 1661 the 'Cart and Whip Act' declared that instead of being executed, Quakers should be tied to a cart and literally whipped out of the colony.[79] Yet the killings of the Quakers suggest that in the 1650s, Massachusetts Puritans were markedly more hostile to pluralism and toleration than Cromwell and other leading English Puritans. In Scotland too, toleration was imposed by the Cromwellian regime in the face of bitter opposition.[80]

The Readmission of the Jews

The relative openness of the Cromwellian regime is illustrated by the informal readmission of the Jews to England in the mid-1650s. The Jews had been expelled from the country in 1290 by Edward I, and it was only with their expulsion from Spain in 1492 and Portugal in 1497 that a small number of Sephardic Jews came to England. To all appearances these *marranos* were practising Catholics and typical Spanish or Portuguese immigrants. Yet contemporary accounts suggest that some, at least, were secretly involved in forbidden Jewish practices like observing the Sabbath and Jewish festivals, and eating unleavened bread at Passover. A number of Jews rose to high positions in their professions. Henry VIII employed nineteen Jewish musicians at court, several Jews deployed their biblical and legal expertise as leading advocates of the king's divorce, and a few became prominent physicians under Elizabeth I. The Portuguese Jew Roderigo Lopez even became the queen's physician, though he was executed in 1594 for plotting with Philip of Spain to poison Elizabeth and overthrow the government.[81]

Despite the presence of these secret Jews in Tudor times, there was no question of tolerating the practice of Judaism in England, and in the first half of the seventeenth century it was commonly accepted that there were no Jews in England. Yet in 1655, Cromwell called a conference at Whitehall to discuss the possibility of a formal readmission of the Jews. As David Katz has shown, the roots of this remarkable development lie in the philo-semitic strain within English Puritanism.[82] Humanists and Protestants had revived the study of Hebrew and eagerly consulted Jewish commentaries on Scripture. More significantly, the seventeenth century had seen the emergence of millenarianism among the Reformed. Like the Jews, millenarian Puritans anticipated a future earthly paradise, and no longer scorned this notion as 'carnal'. They also believed that the millennium would be ushered in by the conversion of the Jews. This 'Judeocentric millenarianism'[83] fostered a new openness to the Jews and led to personal contacts between English Puritans and the Amsterdam rabbi Menasseh ben Israel.[84] Menasseh shared the belief of his Christian millenarian friends that the Messiah was coming soon (though he did not believe that this was the Messiah's second visit), and he saw England as a possible refuge for persecuted Jews. So in October 1655, Menasseh submitted a formal petition for readmission.

Cromwell's response was swift. He arranged a conference on the issue, and invited distinguished delegates, including clergymen, merchants and lawyers. As Katz points out, 'The willingness of the English government to take the political risk of holding a public debate on the Jewish question transforms the English case to one of striking originality and makes it almost unique'. Elsewhere in Europe, Jews often enjoyed a *de facto* toleration, but rulers tried to avoid making 'a public declaration of support for deicides'.[85] Cromwell's philo-semitic instincts, however, overcame such inhibition, and he seems to have hoped that the conference would agree to a formal readmission.

The Whitehall Conference lasted from 4 to 18 December 1655. There were three distinct factions involved: opponents of readmission, who were led by the London merchants and supported by the vociferous Presbyterian pamphleteer William Prynne; a middle group, who favoured readmission if strict conditions were imposed on the Jews; and a strongly millenarian philo-semitic faction who believed that the English had a solemn duty to readmit God's chosen people. Ultimately, the fierce opposition of the merchants and the conservative clergy proved too strong. Cromwell decided that a formal readmission was out of the question, and he did not even issue a public statement.

Menasseh ben Israel and his supporters were bitterly disappointed. Yet the Whitehall Conference marked a real turning point. For the conference revealed that there were Jews in England after all. Reassured by Cromwell's positive attitude, London's secret Jewish community sent a petition to the Lord Protector in March 1656, asking for protection and permission to build a Jewish cemetery. The response was favourable, and by the time of Cromwell's death, London's Jews had their own cemetery and synagogue. The very informality of the readmission meant that they had been allowed to settle with no conditions being placed on where they lived or worked – in sharp contrast to many Jews elsewhere in Europe. The tiny community had come into the open, and from this point on Jews were to be a permanent feature of English society.

Over the next two centuries, Protestants who anticipated the latter day conversion of the Jewish people continued to play a significant role in defending English Jews.[86] Rather surprisingly, John Locke was one of them. It has been argued that Locke's conversionist attitude toward the Jews fundamentally compromised his tolerationism, since his toleration came with 'Christianising strings attached'.[87] However, Katz, Popkin and Endelman have made a strong case for seeing Protestant conversionists as genuinely philo-semitic. Their view of the Jews was certainly a dramatic improvement on the traditional Christian alternative, which identified the Jews with the Devil. Moreover, secular champions of Jewish toleration have also been accused of attaching 'secularising strings' of their own, by expecting Jews to assimilate and convert to rationalism.[88] Indeed, a millenarian like Henry Jessey showed a deep appreciation of Judaism and the Hebrew Scriptures that contrasts sharply with the contempt expressed by later Deist tolerationists.[89] And although Jessey expected the conversion of the Jews, his insistence on their unique status as God's chosen people implies that he envisaged their perpetual distinctiveness rather than assimilation. Most importantly, the philo-semitic commitment to Jewish toleration was firm. The conversion of the Jews was to be an uncoerced millennial miracle, and when English Jews failed to convert, millenarians did not turn against them but simply concluded that the millennium had yet to dawn.

The fortunes of Catholics

Persecution of Catholics died down after the anti-popery campaign of the early 1640s. But the draconian legislation against them remained on the statute books, and two Catholic priests were put to death in the 1650s: Peter Wright was executed at Tyburn in 1651 and John Southworth was hanged, drawn and quartered before a huge crowd in June 1654. However, it seems that the government intended to avoid executing Southworth, only to find that he refused to accept the escape route they offered. He had already been exiled for his activities as a missionary priest in the 1620s, and warned that he would be put to death if he ever returned to England. By returning and by insisting that he was the priest John Southworth, he put the government in a very awkward legal corner; given the clarity of the Elizabethan statutes, it felt that it had no choice. Yet Cromwell protested against the execution, and when Southworth's body had been quartered, he paid a surgeon to sew the pieces together, so that it could be returned to Douai for a Catholic burial.[90]

Moreover, Southworth's fate was exceptional, and otherwise the 1650s were a mild decade for English Catholics. When eight priests were arrested in Covent Garden in 1657, they only suffered the satire of Cromwell and his men, some of whom tried on their 'popish vestments' for themselves and provoked 'abundance of mirth'. Cromwell assured Cardinal Mazarin that he would try to establish some kind of official toleration for the Catholic population, and though this never came to pass, Aveling has written that 'Catholic congregations functioned quietly and almost unnoticed' in this period. Although Catholics continued to face financial penalties for their activities – despite the repeal of recusancy legislation – they were often protected from the full weight of prosecution, and Cromwell's own secretary, John Rushworth, was heavily involved in assisting Catholic gentry in preserving their estates. Cromwell himself dined with leading Catholics like Lord Arundell and Lord Brundenell and the natural philosopher Sir Kenelm Digby.[91] Most remarkably, perhaps, the Catholic Lord Baltimore was reinstated as proprietor of the colony of Maryland in 1657, several years after he had been ousted by militant Puritans.[92] Cromwell's refusal to ratify the action of these extremists possibly reflects his social conservatism, but it also illustrates the breadth of his sympathies. Considering the brutal anti-popery of 1641–6, the mildness with which English Catholics were treated in the 1650s is one of the most surprising features of the Puritan Revolution.

In Ireland, however, the Puritan regime took a far harsher line against Catholic dissent. When the conquest was completed, the authorities 'adopted a punitive policy which intended to force the Irish Catholics to renounce their religion under threats'.[93] Parliamentary commissioners were instructed to enforce existing anti-Catholic laws, and in 1654 Elizabethan and Jacobean laws against Catholic priests were revived. In 1657 an oath of abjuration was imposed which required all Catholics to renounce the pope's temporal and spiritual power along with other doctrines or to face transplantation to Connaught. Most lay Catholics avoided removal, but several thousand do seem to have converted to escape harsh punishment, though they quickly reconverted after the Restoration. Priests were executed, imprisoned or exiled, with the result that their numbers were greatly reduced.

The survival of Anglicanism

Finally, we must not forget that Prayer Book Anglicanism survived throughout the 1640s and 1650s. Because Anglican worship 'had sunk deep roots in popular culture', many parishioners were willing to support clergymen who continued to use the Book of Common Prayer and the traditional communion service.[94] The Puritan attempt to purge the church of popish corruption enjoyed limited success. Whilst the Puritan Sabbath was widely ignored, the traditional Christmas was enthusiastically celebrated despite Puritan attempts to suppress it. Babies continued to be baptised according to the Book of Common Prayer and couples continued to be married by it.[95] Remarkably, Cromwell's own daughters were married in public according to the new regulations of 1653, and then 'in private married by ministers ordained by bishops and according to the form of the Book of Common Prayer'.[96] The minister who probably officiated at Mary's private wedding, Dr John Hewett, was an overt Anglican and royalist, but Cromwell himself accepted these arrangements, demonstrating the lengths to which his tolerance could stretch.[97]

The experience of Prayer Book Anglicans during the 1650s is illuminated by the diary of John Evelyn. Even in the late 1650s, Evelyn had no difficulty in finding Prayer Book services. However, he lamented the fact that for 'the first time the Church of England was reduced to a chamber and a conventicle; so sharp was the persecution'. He records that on Christmas Day 1657, soldiers interrupted the worship just as the congregation was taking the sacrament. 'The miscreants held their muskets against us, as if they would have shot us at the altar', wrote Evelyn, but they were allowed to finish Communion before being arrested. After being interrogated by leading officers, some of the worshippers were released and others were put in prison for a night for celebrating a prohibited festival and using the Book of Common Prayer.[98] The incident is a reminder that the government did not always turn a blind eye to illegal worship, but it also contrasts sharply with the much more severe treatment of Separatists under Elizabeth and the early Stuarts. Yet for Anglicans the situation seemed bleak. Evelyn mentions 'a collection for persecuted and sequestered Ministers of the Church of England, whereof divers are in prison', and remarks, 'A sad day! The Church now in dens and caves of the earth.'[99]

The unwillingness of the Cromwellian regime to grant an official toleration to an episcopal church might seem surprising, given that it tolerated a variety of Protestant sects. But unlike the gathered congregations, Prayer Book Anglicanism was a serious rival to the Cromwellian established church; it had great popular appeal and it was not content with sectarian status. Anglicans saw themselves as the true national church, and the regime probably felt that open Prayer Book services would draw people away from their parish churches and undermine the stability of the Puritan regime. The fortunes of prelacy were bound together with those of royalism; to allow the former to flourish was to invite the latter to strike back.

The impact of the Puritan Revolution

For all its ambiguities, the Puritan Revolution has an important place in our story. Firstly, the Revolution saw the beginning of England's great toleration debate. Before 1640, debate had focused on the range of practice and opinion that could be tolerated *within* the established church, and almost everyone agreed that heretics, recusants and schismatics should be punished in some way. In 1644, however, this consensus was noisily challenged, and for the rest of the century a minority of voices kept up a steady assault on the principle of religious coercion. Secondly, the Revolution ensured that England became a remarkably pluralistic religious culture. Before 1640, only a tiny minority of Protestants dared to meet outside the established church. But in the twenty years that followed, the Protestant sects were given enough time to put down deep roots; the persecution of dissent during the Restoration was simply unable to reverse this. Most of the nonconformist denominations of the eighteenth and nineteenth centuries (including Presbyterians, Congregationalists, Baptists and Quakers) could look back on the Puritan Revolution as the time when they became firmly established. The same applies to England's Jewish community.

Thus what began as a traditional religious war concluded by outlining the shape of the pluralistic future. In 1642, it looked as if Puritans were trying to promote the theocratic uniformity associated with Calvin's Geneva or Presbyterian Scotland. By the 1650s, it was obvious that they had created something much closer to the Dutch republic. The Leveller tolerationists had attacked 'the monopolising patentee-Clergy' for creating a 'Monopoly of the Spirit' instead of allowing 'free trading of truth'.[100] But during the Interregnum, English religion was largely deregulated, and monopoly gave way to an unprecedented measure of free trade. To use the terminology coined by sociologists of religion, the national church ceased to be a compulsory, monopolistic 'church' and became a voluntary 'denomination'. It was not disestablished, of course, and it retained the largest stalls in the market place as well as substantial government subsidies. But though religious radicals complained bitterly at the continuance of tithes and a state church, the Church of England's competitors were no longer prosecuted for peddling their merchandise. The only traders who were not officially tolerated were Catholics and Anglicans, both suspected of wanting to re-establish their own lost monopolies. It is hard to disagree with C. H. Firth's verdict that 'Cromwell's was the most tolerant government which had existed in England since the Reformation'.[101] Although Restoration Anglicans tried hard to force the sects to shut up shop, they had little success. The Church of England after 1689 was to follow in the footsteps of the national church of the 1650s. Monopoly was replaced by competition.

Notes

1   See D. Underdown, *Fire From Heaven: Life in an English Town in the Seventeenth Century* (London, 1992), pp. 197–8.

2 J. Morrill, *The Nature of the English Revolution* (Harlow, 1993), p. 394.

3 See C. Russell, 'The parliamentary career of John Pym, 1621–29', in his *Unrevolutionary England* (London, 1990), p. 227.

4 See S. R. Gardiner, ed., *The Constitutional Documents of the Puritan Revolution, 1625–1660* (Oxford, 1889), pp. 137–44.

5 See B. Mac Cuarta, ed., *Ulster 1641: Aspects of the Rising* (Belfast, 1993), xvi–xvii.

6 See N. Canny, 'Religion, politics and the Irish rising', in J. Devlin and R. Flanning, eds, *Religion and Rebellion* (Dublin, 1997), pp. 40–70, esp. p. 52.

7 Voltaire, *The Calas Affair: A Treatise on Tolerance*, trans. B. Masters (London, 1994), pp. 67, 24–5.

8 Mac Cuarta, ed., *Ulster 1641*, p. 137.

9 See R. Clifton, 'The popular fear of Catholics during the English Revolution', *Past and Present* 52 (1971), 23–55.

10 See A. Fletcher, *The Outbreak of the English Civil War* (London, 1981), pp. 140–1.

11 See H. Trevor-Roper, 'The Fast Sermons of the Long Parliament', in his *Religion, the Reformation and Social Change* (London, 1967), ch. 6; and C. Hill, *The English Bible and the Seventeenth-Century Revolution* (London, 1993), ch. 3.

12 C. Burgess, *The First Sermon, November 17 1640* (1641), pp. 40, 68–9, 67.

13 C. Hibbard, *Charles I and the Popish Plot* (Chapel Hill, NC, 1983), p. 214.

14 Gardiner, ed., *Constitutional Documents*, p. 219.

15 Ibid., p. 229.

16 Fletcher, *The Outbreak of the English Civil War*, p. 417.

17 J. Aubrey, *Brief Lives*, ed. A. Powell (London, 1949), pp. 213–14.

18 C. Russell, 'Issues in the House of Commons 1621–29: predictors of Civil War allegiance', *Albion* 23 (1991), 23–39.

19 See esp. W. Hunt, *The Puritan Moment: The Coming of Revolution in an English County* (Cambridge, MA, 1983); J. Eales, *Puritans and Roundheads: The Harleys of Brampton Bryan and the Outbreak of the English Civil War* (Cambridge, 1990).

20 M. Stoyle, *Loyalty and Locality: Popular Allegiance in Devon during the English Civil War* (Exeter, 1994), pp. 254–5.

21 See Morrill, 'The religious context of the English Civil War', in *The Nature of the English Revolution*, ch. 3.

22 See D. Crouzet, *Guerriers de Dieu: La Violence au Temps des Troubles de Religion, vers 1525–vers 1610*, 2 vols (Seyssel, 1990).

23   I. Gentles, 'The iconography of revolution: England 1642–49', in I. Gentles, J. Morrill and B. Worden, eds, *Soldiers, Writers and Statesmen of the English Revolution* (Cambridge, 1998), pp. 91–113.

24   Richard Baxter, *A Holy Commonwealth*, ed. W. Lamont (Cambridge, 1994), pp. 22–5.

25   C. Russell, 'The slumbering hatreds of the English', *Independent*, 18 August 1992, quoted in N. Davies, *Europe: A History* (London, 1997), p. 552.

26   I. M. Green, 'The persecution of "scandalous" and "malignant" parish clergy during the English Civil War', *English Historical Review* 194 (1979), 507–31. Green draws on the classic account by John Walker: A. G. Matthew, ed., *Walker Revised: Being a Revision of John Walker's 'Sufferings of the Clergy during the Grand Rebellion', 1642–1660* (Oxford, 1947).

27   *Persecutio Undecima, The Churches Eleventh Persecution* (1648), pp. 4, 21, 2.

28   Green, 'The persecution of "scandalous" and "malignant" parish clergy', quotation on 509.

29   A. Laurence, ' "This sad and deplorable condition": an attempt towards recovering an account of the sufferings of Northern clergy families in the 1640s and 1650s', in D. Wood, ed., *Life and Thought in the Northern Church* (Woodbridge, 1999), pp. 465–88.

30   R. Challoner, *Memoirs of the Missionary Priests* (London, 1924), pp. 378–491.

31   W. K. Jordan, *The Development of Religious Toleration in England*, 4 vols (London, 1932–40), III, pp. 31–3.

32   J. Walter, *Understanding Popular Violence in the English Revolution: The Colchester Plunderers* (Cambridge, 1999), pp. 346–9.

33   C. Carlton, *Going to the Wars: The Experience of the British Civil Wars, 1638–1651* (London, 1992), pp. 177–9.

34   M. Tolmie, *The Triumph of the Saints* (Cambridge, 1977), p. 37.

35   R. Acheson, *Radical Puritans in England, 1550–1660* (London, 1990), pp. 35–9.

36   Tolmie, *The Triumph of the Saints*, p. 122.

37   M. Watts, *The Dissenters: From the Reformation to the French Revolution* (Oxford, 1978), pp. 79–81.

38   C. Hill, *Milton and the English Revolution* (London, 1977), p. 65.

39   See Morrill, *The Nature of the English Revolution*, p. 360n.

40   See R. S. Paul, *The Assembly of the Lord: Politics and Religion in the Westminster Assembly and the 'Grand Debate'* (Edinburgh, 1985).

41   Robert Baillie, *Letters and Journals*, 3 vols (1841–2), II, p. 235.

42 *The Writings and Speeches of Oliver Cromwell*, ed. W. C. Abbott, 4 vols (Oxford, 1937–47), I, p. 278.

43 See J. Coffey, 'Puritanism and liberty revisited: the case for toleration in the English Revolution', *Historical Journal* 41 (1998), 961–85; N. Carlin, 'Toleration for Catholics in the Puritan Revolution', in O. P. Grell and R. Scribner, eds, *Tolerance and Intolerance in the European Reformation* (Cambridge, 1995), pp. 216–30.

44 The debates are reprinted in A. S. P. Woodhouse, ed., *Puritanism and Liberty: Being the Army Debates (1647–49) from the Clarke Manuscripts* (London, 1938), pp. 125–78. See also C. Polizzotto, 'Liberty of conscience and the Whitehall debates of 1648–49', *Journal of Ecclesiastical History* 26 (1975), 69–82.

45 Baillie, *Letters and Journals*, II, pp. 211–12.

46 T. Edwards, *Gangraena* (1646), I, pp. 121, 145.

47 See C. Hill, *Antichrist in Seventeenth-Century England* (Oxford, 1971), ch. 3.

48 See, for example, Richard Overton, *The Arraignement of Mr Persecution* (1645).

49 B. Worden, 'Toleration and the Cromwellian Protectorate', in W. J. Sheils, ed., *Persecution and Toleration* (Oxford, 1984), p. 200.

50 See the sympathetic account of T. Reilly, *Cromwell: An Honourable Enemy* (1999). See also I. Gentles, *The New Model Army: In England, Ireland and Scotland, 1645–53* (Oxford, 1992), pp. 357–68.

51 *Writings and Speeches of Oliver Cromwell*, II, p. 127.

52 See R. Karr, ' "Why should you be so furious?": the violence of the Pequot war', *Journal of American History* 85 (1998), 876–909.

53 See A. Fletcher, 'Cromwell and the godly nation', in J. Morrill, ed., *Oliver Cromwell and the English Revolution* (Harlow, 1990), pp. 210–11.

54 *Writings and Speeches of Oliver Cromwell*, I, p. 377.

55 See Archibald Johnston of Wariston, *Diary*, ed. J. D. Oglivie (Edinburgh, 1940), III, p. 102.

56 R. W., *The Fourth Paper, Presented by Major Butler* (London, 1652), preface.

57 *Writings and Speeches of Oliver Cromwell*, I, p. 677.

58 Ibid., III, pp. 436–7.

59 Ibid., pp. 586, 459.

60 See Worden, 'Toleration and the Cromwellian Protectorate', pp. 199–233.

61 See J. C. Davis, 'Cromwell's religion', in Morrill, ed., *Oliver Cromwell*, pp. 181–208.

62 See A. L. Morton, *The World of the Ranters* (London, 1970); J. C. Davis, *Fear, Myth and History: The Ranters and the Historians* (Cambridge, 1986); L. Levy,

Blasphemy: Verbal Offense against the Sacred, from Moses to Salman Rushdie (Chapel Hill, NC, 1993), ch. 8.

63 Gardiner, *Constitutional Documents*, pp. 391–4.

64 *The Ranters Recantation*, reprinted in Davis, *Fear, Myth and History*, p. 182.

65 A. Hessayon, ' "Gold tried in the fire": The prophet Theauraujohn Tany and the Puritan Revolution' (unpublished PhD thesis, University of Cambridge, 1996), pp. 201, 223n.

66 Jordan, *The Development of Religious Toleration*, III, p. 142.

67 C. Polizzotto, 'The campaign against "The Humble Proposals" of 1652', *Journal of Ecclesiastical History* 38 (1987), 569–81.

68 Gardiner, *Constitutional Documents*, p. 416.

69 *Writings and Speeches of Oliver Cromwell*, III, p. 834.

70 See Jordan, *The Development of Religious Toleration*, III, pp. 203–8; H. J. McLachlan, *Socinianism in Seventeenth-Century England* (Oxford, 1951), ch. 10.

71 George Fox, *Journal*, ed. N. Penny (London, 1924), pp. 72–6.

72 B. Reay, *The Quakers and the English Revolution* (London, 1985), p. 52.

73 *An Account of the Travels, Sufferings and Persecutions of Barbara Blaugdone* (1691), reprinted in M. Garman *et al.*, eds, *Hidden in Plain Sight: Quaker Women's Writings, 1650–1700* (Wallingford, PN, 1996), pp. 275–84.

74 Reay, *The Quakers and the English Revolution*, pp. 62, 51.

75 Ibid., pp. 15, 52.

76 The best study of the Nayler case is now L. Damrosch, *The Sorrows of the Quaker Jesus: James Nayler and the Puritan Crackdown on the Free Spirit* (Cambridge, MA, 1996).

77 Levy, *Blasphemy*, p. 191.

78 *Diary of Thomas Burton*, ed. J. T. Rutt, 4 vols (1828), I, pp. 99–101.

79 Levy, *Blasphemy*, pp. 255–9. See also C. Pestana, *Quakers and Baptists in Colonial New England* (New York, 1991).

80 See the 'Declaration of the Protesters in reference to the English actings amongst us, 17 March 1653', in W. Stephen, ed., *Register of the Consultations of the Ministers of Edinburgh and some other Brethren of the Ministry*, vol. I: 1652–7 (Edinburgh, 1921), pp. 13–36.

81 D. S. Katz, *The Jews in the History of England, 1485–1850* (Oxford, 1994), pp. 1–106.

82 D. S. Katz, *Philo-Semitism and the Readmission of the Jews to England, 1603–55* (Oxford, 1982).

83 D. S. Katz, 'Menasseh ben Israel's Christian connection: Henry Jessey and the Jews', in Y. Kaplan, H. Mechoulan and R. H. Popkin, eds, *Menasseh ben Israel and his World* (Leiden, 1989), p. 126.

84 See Kaplan *et al.*, eds, *Menasseh ben Israel*.

85 Katz, *The Jews in the History of England*, p. 107.

86 See T. Endelman, *The Jews in Georgian England, 1714–1830* (Ann Arbor, MI, 1999), ch. 2: 'Philo-Semitism in Anglo-Christianity'; and W. D. Rubenstein and H. L. Rubenstein, *Philosemitism: Admiration and Support in the English-Speaking World for Jews, 1840–1939* (London, 1999).

87 See N. Matar, 'John Locke and the Jews', *Journal of Ecclesiastical History* 44 (1993), 56.

88 See Z. Bauman, *Modernity and the Holocaust* (Cambridge, 1989); and the critique by D. Feldman, 'Was modernity good for the Jews?', in L. Marcus, B. Cheyette, and H. Bhabha, eds, *Modernity, Culture and 'The Jew'* (Cambridge, 1998), ch. 10.

89 Compare Katz, 'Menasseh ben Israel's Christian connection', with Endelman, *The Jews in Georgian England*, pp. 96–7.

90 John Morrill, 'Oliver Cromwell and the boundaries of Christian liberty', unpublished paper. See *Writings and Speeches of Oliver Cromwell*, III, pp. 320–1.

91 H. Aveling, *The Handle and the Axe* (London, 1976), pp. 175–6.

92 See R. Middleton, *Colonial America: A History, 1607–1760* (Oxford, 1992), pp. 78–9.

93 T. Barnard, *Cromwellian Ireland: English Government and Reform in Ireland, 1649–60* (Oxford, 1975), pp. 172–3.

94 J. Morrill, 'The church in England, 1642–49', in his *The Nature of the English Revolution*, ch. 7.

95 C. Durston, 'The failure of cultural revolution, 1645–60', in Durston and J. Eales, eds, *The Culture of English Puritanism* (London, 1996), ch. 7.

96 The Earl of Clarendon, *The History of the Rebellion and Civil Wars in England*, ed. W. Dunn Macray, 6 vols (Oxford, 1888), VI, p. 34.

97 R. Sherwood, *Oliver Cromwell: King in All But Name* (Stroud, 1997), p. 118.

98 *The Diary of John Evelyn*, ed. A. Dobson (London, 1908), pp. 191, 195–6.

99 Ibid., p. 198.

100 See A. Houston, ' "A way of settlement": the Levellers, monopolies and the public interest', *History of Political Thought* 14 (1993), 387–96.

101 Cited in G. Nuttall, *The Holy Spirit in Puritan Faith and Experience* (Oxford, 1946), p. 128.

CHAPTER 7

The Restoration, 1660–88

W. K. Jordan's study of the development of religious toleration in England concludes in 1660. By this date, Jordan suggests, 'the mass of men in England . . . had conceded the case for religious toleration with very few reservations'.[1] His assessment fits neatly with a popular image of the Restoration as the era of the Royal Society, the Merrie Monarch, the Commercial Revolution and bawdy theatre. Unfortunately, it fits less well with reality. During the Puritan Revolution, tolerationists had been very vocal, but in 1660 they were still a small minority whose ideas had made little headway among mainstream Anglicans or Presbyterians. When the king returned, 'the mass of men' were probably more inclined to support the reimposition of uniformity than the maintenance and extension of toleration. If Restoration England did not see a return to the burning of heretics, it did witness persecution on a grand scale.

The Restoration and the 'Clarendon' Code

In April 1660, on the eve of the Restoration, Charles II issued the Declaration of Breda.[2] He sought to reassure his old enemies that his rule would be marked by clemency, and promised a 'liberty to tender consciences', to be confirmed by Parliament on his restoration. Although this irenic gesture made political sense, there is little reason to doubt Charles's sincere support for toleration. The young king was no bigot, and he recognised the need to attract a broad range of support. He was restored in May, and over the next twelve months he did 'all that he could to bring about a compromise settlement of the church'.[3] Although some of his close advisors were opposed to concessions to the Puritans, the Privy Council was dominated by men like Monck who wished to see both Presbyterians and Episcopalians accommodated within a broad national church. Others like Anthony Ashley Cooper were probably committed to going further and securing toleration for minorities who did not join the church. In the second half of 1660, some 700 Quakers were released from prison, and Charles assured one Quaker leader, 'you shall none of you suffer for your opinions or religion, so long as you live peaceably'.[4] The Presbyterians seemed in an especially strong position, for they had supported the Restoration and had every intention of remaining within the national church. In October, Presbyterian and Episcopalian leaders met for negotiations at Worcester House, and Charles issued the Worcester House Declaration, announcing that the restored church would be governed by bishops in conjunction with presbyters and would allow considerable latitude in ceremonial matters. Presbyterians like Richard Baxter and Edmund Calamy were offered bishoprics, and though they refused they did suggest the names of other divines who might be willing to accept. An unprecedented window of opportunity had been opened for a moderate and tolerant church settlement.

Ultimately, however, this was an opportunity wasted. On 28 November, the Convention Parliament voted by a narrow majority against passing the Declaration into law. In January 1661, a Fifth Monarchist rising in London created a new panic about Puritan fanaticism and subversion. A royal proclamation prohibited meetings of 'Anabaptists, Quakers and Fifth Monarchy Men', and more than 4000 Quakers and Baptists were arrested and imprisoned in the space of a few weeks. Even non-sectarian Puritans were vulnerable. Many Anglicans had no desire to offer a generous settlement. They had bitter memories of the Puritan takeover and the expulsion of Anglican parish clergy, and they wanted revenge. A popular backlash against Puritans had been building up for years, and it was now unleashed. Between May and December 1660, almost 700 Puritan ministers lost their livings in parishes the length and breadth of England, most being replaced by the sequestrated clergy of the 1640s. At the Savoy Conference in April 1661 the Presbyterian spokesman Richard Baxter infuriated Anglicans by insisting on wholesale liturgical changes. He was driving a hard bargain just as the Puritan position was becoming hopelessly weak. In May 1661, when the Cavalier Parliament assembled, hardline Anglicans were in the ascendancy, and during the months that followed, these conservatives set about 'framing their measures to extirpate Puritanism'.[5]

The Cavalier Parliament's laws against Dissent became known in the nineteenth century as the Clarendon Code. This is something of a misnomer, since Sir Edward Hyde, the Earl of Clarendon, was not the mastermind behind the legislation, and historians are divided over his attitude towards it. Whatever his personal role, the real movers in the campaign against Dissent were the Anglican gentry, who hated what Puritanism had done, feared what it could do, and saw the episcopal Church of England as a bulwark against rebellion and schism.[6]

In December 1661, Parliament passed the Corporation Act, requiring all holders of municipal office to take oaths of allegiance and supremacy, abjure the Solemn League and Covenant, and take communion in the Church of England. For many conscientious Dissenters, this was impossible, and they were excluded from public office. To add insult to injury, some were elected to offices by Anglican colleagues and then fined for failing to serve. In 1662, the Quaker Act declared that anyone who refused to swear a legally tendered oath or who met with five or more Quakers would be fined, imprisoned, and on a third conviction, transported.

A new Act of Uniformity was also passed in 1662, requiring all clergy to be episcopally ordained, to renounce the Solemn League and Covenant and to assent to the new Prayer Book. Although the king tried to delay or neuter the original bill, his efforts were to no avail. More than 1000 Puritan clergy – including a third of the London ministers – were forced out of their churches, bringing the number of those ejected in England and Wales since 1660 to just over 2000, a total which included around 200 lecturers, college fellows and schoolmasters.[7] The prospects for a broad and comprehensive church settlement had been shattered. The ejected ministers, like the ousted Puritan clergy of the 1630s and their Anglican counterparts in the 1640s, often had to face considerable hardship. Since the great majority of them were Presbyterians who wanted desperately to be part of the national church, the pain of separation was intense. Many Presbyterians and Congregationalists continued to attend their parish church as well as their own illegal conventicles, and they did not give up hope of reconciliation. However, the number of people who worshipped as nonconformists outside the national church was now far larger than ever before. Estimates vary, but the total was probably at least a quarter of a million. Half of these were Presbyterians, with the rest being Congregationalists, Quakers and Baptists.[8]

The legislation of 1661–2 was not what the king had in mind. Despite his libidinous lifestyle and worldly outlook, Charles seems to have been genuinely attracted to Catholicism, and at least in the early years of his reign wanted to grant considerable freedom to both Catholics and Dissenters. In December 1662, he attempted to override the new legislation by issuing a Declaration of Indulgence, in which he proposed allowing Protestant Dissenters to apply for licences to worship publicly and Catholics to worship freely in private domestic meetings. These provisions, however, were subject to the agreement of Parliament, and when the Cavalier Parliament protested loudly, the king had little option but to back down.

If the Uniformity Act was aimed at clergy, and the Corporation Act at magistrates, the Conventicles Act (1664) hit the laity too. It made it illegal for anyone over the age of sixteen to attend a meeting of five or more people for worship outside the household without using the Anglican Prayer Book and liturgy. Those who broke the law would be fined or imprisoned for their first and second offences, and transported for seven years for a third offence. The act expired in 1669, but a Second Conventicles Act was passed in 1670, which greatly increased the fines on preachers at conventicles to £20 for the first offence, and a potentially crippling £40 for subsequent offences. Officials who failed to enforce it were to be subject to prosecution, whilst informers would be rewarded with one-third of the fines. Andrew Marvell described it as 'the Quintessence of arbitrary Malice'. In 1665, after ejected ministers had reoccupied pulpits abandoned by churchmen during the Great Plague, Parliament passed the Five Mile Act. It prohibited Dissenting ministers and preachers from coming within 5 miles of their former parish or of any corporate town. Although the Act of Uniformity did not explicitly forbid ejected clergy from ministering outside the estab-lished church, the Conventicles Act declared that they could only ever address small groups of people, and the Five Mile Act was designed to stop them gathering a congregation of former parishioners or establishing con-gregations in corporate towns.

As well as being prosecuted under the 'Clarendon Code', Dissenters could also fall victim to older legislation. The Elizabethan Act of Uniform-ity (1559) and the Act against Popish Recusants (1593) were both employed against those who failed to attend weekly parish worship. An Act for Retaining the Queen's Subjects in their Due Obedience (1593) continued to be invoked because its penalties of banishment and death for persistent offenders were harsher than those of the Clarendon Code. In 1660, the Bedford tinker and lay preacher John Bunyan was arrested and imprisoned for open-air preaching under this act; refusing to conform, he spent most of the next twelve years in gaol. In 1664, twelve General Baptists were even sentenced to death under the same act, and were only saved from the same fate as Barrow, Greenwood and Penry by a royal pardon.[9]

The persecution of Dissent

Anglican persecutors could now appeal to 'a formidable legal arsenal which, potentially, made possible a Puritan holocaust'.[10] Although the worst possib-ilities were never realised, the Restoration did witness a persecution of Protestants by Protestants without parallel in seventeenth-century Europe.

Dissenters were arrested, prosecuted and imprisoned in their thousands. Hundreds of meetings were violently broken up, and Dissenters were harassed by organised gangs and angry mobs. The statistics for the Quakers alone are breathtaking: well over 15,000 were prosecuted by imprisonment or otherwise, 450 died in gaol, and 200 more were sentenced to banishment. In addition to these threats, Dissenters also had to pay fines which were heavy and sometimes crippling.

The overall scale of the persecution should not obscure significant variations. No dissenting group was persecuted as harshly as the Quakers, and the respectable Presbyterians suffered far less. Richard Baxter noted with a touch of *Schadenfreude* that by absorbing all the energies of the persecutors 'the fanatics called Quakers did greatly relieve the sober people for a time'.[11] As the most extreme of the Protestant sects, Quakers provided persecutors with ample excuses for repression. They could be prosecuted for vagrancy, refusal to take oaths, non-payment of tithes, unlawful assembly and riot, as well as for recusancy and conventicling. By contrast, some prominent Nonconformist divines, like the Congregationalist John Owen, escaped imprisonment altogether. Many Presbyterians did not experience heavy persecution until the 1680s. Yet it is worth noting that of the divines ejected from the Church of England in 1660–2, no fewer than 215 were gaoled. It is hard to agree with C. E. Whiting's remark that 'the Long Parliament had been more severe to the Churchmen than the Churchmen were to the Dissenters'.[12]

Persecution also varied considerably depending on the attitudes of local officials. Craig Horle has argued that even the persecution of the Quakers was 'sporadic and capricious'. Enforcement of the penal laws was patchy, and far from being content with passive suffering, Quakers became increasingly active and sophisticated in organising legal resistance to persecution.[13] Anthony Fletcher has suggested that 'In the countryside, as opposed to the towns, the Conventicle Acts, it would seem, were not systematically enforced in the 1660s and 1670s. The story is rather one of localised battles between particular groups of dissenting congregations and either individual JPs or a few strongly motivated justices.'[14] His view is confirmed by Richard Greaves who suggests that 'persecution was often sporadic and penalties relatively light'. In Chester, the number of prosecutions was high, but justices tended to impose small fines. In Great Yarmouth, Presbyterians and their allies even gained control of the town council in 1666. Elsewhere, magistrates were often either lax or positively sympathetic to the Dissenters' plight.[15] The advocates of persecution often bemoaned this situation. In October 1666, the bishop of Gloucester wrote to local justices charging them with negligence, and reminded them 'that execution is the life of the law, and it lives when executed by your hands, without it tis but a dead

Table 7.1 Numbers of Quakers in prison, 1661–85[16]

1661	4257
Oct 1662	1300
Mar 1672	500
Aug 1683	1000
Mar 1685	1460

letter'.[17] At the Quarter Sessions in Nottingham in 1669, Justice Peniston Whaley complained that 'the laws [against Dissent] have not been executed', and blamed this on negligent Constables who had been appointed because more suitable men were unwilling to do their civic duty. Nottinghamshire Quakers blamed most of their sufferings in the 1660s and 1670s on the activism of Whaley and and his fellow Justice Robert Thoroton.[18] As in the case of witch-hunts, individual magistrates could make all the difference. Whilst the eminent jurist Matthew Hale played a key role in the trial and execution of two Suffolk 'witches' in 1662, he was more famous as the sympathetic judge who used his influence to protect Dissenters.[19]

As well as varying from place to place according to the attitude of local officials, persecution also varied from time to time. The fluctuations of national politics meant that periods of repression were followed by periods of relief, as Table 7.1 illustrates. In the years between 1660 and 1665 the restored Anglican royalists were particularly harsh. Besides taking their opportunity for revenge on their Puritan oppressors, they were also alarmed by the failed Fifth Monarchist rising of January 1661, the northern rebellion of 1663, and subsequent rumours of radical plots. There was a real fear of Dissenters, and particularly of the large number of disbanded soldiers who had zealously supported the old regime. Thousands of Dissenters were imprisoned, and many were also subjected to heavy fines, confiscation of goods, and physical violence.[20]

Persecution abated somewhat in the mid-1660s, as the success of the Restoration became clear and fear of Dissent declined. After 1667, the influence of the Cabal – a group of government ministers none of whom was a rigid Anglican – encouraged a more lenient policy toward Dissent. The debate over toleration, so prominent in the 1640s and 1650s, acquired a new lease of life, and between 1667 and 1673 a spate of tolerationist works appeared by authors like Locke, Owen, Penn, Bethel, Marvell and Milton.[21] In 1668, the Bawdy House Riots saw London crowds attacking brothels in order to protest against a government which had tolerated prostitution whilst persecuting devout believers.[22] There was a renewal of persecution between May 1670 and April 1671 in the wake of the second

Conventicles Act. Even the eminent nonconformist Richard Baxter was imprisoned at this time.

In 1672, however, the king issued a second Declaration of Indulgence. It arose from his Treaty of Dover with Louis XIV in 1670, when Charles had secretly promised the French king that he would publicly announce his conversion to Catholicism. Although this pledge was never fulfilled, the Declaration did extend toleration to Catholics. The preamble declared that there was 'very little fruit of all those forcible courses' pursued over the past decade, and proposed measures for 'quieting the minds of our good subjects' and neutralising the potential threat posed to the government by persecuted conventicles. The penal laws against both Dissenters and Catholic recusants were to be suspended immediately; Dissenters were to be allowed to worship at licensed houses with licensed ministers, while Catholics were permitted to hold services in private.[23] Altogether 1610 preachers took out licences (939 as Presbyterians, 458 as Congregationalists or Independents and 210 as Baptists), and many nonconformist householders had their houses licensed for worship.[24] In some places Dissenters even erected their own meeting houses and chapels, and the king pardoned 491 imprisoned Dissenters, including John Bunyan. Although the Indulgence was only in operation for a year, it allowed Dissenters vital breathing space. According to Norman Sykes, 'Protestant Dissent had received such a fillip as to ensure the eventual failure of a policy of persecution'.[25] It also confirmed the depth of Presbyterian alienation from the Church of England, and made comprehension less likely in the future.

Many Anglicans, however, were appalled by the Declaration. In 1673 the king was forced to withdraw it and Parliament passed the first Test Act, requiring all holders of civil and military offices to take oaths of supremacy and allegiance, sign a declaration against transubstantiation, and receive Anglican communion. This latter clause hit Dissenters as well as Catholics, since it meant that to hold civil office they would have to practise 'occasional conformity'. However, the Act did not apply to MPs, and a second Test Act (1678) which did include MPs was only directed against Catholics. Consequently, when persecution was renewed in the mid-1670s, Dissenters campaigned for the election of their own candidates to Parliament. With one or two exceptions, they were unsuccessful, and the Cavalier Parliament (1661–79) never contained more than a small number of Dissenters, most of them Presbyterians who avoided attending public nonconformist services.[26] Dissenters continued to depend heavily on sympathetic Anglicans, and it was not until the late 1670s that they were able to find respite from persecution.

Ironically, the relief Dissenters enjoyed between 1678 and 1681 came at the expense of the Catholics. Spurious claims of a 'Popish Plot' to replace

Charles II with his Catholic brother James rocked the nation, and Dissenters were suddenly seen as allies against the Catholic threat. Although the years between 1678 and 1686 saw the last severe religious persecution in English history, the repression up until March 1681 was almost entirely focused on the Catholic community. Dissenters, by contrast, enjoyed considerable freedom. When the Cavalier Parliament was dissolved in 1679, new elections were held and as many as 42 Dissenter MPs were elected. Dissenters threw their weight behind Shaftesbury's campaign to exclude James from succession to the throne, and attempts were made to pass toleration and comprehension bills. Roles were now reversed, for whereas Parliament was now sympathetic to Dissent, the king was angry at the support nonconformists gave to Shaftesbury and refused to sign a bill to repeal the notorious anti-Separatist Act of 1593.

The failure of the Exclusion movement by 1681 marked the beginning of the 'Royalist reaction' or 'Tory revenge'. Between 1681 and 1686, Dissenters were to face persecution worse than anything they had encountered since the early 1660s, the other period when they had been seen as a genuine political threat. Massive fines were imposed on ministers and laity alike and hundreds of Dissenters were imprisoned. In Bristol, for example, a mob wrecked Dissenting meeting houses and forced members to meet in secret in fields and woods. One Quaker merchant in the city was sentenced to death under the 1593 Act and was only reprieved because William Penn brought the case to the attention of the Duke of York. By June 1682, no fewer than 150 Bristol Quakers were in prison.[27] In London, over 3800 different people were arrested and brought before the courts between 1682 and 1686 for attending Nonconformist conventicles.[28] London Dissent was terrorised by the Hilton gang, a band of over 40 thuggish informers who infiltrated meetings, gathered incriminating information, participated in prosecutions, and seized Dissenters' goods by force when they failed to pay their fines. By 1684, they had broken up more than 40 meeting houses, and secured the eviction, conformity or imprisonment of a similar number of ministers. The Dissenters they had identified had been fined a total of £40,000.[29]

The king's support for the persecution of the 1680s undermines his reputation as a tolerant monarch. Charles had given personal encouragement to the Hilton gang in 1682: 'intimating his displeasure that the laws against Dissenters were not more vigorously put in execution', he ordered the Hiltons 'to suppress and disturb them'.[30] Although he had acted in defence of religious minorities in the early years of his reign and in 1672, he was quick to abandon toleration and countenance coercion when it became politically expedient. Ronald Hutton has even compared the deaths of more than 400 Quakers in Restoration gaols to the 300 martyrdoms under Mary, and suggested that if one sees a slow death in a verminous gaol as worse than the quick agony of the stake, then 'the supposedly genial and cynical Charles must rank as the most savage persecutor of all'.[31] This seems grossly unfair to the man responsible for the Declaration of Breda, two Declarations of Indulgence, and the pardoning of Dissenters condemned to death. Whereas Mary was a zealous persecutor throughout her reign, Charles often opposed repression and he had no intention of sending Quakers to their deaths. His harshness towards Dissent after 1681 can be partially explained as his vengeance on those who had come so close to undermining his authority during the Exclusion Crisis.

Yet though the 'Merrie Monarch' was no 'Bloody Mary', the 'Great Persecution' of the Restoration era was to be memorialised in much the same way as the Marian persecution. Dissenters left an extraordinarily rich record of their sufferings in autobiographies, short narratives, letters and catalogues. The Quakers, in particular, compiled 'books of sufferings' which chronicled their treatment by the authorities in painstaking detail. These were later used by the martyrologist Joseph Besse in his two-volume *Collection of the Sufferings of the People called Quakers, 1650–1689* (1753). The Presbyterians also had their martyrologist, Edmund Calamy, who recorded the sufferings of the Puritan clergy in his *Account of the Ejected Ministers* (1702).[32]

The most common punishments imposed on Dissenters were fines and the confiscation of goods. In 1670, for example, the Nottinghamshire Quaker Joseph Walls was subjected to a series of heavy fines and confiscations. He was initially fined £4 10s. for holding a conventicle in his home, and the authorities removed £6 worth of goods. For a second offence, he was fined £30 and had £16 worth of goods confiscated; for a third he 'had six Feeding Beasts and a Bull taken from him'; finally, he was fined £20 for preaching and had a stack of hay distrained.[33] In another Nottinghamshire case in 1676, the Quaker wheelwright Edward Wood of Ekrin was fined £20 for holding a meeting in his house, and had 'six Cows and two Heifers taken from him to the value of 19*l.* 14*s.* 6*d.*', as well as the timber he used to make wheels. Others who had attended the same meeting also paid fines and lost goods: John Cam 'had two Cows, one Horse and a Mare taken from him to the value of 10*l.* 5*s.*', and Thomas Estwood lost 'one great Bible, one Warming-pan, one Pewter-Dish'. Shortly afterwards, Edward Wood was fined again for being at a meeting 'by the High-way-side on the Common, being kept out of their Ordinary Meeting House'.[34] The Quaker blacksmith Edward Richardson of Kilverton fared even worse, when in May 1676 the authorities confiscated hay and corn, bedding, his 'Children's Apparel' and the 'working Tools and Utensils of his Trade'.[35] Far from being nominal penalties, these fines and confiscations were clearly intended to inflict considerable hardship on Dissenters, and even destroy their livelihoods.

However, the experience which dominated the consciousness of persecuted Dissenters was the experience of imprisonment. Conditions in prisons varied enormously. When Baxter was gaoled in 1670 he complained that his sleep was constantly disturbed and that he was not allowed to make visits outside the prison. But he also admitted that 'my imprisonment . . . was no great suffering to me, for I had an honest jailer, who showed me all the kindness he could; I had a large room, and the liberty of walking in a fair garden; and my wife was never so cheerful a companion to me as in prison, and was very much against my seeking to be released, and she had brought so many necessaries that we kept house as contentedly and comfortably as at home, though in a narrower room, and I had the sight of more of my friends in a day than I had at home in half a year'.[36] Baxter's experience was not unique and prison clearly had its consolations. Like the Catholic priests in Wisbech prison in the 1590s, Dissenters often enjoyed close fellowship with fellow believers. Whenever possible, they organised collective acts of worship and preached and exhorted each other. They even boasted that Newgate prison had become a house of prayer instead of a den of thieves. Many prisoners were also allowed out of prison for short periods to visit friends and relatives. John Bunyan was given permission to attend church meetings in 1661, 1668, 1669, and 1670, and he was regularly visited in prison by friends. At one time, he was even able to go on a preaching tour that took him as far as London. He had access to books, and was able to use his plentiful spare time to write a number of works, including the first part of *Pilgrim's Progress* with its famous description of the persecution of Christian and Faithful at Vanity Fair.[37] When the British peace envoy Terry Waite was taken hostage in Lebanon by Islamic militants in the late 1980s, he endured four years of solitary confinement. One day he received a postcard of Bunyan in gaol, and thought: 'My word, Bunyan, you're a lucky fellow, you've got a window out of which you can look and see the sky, and here I am in a dark room; you've got pen and ink and you can write, and I've got nothing; you've got your own clothes and a table and a chair.'[38]

But if prison was not always a hell, it was still a deeply painful experience. In his autobiography, Bunyan described the separation from his wife and children 'as the pulling the flesh from my bones'. Like other dissidents, he knew that his family would suffer for his principles, and he was particularly worried about his young daughter, Mary, who was blind. 'O I saw in this condition I was as a man who was pulling down his house upon the head of his Wife and Children; yet thought I, I must do it, I must do it.'

Preoccupied with fears of the gallows, he imagined himself 'on the Ladder, with the Rope about my neck', addressing the crowd attending his execution. Unsure of his ultimate fate, he prepared himself psychologically for the worst.[39]

Besides inflicting such mental agonies, imprisonment also carried physical dangers. While some prisons were very tolerable, others were appalling. Overcrowding was a common problem, particularly after a fresh drive against Dissenters. Although Joseph Alleine was able to curtain off his own space in Ilchester gaol, and bring his wife and bed from home, he had to share a large room with 50 Quakers, 17 Baptists and 13 ministers, as well as many others. In Newgate prison at the height of the Fifth Monarchist panic in 1661, 100 people were packed into one room with no space to lie down. In hot weather, the filth and stench could be unbearable, and plague was a constant threat. Cold weather brought its own problems. Many prisons had no fireplaces and in those that did the whole room was often filled with smoke. Though George Fox had the constitution of an ox, his health was seriously damaged by three years in gaol. In Lancaster, his clothes and bedding were often wet for days on end, and in Scarborough Castle the rain from the North Sea poured in through an open window and flooded his room. Another Quaker, Edward Burrough, died of fever at the age of 28 in Newgate in 1663, after spending his final days on a damp mattress by an open drain. In Norwich, Quakers were confined in a dungeon 27 steps below ground with little air or light. Elsewhere, John Whiting was shackled to a companion for six weeks, so that his wrists were rubbed raw and he was unable to change his clothes. Vermin were a perpetual nuisance and danger, and the convicted felons in the prison could be equally obnoxious. Usually they were kept in separate rooms, but sometimes they were thrown together with the Dissenters. In Newgate, the Quakers had to share a room with felons who played with the heads of three executed men.[40]

Dissenters also had to face difficult circumstances in the local community. The work of recent social historians, however, tends to suggest that relations between Dissenters and Anglicans were not as poor as was once thought. Like Lollards and Familists before them, Dissenters often participated actively in the day-to-day life of their parish. In the words of Bill Stevenson:

> They served their parishes as constables and overseers of the poor; they witnessed and wrote the wills of non-sectaries; they left money in their wills to the parish poor as well as to their poor brethren; they served on manorial juries; they acted as trustees alongside prominent conformist parishioners for the benefit of the parish poor; they socialised with non-sectaries in alehouses, at fairs, and at weddings; they were helped by

non-sectaries when hounded by the authorities; they received the respect of the conforming community at their funerals; they hired conformists as servants, and as midwives and their attendants; they sometimes chose to be buried amongst conformists; they allowed conformists to be buried in their private burial grounds.[41]

Surprisingly, much of this could be true of Baptists and Quakers as well as of Presbyterians. The minutes of Baptist churches, for example, complain of members who have attended alehouses, fairs and even football matches. In Huntingdon, the Quaker draper John Peacock was parish constable in 1661–2. Although the parish congregation was later urged to stop trading with the excommunicated man, his business continued to flourish. From the 1670s, popular sympathy for Quakers was on the rise, and Quaker sufferings books contained fewer instances of public hostility. When the Quaker Robert Falkner of Somersham, in Huntingdonshire, died in 1675, over 200 people from the local area attended his funeral. At a grass roots level, Stevenson concludes, Restoration England was characterised by a good deal of co-operation and 'Christian neighbourliness'.[42]

But this rather idyllic picture of an integrated society should not obscure the darker reality of social intolerance. As Stevenson himself admits, there was often mutual hostility between Dissenters and Anglicans at a local level, with sectarians seeing themselves in opposition to the world, and local society returning the compliment by making their lives difficult. Religion divided families as well as towns and villages. In Bedfordshire, the young Agnes Beaumont paid the price for attending John Bunyan's church. Rumours were spread suggesting that she had an improper relationship with the preacher, and her father shut her out of the house for attending his services. After sleeping all night in a cold barn, she was only readmitted to the house when she promised to stop going to the meetings. When her father died she was accused of poisoning him. Although a sympathetic coroner and jury cleared her name, her case illustrates the popular intolerance of Dissenters.[43]

In the light of their sufferings, it is surprising that the persecution did not cause an exodus of Dissenters to New England or the Netherlands comparable to that of the 1630s. Only fifteen ministers crossed the Atlantic and just ten settled in the Netherlands.[44] Quakers and Baptists, of course, had no reason to look on New England as a haven, but the Netherlands was friendlier. Instead of fleeing, however, Dissenters generally chose to stay put and face up to persecution. The longing for a theocracy had been displaced by a sense that tribulation was the lot of the godly. Yet in the mid-1670s, Quakers did begin to migrate to the middle colonies of North America. In 1675, around 100 Quakers moved to West Jersey, and by 1682 more than

1400 had migrated there. East Jersey also attracted Quakers, including the theologian Robert Barclay. But the major Quaker colonial initiative was launched by William Penn, the son of Admiral Penn and a man with strong connections to the court. In 1681, he obtained a charter for the new colony from Charles II, and in the following year 2000 settlers left England on 23 ships. According to Ned Landsman, 'The Pennsylvania colonization was the most concentrated colonial venture since the Puritan "Great Migration" to New England of half-a-century before'.[45] By 1686, 8000 settlers had sailed to the colony, though only a minority of these were committed Friends. Penn drew up a Frame of Government (1682) guaranteeing that everyone who believed in one God and lived 'peaceably and justly in civil society, shall, in no ways, be molested or prejudiced for their religious persuasion, or practice, in matters of faith and worship, nor shall they be compelled, at any time, to frequent or maintain any religious worship, place or ministry whatever'.[46]

Pennsylvania stood in stark contrast to England, where persecution enjoyed wide and vocal support. As Mark Goldie points out, 'Scarcely a tremor of embarrassment disturbed the voices of divines who called for "a holy violence", "a vigorous and seasonable execution of penal laws" against the "fanatic vermin" whose conventicles troubled the land'. Anglicans defended persecution with considerable intellectual self-confidence, drawing on both the traditional Augustinian arguments and the newer Erastian claim that the magistrate had every right to determine indifferent matters of faith and worship.[47] The archbishops of Canterbury in this period, Gilbert Sheldon (1663–77) and William Sancroft (1677–90), both backed the strict enforcement of the Clarendon Code. Even for latitudinarian Anglicans, 'liberal comprehension rather than plural toleration was the ideal'. Displaying a firm commitment to national uniformity and abhorrence of 'schism', divines like Edward Stillingfleet wished to see freedom of debate within the church rather than diversity and schism outside it. This combination of ecclesiastical tolerance and civil intolerance sprang from a passionate belief that the church should be the nation at prayer.[48]

Dissenters were not the only ones who felt threatened by zealous Anglicanism. According to John Aubrey, the philosopher Hobbes heard 'a report that the Bishops would have him burn't for a Heretique. So he then feared the search of his papers, and burned the greatest part of these verses.' In October 1666 a Bill against Atheism and Profaneness was debated in Parliament, and it was suggested that Hobbes's *Leviathan* should be burned. The bill was aimed at those who denied the Trinity, the authority of the Bible, the immortality of the soul and the eternal torments of hell, and it declared that second-time offenders could be banished, and that if they returned they could be hanged.[49] This final clause recalled the fate of the

Quakers executed in New England, but in the end the bill was not passed into law. In 1678, an Act concerning Heresy abolished the writ *de haeretico comburendo*, which had been used in the past to secure the execution of heretics and blasphemers. In the future, 'atheism, blasphemy, heresy or schism' could only be prosecuted in the ecclesiastical courts 'by excommunication, deprivation, degradation and other ecclesiastical censures not extending to death'.[50]

Towards an open society?

However, although there was strong support for religious uniformity in this period, there were also signs of a new openness. Latitudinarians may have supported coercive measures for restoring uniformity, but they clearly wanted to embrace Presbyterians as brothers rather than persecute them as schismatics. Despite the calamity of 1662, ecumenical Anglicans continued to press for the Presbyterians to be reincorporated within the Church of England. In 1667, a bill of comprehension was introduced into Parliament which proposed making controversial practices (such as kneeling at communion) optional and giving equal recognition to Presbyterian orders. Although the bill failed, Bishop John Wilkins held a conference with prominent Nonconformists like Baxter in 1668, and Matthew Hale drafted a new bill of comprehension. Parliament responded by asking the king to 'send out a proclamation to put the laws against the nonconformists in execution'. Several years on, in 1674, another moderate bishop, George Morley, introduced a bill into the Lords, suggesting minor concessions that might attract Presbyterians back to the church. Although this bill came to nothing, Latitudinarians like Stillingfleet, Tillotson, and Wilkins maintained their contacts with Dissenters and kept working for comprehension. Their task was made easier by the fact that Presbyterians and Congregationalists often continued to attend the parish church, even whilst belonging to private conventicles. In the parish of St Giles, Cripplegate, Dissenters were members of the vestry and served as churchwardens and common councilmen in the early 1680s. The Latitudinarian vicar of the parish, Edward Fowler, acquiesced in this and protected them from prosecution, incurring the wrath of his Tory parishioners for doing so. Fowler still held out the hope that sober Dissenters would return to the church for good, and preferred to keep the doors of the parish open to them rather than alienating them by persecution.[51]

The choice between comprehension and indulgence has been described as 'the leitmotiv of ecclesiastical politics' between 1660 and 1689,[52] but Fowler provides an example of one who adopted an indulgent policy towards

Dissenters in order to win them back to a comprehensive church. Yet Fowler 'was not against the due execution of the [penal] laws if it was pursued in the spirit of reform rather than revenge'.[53] By contrast, a minority of Anglicans condemned the penal laws and championed toleration. Many Anglicans had played an active part in the religious and political life of Interregnum England, and had opposed the purge of the early 1660s. Anthony Ashley Cooper, the Earl of Shaftesbury from 1672, had been a member of Cromwell's Council of State and tried to use his considerable political influence from the late 1660s to secure toleration for Dissenters. In 1666 he met John Locke, who had been educated at Oxford in the 1650s, and went on to write an *Essay concerning Toleration* (1667). In 1669, they drew up a constitution for Carolina, the new colony of which Ashley Cooper was a proprietor. The Fundamental Constitutions of Carolina made the Church of England the state church (probably against Locke's wishes), but any group of seven or more was free to start its own church, and 'Jews, heathens and other dissenters from the purity of Christian religion' were granted religious freedom.[54] Ashley Cooper and Locke were trying to fashion a society which would stand as a rebuke to England and offer an alternative model for its future.

The willingness of some Anglicans to contemplate toleration reflected the fact that 'the dominance of the Church of England was at best precarious and at worst an illusion'.[55] Despite its many privileges and its persecutions of Dissenters, the Restoration church did not feel confident and in control. Like many persecutors before them, Anglicans complained that they were 'under persecution from the tongues and pens of perverse men'. Such self-pity may itself seem perverse, but it rested on the knowledge that powerful figures like Shaftesbury disliked the church as it stood. The king's Indulgences, the various parliamentary comprehension schemes and the tracts in support of toleration demonstrated that many favoured a broader church and took a more lenient view of Dissent. When the Conventicle Acts were passed in 1664 and 1670, around one-third of the MPs who voted actually voted against the new laws.[56] As we have seen, local magistrates were often unwilling to enforce the penal laws, and Dissenters or their sympathisers held office in many parts of the country. A substantial minority of the clergy only partially conformed to the ceremonies and liturgy of the church, and church attendance and conformity among the laity was far from complete.[57] Dissenters even had the self-confidence to erect their own meeting houses.[58]

The fact was that England was gradually becoming a more open society. Although Dissenters faced persecution, they were also making a substantial contribution to English culture. They were overrepresented among London's printers, and Dissenting preachers published an extraordinary number of works during the 1660s and 1670s. Censorship was a serious problem, with the Surveyor of the Press, Roger L'Estrange, being a fierce opponent of Dissent who frequently refused to license Nonconformist works. Despite the restrictions, however, the prolific Richard Baxter published 32 works between 1662 and 1678 and another 34 between 1679 and 1685. A number of these books became bestsellers: *A Call to the Unconverted* (1658) was to reach its 23rd edition by 1685, selling tens of thousands of copies.[59] Bunyan's *Pilgrim's Progress* quickly became a runaway bestseller too, and was to establish itself as one of the classic works of English prose.

The Jewish community also flourished in Restoration England. When the king returned in 1660, he was presented with several petitions by London merchants who wanted him to expel the Jews. One even made the outlandish claim that under Cromwell the Jews had attempted to buy St Paul's Cathedral in order to turn it into a synagogue. However, these petitions were ignored by Charles, and in 1664 the government promised that they would not be molested. According to the community's rabbi, a written statement from the king had declared that during his lifetime 'they need feel no trepidation because of any sect that might oppose them, inasmuch as he himself would be their advocate and assist them with all his power'. According to David Katz, this amounted to 'a formal statement of toleration'. When the London Jews were being prosecuted in 1674 for meeting to worship, the king intervened to stop all proceedings against them. Their right to live in England had been secured, and in 1677 or 1678 they confirmed their presence and self-confidence by making the first of many annual presentations to the Lord Mayor of London of a silver dish or goblet.[60]

The growing openness of English society at this time has been underlined by Steve Pincus in his study of the dramatic proliferation of coffeehouses. Coffeehouses, which were famed as places of public debate and discussion, dated from around 1650, when the first one had opened in Oxford. By 1663, London alone had over 80 coffeehouses, whilst by the end of the century it had more than 2000. People met there to read newspapers and discuss politics, and High Church Anglicans associated coffeehouses with Puritanism and republicanism; one declared that 'a coffee-house is a lay conventicle, good-fellowship turn'd Puritan'. In the mid-1670s, at the height of their power, conservative Anglicans made a serious attempt to suppress the coffeehouses just as they had suppressed the Declaration of Indulgence, but to no avail. Pincus concludes that 'the revolutionary decades of the midcentury had generated a taste for news that could not be suppressed'. England was developing what the German theorist Jürgen Habermas has called 'a public sphere' in which free discussion was valued and even celebrated.[61]

Thus the persistence of persecution disguised profound changes in society. England was a much more pluralistic society than it had been half a century earlier. Science was flourishing, encouraged by the establishment of the Royal Society in 1663, and the new philosophies of Descartes and Hobbes, widely seen as corrosive to Christian orthodoxy, provoked widespread debate. For all his fear of burning at the stake, Hobbes escaped entirely unscathed. Contemporaries decried the spread of atheism and libertinism, and though their jeremiads should be treated with some care, there is good reason to think that freethinking and Deism were on the increase. The sceptical wit of the playwright Aphra Behn and the poet the Earl of Rochester reflected a growing willingness to question traditional beliefs.[62] Those who supported the use of coercion to reimpose uniformity were arguably fighting a losing battle against powerful social and intellectual trends.

Catholics and the 'Popish Plot'

Yet the religious scepticism and rationalism of Restoration England must not be exaggerated. Anti-popery, which had proved so destructive to the Catholic community in the past, was still very much alive. Between 1678 and 1681, at the height of the 'Popish Plot' scare and the Exclusion Crisis, Catholic priests were subjected to persecution as savage as that of the 1580s or the 1640s.

During the first decade of the Restoration, such a severe persecution of Catholics had seemed unlikely. Anglicans were fixated on the threat posed by Dissent, and fears of Catholic subversion had subsided. The king himself was markedly sympathetic to Catholics. His mother, Henrietta Maria, was allowed an official chapel and priests at St James's Palace, and his Catholic wife, Catherine of Braganza, whom he married in 1662, also kept a chapel of Portuguese, Irish and English priests at Somerset House. In addition, Charles had a predilection for Catholic mistresses. At the start of the reign, prominent Catholics petitioned the House of Lords for relief from the penal laws, and even presented a bill. Although this came to nothing, the king himself issued a Declaration of Indulgence in 1662. The Declaration expressed the gratitude of the Stuarts to 'the greatest part of our Roman Catholic subjects', who had loyally supported the crown when many so-called 'zealous Protestants' had made war on it. Although the penal laws against Catholics had been justified in times of crisis, the king had no wish to pursue 'sanguinary' measures against good subjects. As long as Catholics practised their religion quietly and did not criticise or threaten the established Protestant religion, they would be included in the Indulgence.[63]

The Cavalier Parliament forced Charles to withdraw the Declaration, but the situation of the Catholic community was much better than that of the Dissenters. Between the execution of John Southworth in 1654 and the Popish Plot of 1678, no Catholic was put to death under the penal laws. For a community that had endured a stormy existence, this was a quarter of a century of relative calm. The number of committed Catholics in England and Wales during the Restoration period had stabilised at around 60,000, considerably less than the number of Presbyterians and roughly equal to the number of Quakers. Catholics comprised around 1 per cent of the population, and most of the time they were regarded as an unthreatening minority. Catholic landowners among the gentry and aristocracy continued to provide security and support for their co-religionists and enjoyed a generally amicable relationship with their Protestant neighbours. There were around 30 Catholic peers, and several of them sat in the House of Lords. Although all public office-holders were required to take the oaths of allegiance and supremacy, this did not prevent a small number of Catholics from qualifying for office; they either took the oaths or the oaths were not tendered. A few Catholics were elected as MPs in the 1660s, and others became army officers or held civilian posts as governors, JPs or sheriffs. There were perhaps around 500 priests in the country, including 150 Jesuits, and in the years before 1678 little was done to arrest or banish them. Catholics had learnt how to survive in a Protestant society; the days of reckless plotting and open proselytising seemed to be over. The community was introspective and politically loyal.[64]

The enforcement of the penal laws was relatively lax in this period. Even at the height of the Popish Plot, there was never 'an all-out persecution of the Catholic peers and gentry in the shires'. Partly this was due to the complexity of the prosecution procedures, but it also reflected the lack of enthusiasm for persecution felt by local officials. Protestants who condemned popery could still enjoy good relations with individual papists. Even if Catholics were convicted, it was by no means inevitable that they would have to pay fines or forfeit land. There were some magistrates who zealously enforced the penal laws, but they seem to have been the exception rather than the rule. 'When the Catholic question did not dominate politics', writes Miller, 'most Protestants were prepared to leave alone the attenuated minority of Catholics in their neighbourhood.'[65]

Yet anti-popery was dormant rather than dead. When the Great Fire of London destroyed much of the city in 1666, rumours of Catholic treachery spread through the city almost as fast as the fire itself. There were claims that Catholics had started the blaze and armed themselves in order to overthrow Protestantism. Even Samuel Pepys, who had a Catholic wife and a Catholic music teacher, found such claims convincing. Panic spread throughout the country, and there were riots in several towns. Although the panic subsided, a belief in 'Popish pyromania' was added to the anti-Catholic tradition.[66] By the 1670s, the international situation was making such paranoia respectable again. The power of Catholic France under Louis XIV sent a collective shiver down English Protestant spines. In 1670 Louis signed the Treaty of Dover with Charles, and there were ugly rumours about its secret clauses. Had these been known the outcry would have been extraordinary, for Charles had agreed to go to war against Protestant Holland, grant toleration to Catholics and declare himself a Catholic when circumstances permitted. In 1672, he fulfilled part of the bargain by issuing the second Declaration of Indulgence. The Declaration refused to allow Catholics permission to build 'public places of worship', but it did grant them 'exemption from the execution of the penal laws, and the exercise of their worship in their private houses only'.[67] Once again, Parliament forced the king to cancel the Declaration. By now, MPs were becoming more worried by popery than by Dissent. They tried to create a broad Protestant alliance against popery by introducing a bill for the relief of Dissenters, and they forced the king to agree to a Test Act in 1673 which would exclude Catholics from public office. The Act produced a startling revelation: James, Duke of York, first in line to the throne, was outed as a Catholic. Paradoxically, the conversion of the heir to the throne proved to be something of a disaster for Catholics. 'Without James's conversion', writes John Miller, 'there would have been little persecution of Catholics in the 1670s, no Popish Plot and no Exclusion Crisis.'[68] The horror of James's Catholicism was intensified when he married an Italian Catholic, Mary of Modena, in September. English Protestants contemplated the disturbing prospect of a line of Catholic kings.

In a bid to reassure Anglicans, Charles allied himself with the Earl of Danby, who was committed to bolstering the church by attacking both Catholics and Dissenters. In 1674, all non-householding Catholic recusants in London were ordered to leave the capital during the sitting of Parliament. Yet many Protestants remained deeply apprehensive. Catholicism still appeared to be flourishing at court, and the king was willing to prorogue Parliament for long periods. He now had at his disposal a substantial standing army, numbering 20,000 men by 1678. In the light of his close relations with Louis XIV, these developments seemed ominous. Catholic France seemed to pose a threat to European Protestantism as great as that posed by Hapsburg Spain at the time of Elizabeth. When Andrew Marvell published his *Account of the Growth of Popery and Arbitrary Government* in 1677, he touched raw nerves. He wrote that 'there has now for diverse years a design been carried on to change the lawful government of England into an absolute tyranny, and to convert the established Protestant religion into downright Popery'.

The idea of a Counter-Reformation design against English Protestantism was far from absurd, and we should resist the temptation to treat Protestant fear as irrational paranoia. Militant Catholicism had delivered some crushing blows against continental Protestantism since the 1590s, in Bohemia, the Palatinate, Hungary, Poland, Bavaria, Germany, and France.[69] But in 1678, paranoia about popery played into the hands of one of the most disreputable and accomplished conmen in English history, Titus Oates. Oates was the son of a Baptist preacher, but he had been received into the Catholic church and had spent time in Jesuit colleges in Spain and France. In July 1678, he returned to England, and announced that he had gathered evidence of a 'Popish Plot' to assassinate the king and extirpate English Protestantism. Although his tale has been accurately described as 'an amazing tissue of lies stuck together by just a few strips of truth',[70] it was given credibility by two events: the discovery that Edward Coleman, former secretary to the Duke of York, had corresponded with Jesuits and French agents to overthrow Protestantism with French help; and the mysterious murder of Sir Edmund Berry Godfrey, the JP who had taken Oates's depositions. For Protestants reared on stories of the Marian persecution, the St Bartholomew's Day massacres, the Spanish Armada, the Gunpowder Plot, the Irish rebellion, and the Great Fire, these two events were shocking evidence of yet another bloody popish conspiracy to destroy the Reformed religion. The Jesuits were quickly blamed for Godfrey's murder, and the Cavalier Parliament declared that 'there hath been and still is a damnable and hellish plot contrived and carried on by the popish recusants for the assassinating and murdering the King, and for subverting the government, and rooting out and destroying the Protestant religion'.[71] A Second Test Act (1678) excluded Catholics from Parliament by requiring all MPs to make a declaration against Catholicism, repudiating transubstantiation and 'superstitious and idolatrous' Roman rites.

In late 1678 and early 1679, England was seized by an anti-popish panic comparable to that which followed the Irish massacres of 1641. There were rumours that the Catholics had armed themselves, that French and Spanish troops had landed, that the papists were about to set fire to London once again. The houses of Catholics were searched, trained bands were mobilised, and Jesuits were arrested. Proclamations were issued commanding the enforcement of the penal laws, and a Second Test Act was passed excluding Catholics from Parliament. Hundreds of papists were convicted of recusancy and fined accordingly. Pope-burnings were held in London and around the country, especially on 5 and 17 November, the anniversaries of the

Gunpowder Plot and the coronation of Elizabeth I respectively. One report suggested that a crowd of 200,000 people attended the burning of an effigy of the pope at Temple Bar in 1679. Publishers rushed out histories of popish plots, and sets of playing cards were issued which depicted Catholic atrocities.[72]

The crisis produced a new spate of Catholic martyrdoms. In November 1678, Edward Coleman was executed for treason. Although almost a quarter of a century had passed since the last Catholic martyrdom, a new wave of savage persecution was about to hit the missionary priests. Of the 600 or 700 Catholic missionaries in England, around 100 were arrested; 23 died in gaol, and 18 were executed, some for plotting but most under the Elizabethan statute making ordination abroad a treasonable offence.[73]

The irony of this persecution was that a good many who fanned the flames of intolerance were committed tolerationists. If the Tories were the party of intolerant Anglicanism, the Whigs were the party sympathetic to Dissent. They campaigned for the repeal of the draconian 1593 statute against seditious sectaries and favoured policies of comprehension and toleration. It was no coincidence that Dissenters themselves were heavily involved in the Whig propaganda campaign.[74] Yet there was a definite tension between the liberalism of Whig ideology and the thoroughly illiberal repression of the Popish Plot scare. Locke, Marvell, Sidney and Penn genuinely believed in toleration and cannot be held personally responsible for the execution of Catholic priests, but their association with the visceral anti-Catholicism of 1678–9 reminds us of what Richard Ashcraft calls 'the darker side of liberalism'; the Whig campaign for toleration of Dissenters was 'dependent upon a set of specific prejudices, erroneous beliefs, and an attitude fed more by conspiratorial fear than rational judgement'.[75] Shaftesbury's exploitation of Oates's fantasies and his willingness to stand by as Catholics were executed also appear profoundly cynical. Yet the heart of the problem was that Protestant tolerationism had its roots in anti-popery and anti-clericalism – persecution had been identified as a hallmark of the popish Antichrist. For this very reason anti-popery was reaffirmed by tolerationists. Instead of encouraging a new understanding of Catholicism, tolerationism reinforced the idea that there was something inherently oppressive and violent about popery. Tolerationists really did see Catholicism as a tyrannical force hell-bent on destroying Protestantism. In his 'Critical Notes' of 1681, Locke was willing to contemplate a 'regulated toleration' for Catholics, but he was convinced that the Catholic powers had 'an unalterable designe to destroy us'.[76]

In England, however, fear of popery had always jostled with fear of Puritan subversion. The Whigs' willingness to ride the wave of anti-popery ultimately backfired, and the identification of Whigs and Dissenters proved damaging to both. Tory Anglicans were able to exploit memories of 1642, when Puritan anti-popery had led England into civil war. As the crisis wore on, popular opinion began to flow back towards the Tories, who portrayed themselves as the supporters of law and order against the sedition and anarchy of Dissent. By mid-1681, Charles was able to regain control of the political situation, and Shaftesbury was imprisoned for treason.

The failure of Exclusion and the subsequent royalist reaction after 1681 was as beneficial to Catholics as it was detrimental to Dissenters. Once again, militant Protestants had used anti-popery to challenge the crown. Tory Anglicans reminded themselves that Puritan plots were more of a threat than papist ones, and the pressure on Catholics dropped considerably. In Middlesex in 1679, 70 per cent of those arrested for recusancy had been Catholics; by 1683, the figure was only 6 per cent, as the authorities concentrated their fire on Dissenters.[77] The number of priests arrested declined, though a significant number of Catholics remained in prison. Most significantly, however, the execution of Oliver Plunkett on 1 July 1681 was to be the last martyrdom of a Catholic on English soil. As Richard Challoner later put it, the Catholics were still to be 'exposed to some passing storms, yet by God's mercy the persecution has never raged so far as to come to blood'.[78]

Catholicism and toleration under James II, 1685–8

When James II became king in February 1685, he was England's first openly Catholic monarch since Mary I. He had come to the throne thanks to the support of conservative Anglicans, who had fervently opposed the policy of Exclusion. He was to lose his crown because he alienated these very supporters by his autocratic attack on Anglican dominance.

From the outset of his reign, James applied all his energies to securing civil equality for his fellow Catholics throughout the British Isles. He was determined that Catholics should no longer be excluded from public life. Although his commitment to toleration may well have been sincere, he probably expected his policies to lead his subjects back to the true faith. Hitherto, they had been driven from Catholicism by fear and embraced Anglicanism for its civil advantages; once these motives were removed, and Catholicism was placed on a level playing field with Protestantism, the truth would prevail. So it was that Catholics were appointed as members of the Privy Council, as officers in the army, as fellows at Oxbridge colleges, and as magistrates on county benches. In addition to this 'massive affirmative action programme',[79] James also made great efforts to persuade Parliament to repeal the laws against Catholics. Parliament, dominated as it was by Tory Anglicans, was unreceptive, and in November 1685 it protested loudly against the commissioning of Catholic army officers. In their pulpits, Anglican preachers openly denounced the preferment of Catholics, despite James's attempts to silence them. The king and the Anglican royalists were at loggerheads and James began to turn towards another group who might be more supportive – the Dissenters.

During the first year of his reign, James had done little to help Dissenters or end the period of 'Tory revenge'. The Exclusion Crisis had persuaded him that Dissenters were political subversives, and that their public meetings were a threat to the monarchy. The involvement of Dissenters in the Rye House Plot of 1683, and the Monmouth rebellion of 1685, only reinforced his conviction that Dissent was 'faction and not religion'. One hundred and fifty people were executed for their part in the Monmouth rebellion, including a high number of Dissenters. One woman, the Baptist Elizabeth Gaunt, who had merely sheltered one of the rebels, was burned at the stake at Tyburn.[80] Moreover, Dissenters who were not implicated in the rebellion continued to experience persecution.

In 1686, however, the king's policy took a sharp new turn. Exasperated by Anglican intransigence, James decided to woo the Dissenters. In March, he issued a pardon to Dissenters imprisoned under the penal code. In the months that followed, many Dissenters were released from prison, including around 1200 Quakers. Then, in April 1687, James issued a Declaration of Indulgence, which suspended the penal laws (thus confirming the cessation of persecution) and the Test Acts (so opening public office to both Catholics and Dissenters). The preamble explained the king's thinking:

> We cannot but heartily wish, as it will easily be believed, that all the people of our dominions were members of the Catholic Church. Yet we humbly thank Almighty God it is, and hath of long time been, our constant sense and opinion (which upon divers occasions we have declared) that conscience ought not to be constrained, nor people forced in matters of mere religion; it has ever been directly contrary to our inclination, as we think it is to the interest of government, which it destroys by spoiling trade, depopulating countries, and discouraging strangers; and finally, that it never obtained the end for which it was employed. And in this we are the more confirmed by the reflections we have made upon the conduct of the four last reigns [of Elizabeth, James, Charles I and Charles II]; for after all the frequent and pressing endeavours that we have used in each of them, to reduce these kingdoms to an exact conformity in religion it is visible the success has not answered the design, and that the difficulty is invincible.[81]

The Declaration completed James's dramatic policy shift. 'In little over a year', writes John Miller, 'England had passed from a vigorous persecution (of Dissenters) to the most complete toleration it had ever known.'[82] Around 80 addresses of thanks were sent to the king by grateful Presbyterians, Congregationalists, Baptists and Quakers. Yet many Dissenters were deeply suspicious of the intentions of a Catholic monarch who was introducing toleration through the use of his royal prerogative. They feared that James was introducing absolutist government and using toleration to prepare the ground for a restoration of Catholicism. The Revocation of the Edict of Nantes by Louis XIV in 1685 had rekindled Protestant fears of popery and arbitrary government. As a result of the Revocation, around a quarter of a million Huguenot refugees departed from France, with up to 50,000 emigrating to Britain. Those who remained were subjected to forcible conversion or fierce persecution.[83] Although on the surface, James's policy of toleration was the exact opposite of Louis XIV's, his authoritarian style provoked fears that he was walking in the footsteps of the French king. First he would establish his own absolute authority, then he would persecute his Protestant subjects. The Marquis of Halifax warned Dissenters that James was simply hugging them now in order to squeeze them later.

The king's complete lack of sensitivity to such fears was remarkable. Throughout 1687 and 1688 he continued his policy of pushing Catholics into positions of power. In Ireland, Catholics controlled the army and occupied most of the high offices of state. In England, Lord Belasyse was made First Lord of the Treasury, Lord Tyrconnel was appointed Lord-Lieutenant of Ireland, and Lord Arundel became Lord Privy Seal. James also sought to impose a Catholic president on Magdalen College, Oxford, and, most provocatively, appointed a Jesuit priest, Father Petre, to the Privy Council. In July 1687 he dissolved Parliament, gave the papal nuncio a public reception, and began a campaign to purge Anglican office-holders and replace them with Catholics and Dissenters. Whig coups were taking place in borough corporations across the land, and many Dissenters were actively engaged in exposing and shaming their former persecutors through the Commission of Enquiry.[84] By early 1688, James had sacked three-quarters of all JPs, all the Tory ministers he had inherited from Charles, and most of the lords-lieutenant. If Anglicans would not support his programme, he would drive it through without them. In April 1688, he reissued his Declaration of Indulgence, adding that a Parliament would be summoned in November to enact it. In May, the clergy were ordered to read the Declaration in church services, and bishops were told to distribute it in their dioceses.

For Anglican royalists this was too much to take. The archbishop of Canterbury and six bishops petitioned the king, refusing to comply with his order and declaring that the suspending power used by the king was illegal. The bishops were imprisoned in the Tower, and tried at the King's Bench in June for seditious libel, only to be found not guilty. Their acquittal was a blow to James, but the birth of a son to the king and his wife was an even greater blow to English Protestants. They now faced the possibility that far from being a short and troublesome interlude, James's reign might inaugurate a long line of Catholic despots. The sense of panic had intensified to the point at which some Anglicans were willing to take drastic action. Seven disaffected notables, including Danby and the bishop of London, sent an invitation to William of Orange to intervene by force. William was married to the king's daughter, Mary, and he also had a powerful strategic interest in intervention, since he was desperate for England's support in any future war with Louis XIV. On 30 September, he issued a Declaration explaining why he had decided to invade.

In November, William invaded. Panicked by desertions from his army, James failed to offer any military resistance. Fearing for his life, he left London on 11 December and then sailed for France. His denouement had been extraordinarily swift. Just two months later, in February 1689, the Prince of Orange was crowned William III and his wife (James's eldest daughter) became Mary II.

Both contemporary observers and historians have been divided in their attitudes to James. For some, like William Penn and several members of John Locke's circle, the king was a sincere believer in toleration.[85] He had declared himself opposed to persecution for conscience's sake, and he did not hesitate to condemn Louis XIV's persecution of the French Huguenots as 'unchristian'. For others, like Halifax, James was a Catholic bigot, who simply used toleration as a means to the end of re-Catholicising England. Far from being concerned with the welfare of Dissenters, he simply wanted to divide Protestants in order to impose Catholic rule.

Neither picture is entirely convincing. During his time in Scotland in the early 1680s, James had sanctioned a fearsome repression of militant Covenanters, and in England too, he had supported the persecution of Dissenters. Of course, both Scottish Covenanters and English Dissenters had been involved in their fair share of plotting against the government, and James certainly felt that their public meetings were a threat to the state. Yet he failed to see that the seditious tendencies of some Dissenters were related to the repression they continually suffered. His sudden conversion to a policy of toleration for Dissenters in 1686–7 does seem to be the product of convenience more than principle, since he was looking for new allies in his campaign against Anglican dominance. For him, toleration was not so much a pathway to a pluralist society, but the means by which England would be returned to the Church of Rome. But many tolerationists in the seventeenth and eighteenth centuries (Protestants and Deists alike) were convinced that in a free market of ideas their own beliefs would prevail. There is good reason to think that James was sincere in his conviction that 'conscience ought not to be constrained, nor people forced in matters of mere religion'. In the words of John Miller, 'his aim was to improve the position of Catholicism in England by peaceful means. There was not the slightest possibility of imposing Catholicism by force.'[86]

James was a man of mixed motives, profoundly autocratic reflexes and extraordinary naivety. Had he pursued a less confrontational approach he may well have achieved more for his fellow Catholics. But the fact remains that it was his Declaration of 1687, rather than the Toleration Act of 1689, that marked the end of large-scale religious persecution in England. For a brief period he had introduced an official toleration that was greater than any experienced before the nineteenth century. As Mark Goldie has written with reference to his policy of appointing Catholics to Oxford and Cambridge, 'Whatever James's ultimate allegiance to a Counter-Reformation vision of the English Church restored to Rome, for the duration he was, paradoxically, committed to the principles which modern liberals and secul16arists hold dear: a university open to a plural society, unencumbered by the strictures of the Anglican Establishment'.[87] Although many Anglicans howled in protest at the king's arbitrary government, their real objection was to the erosion of their own hegemony. Ironically, by uniting Anglicans and Dissenters against him, James had unintentionally paved the way for the Toleration Act of 1689.

Notes

1   W. K. Jordan, *The Development of Religious Toleration in England*, 4 vols (London, 1932–40), IV, p. 467.

2   The Declaration and the major pieces of religious legislation from the Restoration period can be found in A. Browning, ed., *English Historical Documents*, VIII: *1660–1714* (London, 1966), pp. 365–400. See also the valuable compendium of information in G. Holmes, *The Making of a Great Power: Late Stuart and Georgian England, 1660–1722* (Harlow, 1993), pp. 453–61.

3   I. M. Green, *The Re-establishment of the Church of England, 1660–1663* (Oxford, 1978), p. 1.

4   W. C. Braithwaite, *The Beginnings of Quakerism to 1660*, 2nd edn (London, 1955), pp. 476–7.

5   Green, *The Re-establishment of the Church of England*, p. 143.

6   Ibid., ch. 9.

7   The classic account is A. G. Matthew, ed., *Calamy Revised: Being a Revision of Edmund Calamy's 'Account' of the Ministers and Others Ejected and Silenced, 1660–1662* (Oxford, 1934).

8   See J. Marshall, *John Locke: Religion, Resistance and Responsibility* (Cambridge, 1994), pp. 33–4. Marshall suggests a total of half a million, but this is probably too high.

9   M. Watts, *The Dissenters: From the Reformation to the French Revolution* (Oxford, 1978), p. 224.

10 M. Goldie, 'The search for religious liberty, 1640–1690', in J. Morrill, ed., *The Oxford Illustrated History of Tudor and Stuart Britain* (Oxford, 1996), p. 300.

11 *The Autobiography of Richard Baxter*, ed. N. H. Keeble (London, 1984), p. 189.

12 C. E. Whiting, *Studies in English Puritanism, 1660–1688* (London, 1931), pp. 4–5.

13 C. Horle, *The Quakers and the English Legal System, 1660–1688* (Philadelphia, 1988), preface.

14 A. Fletcher, 'The enforcement of the Conventicle Acts 1664–1679', in W. J. Sheils, ed., *Persecution and Toleration* (Oxford, 1984), pp. 235–46, quotation at p. 245.

15 R. Greaves, *Enemies under his Feet: Radicals and Nonconformists in Britain, 1664–1677* (Stanford, CA, 1990), pp. 132–3.

16 See W. C. Braithwaite, *The Second Period of Quakerism*, 2nd edn (Cambridge, 1961), p. 114.

17 D. L. Wykes, '"They assemble in greater numbers and [with] more dareing than formerly": the Bishop of Gloucester and Nonconformity in the late 1660s', *Southern History* 17 (1995), 24–39, quotation at 28.

18 Joseph Besse, *A Collection of the Sufferings of the People called Quakers*, 2 vols (London, 1753), I, p. 554.

19 G. Geis and I. Bunn, *A Trial of Witches: A Seventeenth-Century Witchcraft Prosecution* (London, 1997), ch. 7.

20 See R. Greaves, *Deliver us from Evil: The Radical Underground in Britain, 1660–1663* (Oxford, 1986).

21 See G. S. De Krey, 'Rethinking the Restoration: Dissenting cases for conscience, 1667–72', *Historical Journal* 38 (1995), 53–83; R. L. Greaves, '"Let truth be free": John Bunyan and the Restoration Crisis of 1667–1673', *Albion* 28 (1996), 587–605.

22 See T. Harris, 'The bawdy house riots of 1668', *Historical Journal* 29 (1986), 537–56.

23 Browning, ed., *English Historical Documents*, VIII, p. 387.

24 See G. Lyon Turner, ed., *Original Records of Early Nonconformity under Persecution and Indulgence*, 3 vols (London, 1911–14), I, pp. 193–623.

25 N. Sykes, *From Sheldon to Secker: Aspects of English Church History, 1660–1768* (Cambridge, 1959), p. 77.

26 Watts, *The Dissenters*, pp. 250–2; D. Lacey, *Dissent and Parliamentary Politics in England, 1661–1689* (New Brunswick, NJ, 1969), chs. 3–6.

27 Watts, *The Dissenters*, pp. 254–5.

28 T. Harris, 'Was the Tory reaction popular? Attitudes of Londoners towards the persecution of dissent, 1681–86', *London Journal* 13 (1987–8), 111.

29 M. Goldie, 'The Hilton gang: terrorising Dissent in 1680s London', *History Today* 47 (1998), 26–32.

30 Ibid., p. 28.

31 R. Hutton, *Charles II: King of England, Scotland and Ireland* (Oxford, 1991), pp. 456–7.

32 See J. R. Knott, 'Joseph Besse and the Quaker culture of suffering', in T. Corns and D. Loewenstein, eds, *The Emergence of Quaker Writing: Dissenting Literature in Seventeenth-Century England* (London, 1995), pp. 126–41; D. L. Wykes, ' "To let the memory of these men dye is injurious to posterity": Edmund Calamy's "Account" of the ejected ministers', in R. N. Swanson, ed., *The Church Retrospective* (Oxford, 1997), pp. 379–92.

33 *A Short Relation of some part of the Sad Sufferings and Cruel Havock and Spoil, Inflicted on . . . Quakers* (1670), in *The Sufferings of the Quakers in Nottinghamshire, 1649–89*, ed. P. J. Cropper (Nottingham, 1892), pp. 6–12.

34 *The Late Sufferings of the People of God called Quakers in Nottingham-shire* (n.d.), in *The Sufferings of the Quakers in Nottinghamshire*, pp. 30–2.

35 Besse, *A Collection of the Sufferings of the People called Quakers*, I, pp. 556ff.

36 *The Autobiography of Richard Baxter*, pp. 207–8.

37 C. Hill, *A Turbulent, Seditious, and Factious People: John Bunyan and his Church* (Oxford, 1989), pp. 120–4.

38 T. Waite, *Taken on Trust* (London, 1993), p. 450.

39 *Grace Abounding with other Spiritual Autobiographies*, ed. J. Stachniewski (Oxford, 1998), pp. 88–93.

40 The material in this paragraph has been drawn from G. Cragg, *Puritanism in the Period of the Great Persecution, 1660–1688* (Cambridge, 1957), ch. 4; Watts, *The Dissenters*, pp. 235–6.

41 B. Stevenson, 'The social integration of post-Restoration dissenters', in M. Spufford, ed., *The World of Rural Dissenters, 1520–1725* (Cambridge, 1995), pp. 385–6.

42 Ibid., pp. 360–87.

43 'The Persecution of Agnes Beaumont', in *Grace Abounding with Other Spiritual Autobiographies*, pp. 193–224.

44 N. Keeble, *The Literary Culture of Nonconformity in Later Seventeenth-Century England* (Leicester, 1987), p. 48.

45 N. Landsman, 'The middle colonies', in N. Canny, ed., *The Origins of Empire* (Oxford, 1998), pp. 359–60.

46 J. F. Maclear, ed., *Church and State in the Modern Age: A Documentary History* (New York, 1995), pp. 51–3.

47 M. Goldie, 'The theory of religious intolerance in Restoration England', in O. P. Grell, J. Israel and N. Tyacke, eds, *From Persecution to Toleration* (Oxford, 1989), p. 330.

48 M. Goldie, 'Sir Peter Pett, sceptical Toryism and the science of toleration in the 1680s', in Sheils, ed., *Persecution and Toleration*, p. 263.

49 P. Milton, 'Hobbes, heresy and Lord Arlington', *History of Political Thought* 14 (1993), 534–79.

50 Browning, ed., *English Historical Documents*, VIII, p. 400.

51 M. Goldie and J. Spurr, 'Politics and the Restoration parish: Edward Fowler and the struggle for St Giles Cripplegate', *English Historical Review* 109 (1994), 572–96.

52 Sykes, *From Sheldon to Secker*, p. 68.

53 Goldie and Spurr, 'Politics and the Restoration parish', p. 585.

54 John Locke, *Political Writings*, ed. D. Wootton (Harmondsworth, 1993), pp. 41–3, 228–9.

55 J. Spurr, 'Religion in Restoration England', in L. Glassey, ed., *The Reigns of Charles II and James II and VII* (London, 1997), p. 98.

56 N. Morgan, *Lancashire Quakers and the Establishment, 1660–1730* (Halifax, 1993), p. 61.

57 Spurr, 'Religion in Restoration England', pp. 100–4.

58 On the history of Dissenting building projects during the Restoration see D. L. Wykes, 'James II's religious indulgence of 1687 and the early organisation of Dissent: the building of the first nonconformist meeting-house in Birmingham', *Midland History* 16 (1991), 86–102.

59 N. Keeble, *Richard Baxter: Puritan Man of Letters* (Oxford, 1982), pp. 18–21, 8.

60 D. Katz, *The Jews in the History of England, 1485–1850* (Oxford, 1994), pp. 140–4.

61 S. Pincus, '"Coffee politicians does create": coffeehouses and Restoration political culture', *Journal of Modern History* 67 (1995), 807–34, quotation at p. 834.

62 C. Hill, 'Freethinking and libertinism: the legacy of the English Revolution', in his *England's Turning Point: Essays on 17th Century English History* (London, 1998), pp. 307–22. See also A. Feldwick and C. J. Nederman, ' "Religion set the world at odds": Deism and the climate of religious tolerance in the works of Aphra Behn', in J. C. Laursen and C. J. Nederman, eds, *Beyond the Persecuting Society: Religious Toleration before the Enlightenment* (Philadelphia, 1998), ch. 9.

63 Browning, ed., *English Historical Documents*, VIII, pp. 373–4.

64 J. Miller, *Popery and Politics in England, 1660–1688* (Cambridge, 1973), pp. 9–12, 64–6, 40.

65 Ibid., ch. 3, quotations from pp. 56, 63.

66 Ibid., p. 105.

67 Browning, ed., *English Historical Documents*, VIII, pp. 387–8.

68 Miller, *Popery and Politics*, p. 93.

69 J. Scott, 'England's troubles: exhuming the Popish Plot', in T. Harris, P. Seaward and M. Goldie, eds, *The Politics of Religion in Restoration England* (Oxford, 1990), pp. 112–15.

70 Holmes, *The Making of a Great Power*, p. 123.

71 J. P. Kenyon, *The Popish Plot* (London, 1972), p. 96.

72 See D. Cressy, *Bonfires and Bells: National Memory and the Protestant Calendar in Elizabethan and Stuart England* (London, 1989), pp. 178–82.

73 See R. Challoner, *Memoirs of the Missionary Priests* (London, 1924), pp. 510–83.

74 T. Harris, *Politics under the Later Stuarts: Party Conflict in a Divided Society, 1660–1715* (London, 1993), pp. 93–4.

75 See R. Ashcraft, 'Religion and Lockean natural rights', in I. Bloom, J. P. Martin and W. L. Proudfoot, eds, *Religious Diversity and Human Rights* (New York, 1996), p. 196.

76 See Marshall, *John Locke*, pp. 110–11.

77 Miller, *Popery and Politics*, p. 191.

78 Challoner, *Memoirs of the Missionary Priests*, p. 583.

79 J. Morrill, 'Politics in an age of revolution, 1630–1690', in *The Oxford Illustrated History of Tudor and Stuart Britain*, pp. 391–2.

80 Watts, *The Dissenters*, p. 257.

81 Browning, ed., *English Historical Documents*, VIII, pp. 395–6.

82 J. Miller, 'James II and toleration', in E. Cruickshanks, ed., *By Force or Default? The Revolution of 1688–89* (Edinburgh, 1989), p. 19.

83 See P. Joutard, 'The Revocation of the Edict of Nantes: end or renewal of French Protestantism?', in M. Prestwich, ed., *International Calvinism, 1541–1715* (Oxford, 1985), ch. 12.

84 M. Goldie, 'James II and the Dissenters' revenge: the commission of enquiry of 1688', *Historical Research* 66 (1993), 53–88.

85 See M. Goldie, 'John Locke's circle and James II', *Historical Journal* 35 (1992), 557–86.

86 Miller, *Popery and Politics*, p. 197. See also Miller's discussion of James's intentions in *James II: A Study in Kingship* (London, 1978), pp. 125–8.

87 M. Goldie, 'Joshua Basset, popery and revolution', in D. Beales and H. Nisbet, eds, *Sidney Sussex College, Cambridge: Historical Essays* (Woodbridge, 1996), p. 119.

CHAPTER 8

1689 and the Rise of Toleration

At the heart of William of Orange's great expedition to England in 1688 there lay a fundamental ambiguity. On the one hand, William had assured the Catholic powers that he would secure toleration for English recusants. He wrote personally to the Emperor to confirm his tolerant intentions. In his first declaration to the English, issued in October 1688, he had declared that he would secure peaceable dissenters 'from all persecution on account of their religion, even Papists themselves not excepted'. Such pledges made political sense, for William was desperate to avoid hostile intervention from Catholic powers. Yet there is every reason to think that William was sincere. According to Jonathan Israel, he was a man of 'decidedly tepid' faith, and he had little sympathy for the hardline Dutch Calvinists who opposed toleration. In his territory of Lingen, he had allowed the Catholic majority considerable religious freedom. The fact that a similar toleration was not granted to English Catholics says far more about English Protestants than it does about William. In Israel's judgement, 'Possibly no other major statesman of early modern times came to be so closely associated with the cause of religious toleration in his own time and made so considerable a contribution to the achievement of religious and intellectual freedom in the Western world as the Stadholder-King, William III'.[1]

However, William also knew that in order to gain British support he had to present himself as a Protestant champion. Catholics in the royal household, including William's chief cook, were quietly put away; the Dutch army left Catholic soldiers behind and conspicuously employed Huguenot officers; and in his propaganda, William assured the English that he would defend the Protestant faith. This message was far more welcome to English Protestants than talk of tolerating Catholics, and William was hailed as a new Moses, a providential deliverer from popish tyranny. In one of history's ironies, the tepid prince was to become 'King Billy', 'the patron saint of the most bigoted of British Protestants'.[2]

1689 and after

The depth of Protestant prejudice against Catholics meant that William's plan to grant them toleration was doomed from the start. Yet he did his best to ameliorate the condition of Catholics. In December 1688, when Protestant mobs in London had hunted for Catholic priests and wrecked chapels, William brought his army into the city and put an end to the violence. In January 1689, he assured the Spanish and Austrian ambassadors that 'although the humours of this nation are somewhat violent and impulsive', he was working tirelessly 'to ensure that in the future Catholics would be treated with the most complete toleration'.[3] He was probably behind the bill introduced in the Lords in December 1689 which aimed to protect private Catholic worship. Although the bill came to nothing, Gilbert Burnet could plausibly claim that since the Revolution 'the Papists have enjoyed the effects of the Tolleration tho they were not comprehended within the Law that was made for it'.[4]

With Protestant Dissenters, the prospects for an official toleration were much better. In 1688, the ice of Anglican intolerance had melted in the heat generated by the conflict with a Catholic king. Anglican leaders had promised freedom of worship to Dissenters in order to guarantee their support against James, and Archbishop Sancroft had instructed his clergy 'to have a very tender regard to our brethren the Protestant Dissenters'.[5] Ironically, William's task of introducing toleration had been made a good deal easier by his predecessor. In March 1689, two bills were introduced into the Convention Parliament by the Secretary of State, the Earl of Nottingham. The first, a Comprehension Bill, proposed to reincorporate Dissenters within the church by making certain alterations to its terms of communion. The second was an Indulgence Bill, based on the Toleration Bill of 1680, and intended to cover the sects who could not rejoin the established church. Neither bill was particularly appealing to conservative Anglicans, who were shocked when the king urged Parliament on 16 March to allow Dissenters to take up public office. The opposition of High Church Tories eventually led to a compromise deal. In mid-April, William abandoned the Comprehension Bill and the proposed repeal of the sacramental test, and the church party agreed to allow the Indulgence Bill to proceed. The compromise ensured the smooth passage of the Bill through Parliament, and on 24 May it became law.[6]

The new law was entitled 'An Act for exempting their Majesties' Protestant subjects, dissenting from the Church of England, from the penalties of certain laws'. Yet as well as exempting Dissenters from the penalties imposed by the Act of Uniformity and the Clarendon Code, it also granted them the freedom to worship publicly in licensed meeting houses. Dissenting ministers were required to take an oath of allegiance and supremacy to the crown, and to subscribe to the Thirty-Nine Articles of the Church of England, with the exception of the articles on church government and (in the case of Baptists) the article on infant baptism. More surprisingly, Quakers – who were suspected of unorthodoxy and identified with the unpopular policies of James II – were included in the Act and allowed to make a declaration of allegiance instead of taking an oath.[7]

For many Dissenters the Toleration Act was a providential deliverance from Anglican oppression. Others, including William III himself, were disappointed. As Mark Goldie explains, 'The Act was a broken-backed remainder of a larger package of reform which came to grief at the hands of High Churchmen'.[8] The Comprehension Bill was sidelined and killed in Convocation, a bitter blow to Presbyterians and Latitudinarians alike. Moreover, the Test and Corporation Acts remained on the statute book, and Nonconformists were excluded from holding public office unless they took Anglican communion. After the shock of James II's reign, Anglicans now secured the restoration of their dominance over public life and the marginalisation of Dissent. Even the Toleration Act itself was strictly limited. In the first place, the new legislation only covered Trinitarian Protestant Dissenters; it explicitly excluded anti-Trinitarians and Catholics, and offered nothing to Jews or atheists. Indeed, Quakers had to go out of their way to persuade Parliament that they did not deny the doctrine of the Trinity. Secondly, although it became known as the Toleration Act, this was not its official title. The term 'toleration' was not even present in the text. In contrast to James's Declaration of 1687, the preamble merely spoke of giving 'some ease to scrupulous consciences in the exercise of religion', and there was no ringing endorsement of liberty of conscience. The Act of Uniformity and the Clarendon Code were not repealed; Dissenters were simply exempted from their penalties. One Whig MP revealed the profoundly limited character of the Act when he declared during the passage of the bill through the Commons that 'the Committee, though they were for Indulgence, were for *no Toleration*'.[9]

Besides being strictly limited, the Toleration Act did not put a stop to the intolerance and prejudice experienced by religious minorities. 'Religious toleration was a chimera of the salons', claims Mark Kishlansky, 'a liberal daydream in a world which, having endured the mass hysteria of the Popish Plot, could be congratulated only on having avoided the mass violence of the Gordon Riots which were still to come. The beliefs of Catholics, Unitarians, deists and atheists were still proscribed, and nonconforming Protestants were still penalized.'[10]

The force of this continuing intolerance can be seen in the reaction to Deism. The 1690s witnessed an unprecedented proliferation of anti-Trinitarian and even Deistic ideas. The expiry of the Licensing Act in 1695 signalled the effective end of press censorship, and in the following year John Toland caused an uproar by publishing *Christianity not Mysterious* (1696). Unlike Arians and Socinians, Deists like Toland were not simply heterodox Christians; rather they had self-consciously stepped outside the Christian tradition, denying the authority of the Bible and the need for revelation. Even a committed tolerationist like Gilbert Burnet now felt that the rising tide of radical ideas needed to be combated by the state. Toland himself escaped punishment by first fleeing to Ireland and then going under cover in England, but his book was burned by the hangman. In 1697 an Edinburgh medical student, Thomas Aikenhead, was less fortunate. He was accused of mocking Christian doctrines like the Incarnation and the Trinity, and despite recanting, was hanged for blasphemy in the Scottish capital, becoming the last person in the British Isles to be executed for his religious ideas.[11] One year later, the English Parliament passed a new Blasphemy Act, directed against those who denied the Trinity, the authority of Scripture, or the truth of the Christian religion. It declared that first-time offenders would be deprived of civil, military or ecclesiastical employment, and those who offended a second time would lose all civil rights and suffer three years' imprisonment.

Although the heresy executions under Elizabeth and James had been long forgotten, the new crusade against blasphemy sent John Locke and his Dutch Arminian friend Philipp van Limborch scurrying back to the history books. In 1699, they swapped findings about 'heretics' burned under Protestant monarchs in England: Bocher, van Parris, Terwoort, Pieters, Hamont, Lewes, Legate and Wightman. Locke and van Limborch were appalled to discover the 'popish' cruelty of a past generation of fellow Protestants, but they also feared that these distant horrors might yet be revived in their own day by Anglican bishops.[12] Though hindsight tells us that the age of burning heretics was over, in 1699 this was far from clear. It comes as something of a surprise to find Daniel Defoe, an ardent supporter of the Toleration Act, praising the Scots for the execution of Aikenhead – though he does complain that in England people deny God with impunity.[13]

But even mainstream Dissenters like Defoe could not feel entirely secure after 1689. Besides suffering excoriating attacks from Anglican pulpits, Dissenters also had to reckon with verbal abuse, harassment, violence and even arson. In Chester in 1692, an arsonist attempted to burn down the meeting house of the respected Nonconformist minister Matthew Henry.[14] High Church Anglicans were appalled by the brazen expansionism of Dissent, and campaigned for the Toleration Act to be either repealed or interpreted in the most restrictive manner possible. In 1702, Defoe published *The Shortest Way with Dissenters*, a brilliant satirical spoof which won the praise of High Churchmen until they discovered that it was a biting parody of their zeal for persecution; Defoe was punished with a spell in Newgate prison. In 1709, Henry Sacheverall, the High Church divine who had provoked the tract, reignited the debate with a vitriolic sermon against Dissenters and toleration. When he was put on trial in the following year for libelling the Revolution and the crown, mobs shouting 'High Church and Sacheverall' attacked and partially destroyed some of the largest Dissenting chapels in London and elsewhere. In 1711, after several unsuccessful attempts, High Church MPs finally passed an Occasional Conformity Act, aimed at preventing Dissenters from taking up public office by simply attending Anglican communion once a year. The Schism Act of 1714 was intended to close down the flourishing Dissenting academies and schools, by banning Nonconformists from teaching. Although both of these Acts were repealed under the Whigs in 1719, they remind us that during the reign of Queen Anne (1702–14), the newly acquired freedoms of Dissenters were still under serious threat.

Even after 1720, Dissenters were still subjected to discrimination and intolerance. The early Methodists, even though they had not formally separated from the Church of England, were quite frequently attacked by hostile crowds, and in 1791 Dissenters like Joseph Priestley were again assaulted by 'Church and King' mobs. In many respects, Dissenters were still second-class citizens. Indeed, Jonathan Clark has argued that far from being a modern, liberal and pluralistic society, eighteenth-century England was a traditional *ancien régime*, a 'confessional state' dominated by the Church of England and Anglican ideology.[15] Though many historians feel that Clark has exaggerated his case, most would agree that he has provided a salutary reminder of the continuing power of the established church and the marginalisation of Dissent. If 1689 marked the end of the persecutory society, it did not mark the beginning of the secular state. Gilbert Burnet, who had been so dismissive of Augustine's theory of religious coercion in 1687, was also the man who orchestrated a propaganda campaign in the 1690s aimed at convincing the English that they still lived in a godly state.[16] Latitudinarian Anglicans may have abandoned the persecution of heretics and Dissenters, but they still saw Christian religion in its Anglican form as the fundamental basis for society and the state. The Test and Corporation Acts were finally repealed in 1828, but a decade later the young High Anglican fogey William Gladstone was still trying to reverse the tide of history by arguing that those who were not communicant members of the Church of England should be excluded from all public service jobs.[17] Gladstone, of course, soon saw the error of his ways and emerged as a great Liberal statesman, revered by Nonconformists. But discrimination persisted. Dissenters could not graduate with degrees from Oxford and Cambridge until 1870.

If Dissenters still faced discrimination, Catholics were in a worse position. As Linda Colley has shown, eighteenth-century Britons defined themselves as a Protestant people, over against the Catholic nations, particularly France. Dissenters were incorporated into this British Protestant identity, but Catholics were the threatening 'Other', especially during the Jacobite rebellions of 1715 and 1745.[18] Until the Catholic Relief Act of 1778, the draconian penal code remained firmly in place and was even augmented by new laws. Although never fully enforced, the Act against Popery (1700) established fines for Catholics who sent their children abroad for education, deprived Catholics of the right to purchase estates, and determined that if they refused the oaths of loyalty to William their inheritance would pass to the Protestant next of kin. This was another intolerant measure supported by Gilbert Burnet, who was convinced that Catholics were bound to be 'ill subjects for a Protestant king'.[19] Popular anti-popish prejudice was fed by sermons, parades, pope-burnings, puppet shows, ballads, almanacs, prints, cartoons and Protestant societies.[20] The passage of the Catholic Relief Act in 1778 unleashed a wave of protests culminating in the Gordon Riots of 1780, 'an outbreak of violence and destruction in the capital unprecedented between the Great Fire and the Blitz'.[21] For an entire week London seemed to be out of control, as Protestant mobs attacked Catholic chapels, houses and schools. Eventually, the riots were quelled by a force of 10,000 troops, but 285 people – nearly all rioters – lost their lives. Edward Gibbon was reminded of the anti-popish mobs of the early 1640s; the rioters, he said, were 'Puritans such as they might be in the time of Cromwell . . . started out of their graves'.[22] The anti-Catholic bigotry of English Protestants was alive and well, and would continue to thrive in the nineteenth century, despite the Second Catholic Relief Act of 1791, and Catholic Emancipation in 1829.[23]

Anti-semitism too was far from dead in eighteenth-century popular culture. Frank Felsenstein claims that 'in the so-called age of Enlightenment', the English nation 'showed a purblind refusal to let go of its primitive [anti-semitic] superstitions with anything like the genial quiescence that many later scholars would have us suppose'.[24] Even if Felsenstein replaces an overly sanguine picture of English attitudes to the Jews with an excessively negative one, he does draw our attention to the reality of prejudice. The Jewish Naturalisation Act of 1753, introduced to enable wealthy foreign-born

Sephardic Jews to become naturalised Britons without converting to Anglicanism, provoked such an outcry that it was repealed in the same year. Only in the second half of the nineteenth century did English Jews achieve full civil equality. In 1858 they were allowed to be elected to Parliament, and in 1870 it became possible for them to take degrees at Oxford and Cambridge. Self-professed atheists had to wait even longer before they could sit in Parliament. The controversial secularist Charles Bradlaugh was elected as MP for Northampton in 1880, but was not allowed to take up his seat because he refused to take the oath; only in 1886, when he finally swore the oath, was he allowed to enter the Commons.

Yet in facing up to the persistence of intolerance in eighteenth- and nineteenth-century England, we should not blind ourselves to the transformation wrought by 1689. In the judgement of Jonathan Israel, 'the Act was a much more fundamental landmark in English history than it is nowadays fashionable to suppose. Except during the Cromwellian Commonwealth, there had never, since the Reformation, been any statutory limitation on the exclusive control exercised by the Established Church over divine worship in England.'[25] Now, however, Nonconformists were legally free to register and build chapels, rebut Anglicans from the pulpit, proselytise openly for their beliefs, officiate at marriages, or baptise infants. They grasped these new opportunities with both hands. In the two decades after 1689, Nonconformists registered thousands of places of worship. Dissenting academies flourished, and Dissenters who were willing to take Anglican communion sometimes occupied high public office. In both 1697 and 1700 the Lord Mayor of London was a Presbyterian, and in Nottingham the mayoralty was occupied by Presbyterians for 66 years of the eighteenth century.[26]

To get things into perspective we must compare the situation in 1690 to that which prevailed half a century earlier. In 1640, the life of a Protestant who separated from the Church of England was fraught with the danger of detection and imprisonment. Many of those who broke with the established church felt that they had little choice but to emigrate to the Netherlands or America. In England itself, no more than a few thousand people dared to join the small number of illegal Separatist and Baptist conventicles. By 1690, however, fifty or a hundred times as many Protestants had separated from the Church of England. Geoffrey Holmes has estimated that by 1715 there were at least 400,000 Dissenters in England and Wales, comprising around 7 per cent of the total population.[27] They were gathered in almost 2000 congregations, some of them very large,[28] and their heavy concentration in certain areas made them even more important. Denominations that did not exist in the 1630s, like the Presbyterians and Quakers, were now a significant force, and Nonconformists were free to meet openly in licensed meeting houses and chapels. 'For the most part', writes Watts, 'Dissenters were now able to go about their daily business without fear of the informer, the constable, and the magistrate.'[29] In 1640 they had been akin to a small band of outlaws; 50 years on, they had become a substantial body of respectable citizens.

Contemporaries were not blind to this transformation, and were less convinced than some revisionist historians of the continuing hegemony of the established church. As Frank O'Gorman explains, 'the ramparts of the confessional state were breached on a number of occasions during this period, and many contemporaries recognized that they lived in a society which in religious terms was becoming pluralistic'.[30] The bitter frustration of High Churchmen was a powerful indicator of the reality of change. Control of the established church had passed to Latitudinarian bishops who had no wish to return to the intolerance of the Restoration era. Even the purveyors of heretical and anti-Christian ideas enjoyed unprecedented scope. It is true that William Whiston was expelled from his Cambridge professorship for his Arian beliefs, and that Isaac Newton wisely decided to keep his own anti-Trinitarian convictions secret, but High Churchmen had good reason to complain that Latitudinarians were failing to suppress 'our new sect of freethinkers'. From the 1690s onwards, Deists like Charles Blount, John Toland, Matthew Tindal, and Anthony Collins were able to publish a series of openly anti-Christian books.[31]

Catholics also enjoyed considerable freedom after 1689. William III had always intended to secure toleration for English Catholics, and although English Protestants would not countenance an official toleration, the king used his influence to restrain them. There was to be no repeat of the anti-Catholic persecution of the Civil War and the Popish Plot. The days of Catholic martyrdoms were ended. John Bossy has gone so far as to suggest that 'English Catholics during the century after 1688 were not on any reasonable judgement an oppressed minority'.[32] The Toleration Act had effectively abolished the offence of recusancy, and this benefited Catholics almost as much as Dissenters. Ostentatious public worship and open proselytisation of Protestants were unacceptable, but so long as Catholics were discreet they could worship with considerable freedom. The community prospered, both numerically and economically. Although anti-popery still exercised considerable popular appeal, it also aroused increasing elite revulsion. According to Haydon, 'Magistrates grew less and less worried about the Papist minority' after the failure of the last great Jacobite rebellion in 1745, and the government showed that it was prepared 'to intervene directly in order to mitigate the lot of Catholics in England'.[33] The Quebec Act of 1774 formally sanctioned the establishment of Roman Catholicism in the colony, and the Catholic Relief Act of 1778 removed restrictions on Catholics holding, leasing and inheriting land. The Second Catholic Relief Act of 1791 introduced a formal toleration of Catholic schools and worship, whilst the Emancipation of 1829 removed almost all disabilities and admitted Catholics to most public offices.

Although England's Jews still encountered much prejudice, they were not forced to live in ghettos or subjected to mob violence, as was the fate of Jews in some other parts of continental Europe. Their freedom of worship was secure, and when an amendment was proposed to the Blasphemy Bill in 1698 allowing Jews to be prosecuted, it was defeated in the Commons by 140 votes to 78. In the following year, William III went to dine at the Richmond home of 'Mr Medina, a rich Jew'. In 1700, the king knighted Solomon de Medina at Hampton Court. David Katz concludes that 'Anglo-Jewry had arrived', and that 'The slings and arrows of revisionism notwithstanding, the Glorious Revolution remains of enormous importance, at least for the permanent establishment of Jewish residence in England'.[34] Todd Endelman agrees, and suggests that despite the persistence of antisemitic stereotypes, 'the conditions of Jewish life in eighteenth-century Britain [were] more tolerable than elsewhere in Europe at this time'. Wealthy Sephardic Jews continued to mix in high social circles, and the acculturation of Anglo-Jewry moved faster than in other countries. For all the furore over the Jewish Naturalisation Bill, there was little threat of persecution.[35]

To French observers, the contrast between English tolerance and French repression was very striking. Voltaire deplored the gulf between France, where Calvinist preachers were still being sent to the galleys in the mid-eighteenth century, and England, where Catholic priests operated quietly but freely. Voltaire's depiction of English pluralism in his *Letters concerning the English Nation* (1733) was idealised in order to shame his own countrymen, but the pluralistic co-operation he witnessed was nevertheless real. The dramatic change of fortune experienced by England's religious minorities constitutes a fundamental turning point in the nation's history. The English state had come to terms with religious pluralism, and the traditional requirement of uniformity had collapsed.

This political change coincided with a corresponding intellectual shift. For more than 1000 years Christians had accepted that the magistrate had the authority and the duty to punish heresy and schism. A venerable tradition of religious coercion had developed, building on the writings of Augustine and the actions of the early Christian emperors. It had proved immensely powerful and resilient, guiding the thinking and actions of countless Christian rulers in many different times and places. Whilst the success of the Reformation meant that it was no longer feasible to enforce uniformity across the whole of western Christendom, it was still possible to persecute dissent within particular territories, and Protestants were as enthusiastic as Catholics about doing so. Yet during the course of the seventeenth century, the consensus on religious coercion broke down. In 1603, English Protestants had believed that the Christian magistrate had a solemn duty to *punish* heresy and schism. By 1689, many had come to the conclusion that this was simply not so. Indeed, a substantial minority of seventeenth-century Protestants had become convinced that the magistrate had a solemn duty to *tolerate* heresy, schism and other faiths. As far as they were concerned, persecution was fundamentally at odds with the teaching and example of Christ and his apostles.

The tolerationist legacy

Eventually, this tolerationist position was to become the new orthodoxy among Christians. Tolerationists had posed as reformers of European Christianity who were calling the church back to its roots. In its own way, their reformation was to be as successful as that of Martin Luther and John Calvin. The eventual triumph of tolerationism constituted a transformation of the Christian tradition every bit as significant as the fragmentation caused by the Reformation. Today, Christians of all denominations look back on the centuries of persecution with a mixture of revulsion and incomprehension. Persecution is seen as antithetical to Christian faith. This tolerationist version of Christianity took a long time to gain general acceptance, and even in 1700 there was still a good deal of enthusiasm for various measures of religious coercion. Yet in England at least, the seventeenth century proved to be the beginning of a critical watershed, dividing a Christianity that persecuted its enemies from a Christianity that eschewed violence and coercion in religion.

The pamphlets of seventeenth-century English tolerationists stand among the finest early modern defences of religious liberty. Although many of the radical Puritan tolerationist writings were not republished, the 'militant anticlericalism' and 'Christian reformism' of Puritans was taken up and secularised by Whigs.[36] Whigs shared the radical Puritan notion that the primitive innocence of the Christian religion had been contaminated by the innovations of priests, and like many sectarian writers during the English Revolution they identified persecution as one of those innovations. It is significant that both *Areopagitica* and *A Letter concerning Toleration* became canonical liberal texts, for the continuity between Milton the Puritan and Locke the Whig was considerable. Both were placed in the pantheon of 'early modern liberalism' alongside Harrington, Sidney, Vane, Ludlow and Marvell, men who had championed the Good Old Cause of civil and religious liberty.[37] When the Deist John Toland published the core Whig texts in the

1690s, he included the writings of Milton, Ludlow and Sidney, but did his best to remove the husk of Puritan divinity lest it hide the kernel of anticlericalism, republicanism and toleration.[38] The Puritan had been transformed into the Whig, and England's Radical Reformation had prepared the ground for the early Enlightenment.

In England itself, the Lockean view on toleration gathered increasing support during the eighteenth century,[39] but the radical Whig and Dissenting tradition was to reach its apogee in the nineteenth century. The principles enunciated by seventeenth-century tolerationists – religious liberty, the separation of church and state, non-discrimination, 'the doctrine of the level playing field', opposition to monopolies, equality of birthright, and government by consent – were taken up and extended by Victorian Liberals.[40] Popular Gladstonian Liberals, as Eugenio Biagini has demonstrated, looked back with admiration on the Puritan Revolution, and Cromwell, Milton, Sidney and Locke were revered as liberal heroes.[41] Many Dissenters campaigned vigorously for disestablishment and religious equality, raised the old Leveller cry of 'free trade in religion', championed Jewish emancipation, and defended the rights of Irish Catholics and atheists. The arguments they used reflected the anticlericalism and voluntarism of Dissenting ecclesiology, and mirrored the arguments of Puritan tolerationists two centuries before.[42]

Yet the brightest future for the radical Puritan–Whig tradition of toleration lay in North America. Already in the seventeenth century, three of England's leading tolerationists had succeeded in establishing pluralistic colonies in the New World. Their achievements cast doubt on the claim that toleration was simply 'a loser's creed', 'a belief only advocated by outsiders'.[43] These tolerationists passed 'the power test', since they did not renege on toleration when they themselves acquired power.[44] In Rhode Island, Roger Williams founded a haven for persecuted minorities which stood in stark contrast to contemporary England and Massachusetts. In the judgement of Henry Kamen, he was 'the first great defender of natural and religious liberty' in American history.[45] John Locke drafted *The Fundamental Constitutions of Carolina* in 1669, and guaranteed toleration for all peaceable religions. Finally, William Penn drew up the constitution of Pennsylvania, and established a colony that was to become a powerful example of a viable pluralistic society. Before long it became home to a bewildering array of religious groups: besides Catholics, Lutherans, Anglicans and Presbyterians, there were Jews, Baptists, Moravians, Mennonites and Swenckfeldians. In his *Traité sur la Tolérance* (1763), Voltaire bolstered the case for toleration by pointing his readers to Carolina and Pennsylvania.[46]

Seventeenth-century English tolerationists also shaped eighteenth-century American opinion through their writings and ideas. The arguments of the

English tolerationist tradition were mediated to Americans in the hugely popular writings of the radical English Whigs Thomas Gordon and John Trenchard, and seventeenth-century tolerationist texts were edited and exported by radical Whig enthusiasts like the Dissenter Thomas Hollis. The architects of the American Revolution – including Jefferson, Madison and Adams – stood self-consciously in the tradition of Milton, Sidney and Locke, and fully shared their anticlerical tolerationism, whilst extending it further to include Catholics and atheists. When Jefferson set out on his campaign against the Anglican establishment in Virginia in 1776, he prepared by reading Locke's *Letter* and Milton's *Of Reformation* and *The Reason of Church Government*.[47] The Baptists and Quakers who agitated for disestablishment in New England and Virginia could also trace their roots back to seventeenth-century predecessors like Williams and Penn. In Virginia, as in Restoration England, persecuted Dissenters and elite liberal Anglicans once again acted together to attack Anglican repression.[48] Indeed, one could argue that the tolerationist tradition of seventeenth-century England reached its fulfilment in the Virginia Statute for Religious Freedom and the First Amendment to the American Constitution. These measures embodied the most radical of tolerationist ideals far more fully than did the Act of Toleration. The English Act signalled the end of the persecutory society, but the American legislation marked the acceptance of the separation of church and state advocated in the previous century by England's most thoroughgoing tolerationists.

Explaining the rise of toleration

Chronicling the ebb and flow of persecution and toleration is a relatively straightforward task. Explaining why persecution declined is more difficult. Historians have often spoken of 'the rise of toleration', but insofar as this suggests a gradual, inexorable growth of religious freedom, it is somewhat misleading. The story of toleration is a story of reversals as well as rises. In England, persecution and anti-popery were as fierce during the Restoration period as they were in the Jacobean, despite the lull during the 1650s. For all the great intellectual and cultural changes of the seventeenth century, there was nothing inevitable about the emergence of toleration.

It is clear, for example, that the relationship between tolerationist ideas and the Act of Toleration was far from straightforward. Contrary to what some traditional historiography has suggested, the 1689 Act was not passed because a rising tide of tolerationist conviction made it inevitable. Radical tolerationists who condemned all forms of persecution were still a small minority. The MPs who passed the Act were willing to grant relief to Dissenters who had stood against popery, but very few were radical tolerationists.[49]

Instead, the Act of Toleration came about in a muddled fashion as a result of a series of political and religious contingencies stretching back half a century. The outbreak of the English Civil War in 1642 prepared the way for two decades of unprecedented religious freedom during which England became a profoundly pluralistic nation. The rigid Act of Uniformity in 1662 forced Presbyterians and Independents out of the Church of England, greatly increased the number of Dissenters, and made religious uniformity more difficult to realise. Charles II's Declaration of Indulgence in 1672 gave Dissenters vital breathing space, and enabled them to reinforce their separate identity by opening licensed meeting places. The conversion of James, Duke of York, to Catholicism gave him a vested interest in toleration, so that after he became king he introduced Indulgences which provided further relief. Yet James's authoritarian policies also forced Anglicans into a Protestant alliance with Dissenters, making Anglican leaders far more open towards their 'separated brethren'. Meanwhile, the aggression of Louis XIV and the military vulnerability of the Dutch republic persuaded William of Orange to take the huge political gamble of sending his army to England. In late 1688, the fragility of James himself allowed William and Mary to take the crown without fighting a battle on English soil. Because the cause of toleration was now associated with a Protestant champion rather than a Catholic absolutist, its credibility and support were greater than they had ever been.

Yet the key role of political contingencies in our story should not obscure the long-term forces which contributed to the breakdown of religious uniformity. Toleration was not a uniquely English development, and if local and contingent factors determined the precise timing and character of particular toleration settlements, the eventual rise of toleration across the continent was arguably the result of longer-term trends. Of course, had Louis XIV rather than William of Orange been victorious in the conflicts of the 1680s and 1690s, the cause of European toleration may well have suffered a very serious setback. But certain trends within European culture make it difficult to see how a policy of religious uniformity could have been sustained over the long term.

Among the forces encouraging the development of toleration was Renaissance humanism. We saw in chapter 1 that the Erasmus of history was a more traditional figure than the Erasmus of modern European mythology. Yet although most Christian humanists did not break with the Augustinian assumption that religious coercion was legitimate, humanism did encourage greater openness in religion. Erasmus provided the inspiration for both

Catholic and Protestant moderates. He stressed devout and practical piety rather than external institutions, dogmas and rituals; agreement on a few basic fundamentals of the faith (never clearly defined), and freedom to disagree on a multitude of secondary matters; the voluntariness of faith; the value of scholarship and intellectual dialogue; and the fallibility of human judgement. These emphases were to inform the writings of intellectuals like Acontius, Chillingworth, and Locke, who in their turn encouraged the development of more tolerant attitudes between Christians.[50] Besides exercising a moderating influence on Christian theologians, however, the Renaissance recovered more of the pagan past. In doing so, it added to the complexity of European intellectual culture, providing resources for sceptical freethinkers and preparing the way for greater pluralism.[51]

On one reading of early modern history, the Reformation shut all the doors that the Renaissance had opened. In 1515, Europe could look forward to a bright future of church reform and intellectual debate; by 1525, the clouds were gathering, and western Christendom was being divided into militant and polarised camps.[52] On this view, the traditional Whiggish connection between Protestantism and progress is profoundly mistaken. As the great liberal Catholic historian Lord Acton had no difficulty demonstrating, the major Protestant Reformers were often zealous advocates of persecution.[53] This book has simply confirmed Acton's argument, for the case of England demonstrates the full persecutory potential of Protestantism. From John Jewel through to Restoration divines, English theologians did not hesitate to champion uniformity and defend persecution. In no other Protestant state were Catholic priests in so much danger, or Protestant minorities imprisoned and exiled in such large numbers.

Yet the contribution of Protestantism to the demise of persecution should not be dismissed. In 1600, Protestants more than matched Catholics in their intolerance, and the broadest toleration was to be found in Poland and France (though the great majority of heresy executions in the sixteenth century had been carried out by Catholic rulers). Yet by 1700, things looked very different. The cause of toleration had foundered in Poland and France, and it was now Protestant nations and intellectuals who were spearheading the move towards greater toleration. In terms of ideas, Protestantism prepared the way for tolerationism by throwing centuries of Christian tradition into question. The Protestant conviction that the Christian church had fundamentally lost its way after the primitive centuries proved uniquely corrosive to the traditional theory of persecution. The fact that Augustine's defence of religious coercion had been the orthodoxy for a millennium did not impress Protestant primitivists. Instead, they were haunted by the belief that the church had been subverted by Antichrist. John Foxe had reminded

English Protestants that persecution was one of the hallmarks of the Beast of Revelation, and in the course of the seventeenth century many came to believe that the Beast could take Protestant as well as popish forms. Ever since the 1520s, radical Protestants had argued that the church must eschew religious violence if it was to recover primitive purity.

There were, of course, Catholics who condemned religious coercion, but Protestants found it easier to repudiate the traditional position and denounce the church's historical record. Radical Protestants made up a quite disproportionate number of early modern Europe's most emphatic tolerationists, and the principle of toleration was vigorously promoted by a variety of dissident Protestants: pacifist Anabaptists, Protestant humanists and mystics, Socinians, the later Dutch Arminians, English Baptists, radical Puritans, Levellers, Quakers, and heterodox Anglicans. For these movements, toleration was not merely a *politique* response to the stubborn reality of pluralism, it was a principled commitment arising out of their theology. It is no coincidence that the two great toleration debates of the seventeenth century occurred in Protestant countries: in the Netherlands from the 1620s, and in England from the 1640s.

Yet the development of tolerationist beliefs might never have occurred had not tolerationists found rich resources within the Christian tradition for mounting a powerful attack on religious coercion and forging a thoroughgoing doctrine of toleration. The simple fact that the New Testament documents had been written by a persecuted sect proved to be immensely important in early modern Europe. The Gospels, the Epistles and the book of Revelation provided ample ammunition for critics of persecution, and they suggested an alternative to the religious uniformity of European Christendom. A. G. Dickens once wrote that 'it would be anachronistic to envisage a kindly Renaissance humanism fighting against an obscurantist Protestant biblicism. During this part of the story the chief hero is not Erasmus of Rotterdam, but the New Testament itself.'[54] He meant that the call for toleration was a call to return to the New Testament pattern, in which the church had been a non-coercive, voluntary community.

The philosopher Jacques Derrida has made a similar point. He writes that 'the concept of tolerance, *stricto sensu*, belongs first of all to a sort of Christian domesticity . . . It was printed, emitted, transmitted and circulated in the name of the Christian faith.' He illustrates his argument with reference to Voltaire, who despite his religious scepticism called on contemporary Christians to live up to the example of primitive Christianity:

> When Voltaire accuses the Christian religion and the Church, he invokes the lesson of originary Christianity, 'the times of the first Christians', Jesus

and the Apostles, betrayed by 'the Catholic, Apostolic and Roman religion'. The latter is 'in all its ceremonies and in all its dogmas, the opposite of the religion of Jesus'.[55]

Voltaire, of course, was far from unique among eighteenth-century Deists in appealing to the New Testament to justify tolerance: Diderot, Frederick II, and Thomas Jefferson all lectured traditional Christians on 'the religion of Jesus'.[56] They would have agreed with Voltaire's startling advice: 'If you want to be like Jesus Christ, better be a martyr than a hangman.'[57] They remind us that the development of the idea of tolerance in the West was predicated on a re-reading of Christianity's foundational texts.

Besides facilitating this re-reading and reinterpretation of the Christian tradition, Protestantism was inadvertently responsible for the growth of religious pluralism in early modern Europe. Ultimately, this development did more than anything else to undermine the enforcement of religious uniformity. We often assume that Protestantism was inherently fissiparous, that Luther's emphasis on the individual conscience, the priesthood of all believers, and the accessibility of the vernacular Bible was loaded with pluralist potential, and the extraordinary diversity of the Radical Reformation tends to confirm this hypothesis. However, magisterial Protestantism strove mightily to stave off schism and fragmentation, and the capacity of the Lutheran state churches to accommodate and contain all but a tiny minority of the population was impressive. In England too, the national church was remarkably successful at maintaining its monopoly before 1640. But the 'half-reformed' character of the Church of England was a constant provocation to Puritans, and the persecution of the 1630s and the confusion of the 1640s unleashed all the fissile potential of the Protestant message. England experienced its own Radical Reformation, as ordinary Protestants separated from the national church to establish pure sectarian communities.

The stubbornness of these new religious movements eventually proved too much for the defenders of uniformity. But the failure of persecution was not inevitable. Protestantism in Spain had been crushed by a few dozen executions in the 1550s,[58] whilst tens of thousands of French Huguenots had returned to the Catholic church in the wake of the massacres of 1572.[59] That this was not the case in Restoration England was partly due to the fact that prison was the worst punishment on offer. Stark terror at the prospect of hideous death never swept through the Dissenting community. Yet we must acknowledge the courage and sheer cussedness of the persecuted. Vast numbers went to prison during the Restoration, sometimes remaining there for years, with hardly a sign of faltering or weakness. In them, Anglican persecution had met its match. To many late-modern secular liberals these dogmatic, stern, passionate 'fundamentalists' seem a strange lot. Yet it was precisely their dogmatic convictions that carried these people through the storms of persecution. England became a profoundly pluralistic nation largely because its Catholic recusants and Puritan minorities were so unwilling to compromise their strongly held beliefs. Their religious dogmatism may seem uncongenial, but without it there would have been little pluralism to tolerate. By separating from the national church and resisting all pressure to rejoin, they changed the issue from one of ecclesiastical tolerance to one of civil tolerance. And once it became clear that uniformity would not be restored by coercion, civil toleration became a cogent solution.

Alongside humanism and radical Protestantism, we must stress the impact of the early Enlightenment. The second half of the seventeenth century has traditionally been identified as a period of profound intellectual change, and if recent scholarship has emphasised the complexity of that change it has not denied its reality.[60] Writing in the light of the new science, the challenge of scepticism, and the catastrophe of the religious wars, early Enlightenment intellectuals mounted a powerful critique of theological dogmatism. In England, Latitudinarians associated with the Royal Society argued that all truth claims were subject to human fallibility, but that one could avoid the abyss of scepticism by finding refuge in probability.[61] John Locke redefined Evangelicals (the traditional term for Protestants) as tolerant, open-minded searchers after truth.[62] Others were more radical still – the biblical criticism of Hobbes, Isaac La Peyrère, Richard Simon and Spinoza raised serious questions about scriptural infallibility, and prepared the ground for the rise of Deism and atheism. Although most intellectuals were still committed Christians, the new vogue for tentative faith undercut the dogmatic foundations of persecution. Enlightenment intellectuals appreciated Montaigne's aphorism (made in relation to witch-hunts) that 'it is taking one's conjectures rather seriously to roast someone alive for them'. In Geneva, where Nicholas Antoine had been burned for heresy as recently as 1632, Enlightenment attitudes were taking root by the 1670s, and Genevan professors openly condemned Calvin for the execution of Servetus.[63] Religious toleration was to become one of the central goals of the Enlightenment project.

At 'the epicentre of the early Enlightenment' was a group of Protestant intellectuals which gathered in the house of the liberal Quaker Benjamin Furly in Rotterdam in the 1680s. Furly's circle included the Arminians Philipp van Limborch and Jean Le Clerc, the moderate Anglicans John Locke and Gilbert Burnet, the future Deists John Toland and Anthony Collins, the Quaker William Penn, the young Anthony Ashley Cooper who as the third Earl of Shaftesbury was to become an influential philosopher, and the French Huguenot Pierre Bayle. This group evenhandedly condemned 'the Spanish and Genevan persecution' and 'Protestant Inquisition', and it campaigned tirelessly in favour of toleration.[64] Furly's remarkable library of more than 4000 volumes was a treasure trove of radical Protestant texts, and it contained the writings of many of the tolerationists mentioned in this book, including Castellio, Franck, Coornhert, Crell, Episcopius, Helwys, Williams, Lilburne, Collier, Fisher, Taylor, More, Bethel, Milton, Marvell, Penn and Barclay.[65] Furly's circle constituted the latest and most influential wave of radical Protestant tolerationism, for it formed a bridge between that tradition and the European Enlightenment. Although it was an *avant garde* in the 1680s, its ideas would eventually enter the mainstream, contributing to the stability of toleration in both England and the Netherlands. The importance of these two nations to the early Enlightenment and to the cause of toleration was considerable. Indeed, Ernest Gellner once claimed that the French *philosophes* were the first Westernisers (or rather Northernisers) intent on emulating the more tolerant societies of England and the Netherlands.[66]

But the growth of intellectual movements like the Enlightenment did not occur in a vacuum, and historians have often suggested that ideological change was driven by material factors, and by changing circumstances and conditions. Christopher Hill, for example, asserts that more tolerant attitudes began to emerge in the seventeenth century because the European understanding of the world was being transformed as a result of the discovery of the New World, the expansion of world trade and the new science.[67] There is something to be said for this, but the impact of global and scientific exploration was not entirely straightforward. The cliché that travel broadens the mind was as problematic in the seventeenth century as it is today, and Anthony Grafton can write emphatically that 'The discovery of the New World did not inculcate humanity and tolerance'.[68] Another historian suggests that increased awareness of other faiths did not lead to a deeper appreciation of them: instead, Judaism, Islam and other religions were merely discussed 'to show that they offered no serious challenges to Christianity'.[69] Moreover, supporters of the Royal Society often took up traditional positions in contemporary debates: Samuel Parker argued for religious uniformity and Joseph Glanvill defended the idea of witchcraft.

Nevertheless, the new discoveries of the early modern period did make the world a more perplexing place, and the study of comparative religion prompted fundamental questions about the uniqueness of Christianity and the historicity of biblical narratives. Many Protestant theologians in the second half of the seventeenth century downplayed the exclusivity of Christianity by arguing that pagans would be saved if they lived according to the 'light of nature'. Deists followed Lord Herbert of Cherbury in favouring a universal 'natural' religion over the 'revealed' religion of Christianity.[70] Growing awareness of the history and beliefs of non-European peoples undermined the claim that all civilisations were theistic, and encouraged the growth of religious scepticism.[71] The discovery of the New World exposed the fallibility of ancient texts, and dealt a severe blow to literalist interpretations of Genesis.[72] Alongside the new science, it increased the readiness of Europeans to engage in empirical investigation and open intellectual debate, practices which eventually fostered greater pluralism and tolerance. In addition, of course, the discovery of America opened up an escape route for persecuted religious minorities that had simply not existed in the Middle Ages.

The invention of the printing press in the late fifteenth century also made an immense contribution to intellectual and religious change. Without it, the success of the European Reformation would be almost inconceivable, and Renaissance and Enlightenment ideas could not have taken hold as they did. In England, the printing press was a significant factor in the growth of religious pluralism. Separatists, Baptists, Independents and Quakers had at their disposal a propaganda tool unavailable to medieval Albigensians, Waldensians and Lollards. Dissenters were able to print their polemical literature in the Netherlands, or use secret presses in England. During the key decades of the mid-seventeenth century, England became a much more pluralistic nation partly because the printing press and the relaxation of censorship allowed religious radicals to propagate their beliefs. Between 1640 and 1660 more than 20,000 pamphlets were published by English presses, many of them advocating novel or heterodox religious ideas, including toleration. Elizabeth Eisenstein has argued that 'From the days of Castellio to those of Voltaire, the printing industry was the principal natural ally of libertarian, heterodox and ecumenical philosophers. Eager to expand markets and diversify production, the enterprising publisher was the natural enemy of narrow minds.'[73] There is good reason to be cautious about this judgement, and historians of the French Wars of Religion, for example, are likely to deliver a far bleaker verdict on the impact of the printing press. But if printing could be used to spread prejudice, its role in the development of religious pluralism was also highly significant.

The growth of urban centres also facilitated the development of pluralism. There were, of course, many rural Dissenters in England, as Margaret Spufford and her students have reminded us. But the importance of London to sectarian minorities should not be underestimated. In 1550, London had a population of 120,000, but by 1700 it was home to almost half a million people, many of them immigrants from the countryside or overseas. Even in 1583, there were already 5650 foreign residents in the city, including French and Dutch Calvinists whose worship differed from that of the established church. During the course of the seventeenth century, London was to welcome many more immigrants, including Jews and Huguenots.[74]

In a city of this size, it was exceedingly difficult to regulate religious practices effectively, and the parish churches did not have the seating capacity to contain the population. In the parish of St Giles, Cripplegate, for example, the church could contain crowds of 5000 people, but the number of inhabitants totalled 30,000. 'The area was a warren of narrow streets, alleys and courtyards', and its 'teeming anonymity' made it 'a haven for Dissenters'. It was home to ejected ministers like Thomas Goodwin, a large number of Dissenting schoolmasters, several thousand Dissenters, numerous conventicles, and a successful Presbyterian academy. Its 'pluralistic urban culture' was the shape of things to come.[75] With the growth of cities, religious uniformity became even harder to enforce than it was already.

The prospects of toleration may also have been helped by rising prosperity in the later seventeenth century. Jean Delumeau and other historians have made a strong case for seeing early modern European religion as 'predominantly pessimistic': many believers were haunted by intense anxiety and despair, and by the fear of judgement. The credibility of this 'discourse of fear' rested in part on 'a series of vast collective disasters that besieged Europeans from the Black Death to the end of the Wars of Religion'.[76] In this context, the belief that heresy must be purged in order to avert divine judgement from the land seemed entirely plausible. Indeed, one could argue that the severity of the Christian magistrate and the contemporary vision of a wrathful God reflected the miseries and woes of daily life.

But the final decades of the seventeenth century saw an unprecedented economic boom. In the twenty years before 1689, England experienced a 'commercial revolution', as trade flourished, real incomes rose, and standards of living improved markedly. In addition, the threats from plague and harvest failure diminished.[77] It would be foolish to suggest that the new prosperity automatically snuffed out prejudice and persecution, but it probably made a significant impact on religious mentalities. The profound pessimism and anxiety of much sixteenth- and seventeenth-century religion thawed from the late seventeenth century, and the tendency to look for scapegoats to blame for misfortune declined.[78] The new bourgeois religion of men like Locke placed the accent on reasonableness and offered a rosier outlook on this life and the next. Even eighteenth-century Evangelicalism, so often interpreted as a reaction to the new outlook, was influenced by Enlightenment optimism, and John Wesley was 'genuinely and passionately opposed to physical persecution'.[79] Prosperity and toleration were now seen as twins rather than as mortal enemies. The economic vigour of the pluralistic Netherlands was hailed as living proof of this, whilst the decline of Spain was attributed to the malign effects of the Inquisition and the expulsion of religious minorities. In his second Declaration of Indulgence in 1688, James II had suggested that his policy would be welcomed by 'whoever is concerned for the increase of the wealth and power of the nation'. By permitting liberty of conscience, the three kingdoms could steal a march on 'some of our neighbours'.[80]

James's picture of a wealthy, powerful and pluralistic Britain climbing rapidly up the international league tables was to prove prophetic. The expansion of the English economy underpinned England's rise to Great Power status, and this in turn helped to ensure the stability of toleration after 1689. Throughout the period from the 1560s to 1688, English Protestants had been periodically gripped by fear of Catholic risings and invasions, and the Catholic community had experienced persecution as a consequence. By the 1690s, however, England had a powerful army and navy in Protestant hands. Although the Jacobite rebellions of 1715, 1722 and 1745 reactivated the old sense of vulnerability, Protestant England was far more secure and self-confident in the eighteenth century than it had been before. Toleration allowed Dissenters to feel part of the Protestant nation, and the old fear of Puritan subversion faded too. The demise of persecution was intimately bound up with the decline of these fears.

Finally, we must mention the impact of Europe's catastrophic religious wars. It is a truism to suggest that exhaustion set in after the wars of religion, and that Europeans concluded that toleration was the only way out of the impasse. Thus the French Wars of Religion concluded with the Edict of Nantes (1598), and the Thirty Years War with the Treaty of Westphalia (1648). However, the Treaty of Westphalia did not stop the enforcement of uniformity within particular territories; it simply signalled an end to confessional wars between different states. Moreover, defenders of religious uniformity in England and elsewhere argued that the religious wars illustrated the perils of division and the value of unity. Even in France, many Catholics continued to hold on to the ideal of religious unity, and Louis XIV seized the opportunity to enforce it in the 1680s. Indeed, religious wars could intensify hatreds. In Restoration England, the persecution of Dissenters was justified by pointing to their role in the war against the king and the church.

Tolerationists, by contrast, drew the opposite lesson from religious wars, claiming that they demonstrated the tragic futility of persecution. They insisted that the enforcement of uniformity was bound to fail, and would only lead to rivers of blood. By the late seventeenth century, this interpretation of recent European history was looking increasingly plausible, and a more secularised vision of government began to evolve. With foreign policy being run along essentially secular lines and determined by considerations of national interest rather than confessional allegiance, the notion of applying the same approach to the domestic arena gained credence. The divisive potential of religion encouraged thinkers like Locke to look for an anthropological rather than a theological foundation for the political order. The later seventeenth century saw a growth in theories of natural law, natural morality, and natural religion. Instead of grounding government in theological agreement, Locke grounded it on the idea of contract. By providing alternative foundations for political life, the new ideas undermined the notion that religious unity was essential to the viability of a nation-state. Indeed, some historians have dared to speak of 'secularisation' in the seventeenth century, arguing that religion was becoming a matter of 'private faith', and ceasing to be the foundation of society.[81]

And yet we have to end on a note of caution. In identifying such grand processes, we run the risk of modernising a past that still remained profoundly traditional, and making the triumph of religious liberty appear effortless and inexorable. Here was no easy-to-make recipe – take a printing press, add some urbanisation and a pinch of world travel, mix in a few ounces of economic prosperity, and watch the toleration rise. Traditional habits and beliefs died hard, and recent historians have rightly insisted that the progress of toleration across Europe was uneven, fragile, reversible, contingent, and painfully slow. In the early eighteenth century, radical tolerationism was still a minority opinion. It was perfectly possible to inhabit the brave new world of printing, science, urbanisation, religious pluralism, commercial prosperity and global exploration, and still remain wedded to traditional ideals of religious uniformity and coercion. Indeed, the history of the twentieth century and the resurgence of religious nationalism over the last three decades make it hard to believe that modernisation necessarily fosters greater toleration.

We have already seen that the Act of Toleration itself was more the result of short-term political contingencies than of long-term ideological change. And Richard Ashcraft argues that the Lockean theory of natural rights and religious toleration was not so much the by-product of general socio-economic trends, but the fruit of bitter political struggles, of English anti-Catholicism, and of 'a radicalized version of [Protestant] Christianity'. Ashcraft's conclusion is a fitting way to end our study:

If we continually insist upon rooting human rights in such impersonal phenomena as industrialization, urbanization, or secularization, we may come to believe that these rights are as stable or as far beyond the capabilities of organized human action as the social forces with which we have identified them. To see such rights as the products of the cultural prejudices of the community, or a fragile political alliance, or fear of a common enemy, etc., may place these rights within a less attractive framework, but, at the same time, it reinforces our consciousness that such rights are impermanent, that they are products of a political struggle, and that organized human action is necessary to guarantee their preservation.[82]

Notes

1   J. Israel, 'William III and toleration', in O. P. Grell, J. I. Israel and N. Tyacke, eds, *From Persecution to Toleration: The Glorious Revolution in England* (Oxford, 1991), pp. 129–69, quotations at pp. 131, 129.

2   H. Trevor-Roper, 'Religious toleration after 1688', in his *From Counter-Reformation to Glorious Revolution* (London, 1992), p. 270.

3   Israel, 'William III and toleration', p. 150.

4   C. Rose, *England in the 1690s* (Oxford, 1999), pp. 26–7.

5   Quoted in M. Watts, *The Dissenters: From the Reformation to the French Revolution* (Oxford, 1978), p. 259.

6   See J. Spurr, 'The Church of England, comprehension and the Toleration Act of 1689', *English Historical Review* 104 (1989), pp. 927–46.

7   See D. L. Wykes, 'Friends, Parliament and the Toleration Act', *Journal of Ecclesiastical History* (1994), 42–63.

8   M. Goldie, 'John Locke, Jonas Proast and religious toleration, 1688–1692', in J. Walsh, C. Haydon and S. Taylor, eds, *The Church of England, c.1689–c.1833* (Cambridge, 1993).

9   G. Holmes, *The Making of a Great Power: Late Stuart and Early Georgian England, 1660–1722* (London, 1993), p. 352.

10 M. Kishlansky, *A Monarchy Transformed: Britain, 1603–1714* (London, 1996), p. 341.

11 See M. Hunter, ' "Aikenhead the atheist": the context and consequences of articulate irreligion in the late seventeenth century', in his *Science and the Shape of Orthodoxy: Intellectual Change in Late-Seventeenth-Century Britain* (Woodbridge, 1995), ch. 15.

12 *The Correspondence of John Locke*, ed. E. S. De Beer, 8 vols (Oxford, 1978–), VI, pp. 641, 689, 695–701, 726–31, 763.

13 See *Defoe's Review*, ed. A. W. Secord, 22 vols (New York, 1938), XII, p. 265.

14 D. Wykes, ' "So bitterly censur'd and revil'd": religious dissent after the Toleration Act (1689)', unpublished paper.

15 J. Clark, *English Society, 1688–1832* (Cambridge, 1985).

16 See A. Claydon, *William III and the Godly Revolution* (Cambridge, 1996).

17 See R. Jenkins, *Gladstone* (London, 1995), p. 54.

18 L. Colley, *Britons: The Forging of a Nation, 1707–1837* (London, 1992), ch. 1.

19   See R. K. Webb, 'From toleration to religious liberty', in J. R. Jones, ed., *Liberty Secured? Britain before and after 1688* (Stanford, CA, 1992), pp. 160–1.

20   See C. Haydon, *Anti-Catholicism in Eighteenth-Century England, c.1714–80* (Manchester, 1993).

21   J. Stevenson, *Popular Disturbances in England, 1700–1832* (London, 1992), p. 106.

22   Haydon, *Anti-Catholicism*, p. 240.

23   See J. Wolffe, *The Protestant Crusade in Great Britain, 1829–60* (Oxford, 1991).

24   F. Felsenstein, *Anti-Semitic Stereotypes: A Paradigm of Otherness in English Popular Culture, 1660–1830* (Baltimore, MD, 1995), pp. 1–2.

25   Israel, 'William III and toleration', p. 153.

26   Watts, *The Dissenters*, pp. 482–3.

27   Holmes, *The Making of a Great Power*, pp. 353, 459–61.

28   Watts, *The Dissenters*, p. 269.

29   Ibid., p. 264.

30   F. O'Gorman, *The Long Eighteenth Century* (London, 1997), p. 169.

31   Goldie, 'John Locke, Jonas Proast and religious toleration', pp. 143–71, quotation from p. 167. See also J. Champion, *The Pillars of Priestcraft Shaken: The Church of England and its Enemies, 1660–1730* (Cambridge, 1992).

32   J. Bossy, 'English Catholics after 1688', in Grell, Israel and Tyacke, eds, *From Persecution to Toleration*, p. 370.

33   Haydon, *Anti-Catholicism*, pp. 165, 173.

34   D. Katz, *The Jews in the History of England, 1485–1850* (Oxford, 1994), p. 188.

35   T. Endelman, *The Jews of Georgian England, 1714–1830: Tradition and Change in a Liberal Society* (Ann Arbor, MI, 1999), xx–xxi.

36   M. Goldie, 'Priestcraft and the birth of Whiggism', in N. Phillipson and Q. Skinner, eds, *Political Discourse in Early Modern Britain* (Cambridge, 1993), pp. 209–31, quotations from p. 211.

37   See A. Patterson, *Early Modern Liberalism* (Cambridge, 1997).

38   See Edmund Ludlow, *A Voyce from the Watch Tower*, ed. A. B. Worden (London, 1978). See also N. von Maltzahn, 'The Whig Milton, 1667–1700', in D. Armitage, A. Himy, and Q. Skinner, eds, *Milton and Republicanism* (Cambridge, 1995), ch. 12.

39   See A. Sell, *John Locke and the Eighteenth-Century Divines* (Cardiff, 1997), ch. 5.

40   See C. Russell, *An Intelligent Person's Guide to Liberalism* (London, 1999), pp. 24–6, 37–8, 47–53, 83–6.

41   E. Biagini, *Liberty, Retrenchment and Reform: Popular Liberalism in the Age of Gladstone* (Cambridge, 1992), ch. 1.

42   T. Larsen, *Friends of Religious Equality: Nonconformist Politics in Mid-Victorian England* (Woodbridge, 1999), ch. 4; Biagini, *Liberty, Retrenchment and Reform*, ch. 4.

43   O. P. Grell, 'Introduction', in Grell and R. Scribner, eds, *Tolerance and Intolerance in the European Reformation* (Cambridge, 1995), p. 4.

44   J. Lecler, *Toleration and the Reformation*, 2 vols (London, 1960), II, p. 483.

45   H. Kamen, *The Rise of Toleration* (London, 1967), p. 187.

46   Voltaire, *The Calas Affair: A Treatise on Tolerance*, trans. B. Masters (London, 1994), pp. 28–9.

47   See Patterson, *Early Modern Liberalism, passim* and p. 239; R. Greaves, 'Radicals, rights, and revolution: British Nonconformity and the roots of the American experience', *Church History* 61 (1992), 151–68; and *The English Libertarian Heritage: From the Writings of John Trenchard and Thomas Gordon in 'The Independent Whig' and 'Cato's Letters'*, ed. D. L. Jackson (San Francisco, 1994), esp. pp. 2–30.

48   See R. Isaac, *The Transformation of Virginia, 1740–90* (Chapel Hill, NC, 1982), chs. 11–12; and *idem*, '"The rage of malice of the old serpent devil": the Dissenters and the making and remaking of the Virginia Statute for Religious Freedom', in M. Peterson and R. C. Vaughan, eds, *The Virginia Statute for Religious Freedom* (Cambridge, 1988), pp. 139–69.

49   See G. Schochet, 'The Act of Toleration and the failure of comprehension', in D. Hoak and M. Feingold, eds, *The World of William and Mary: Anglo-Dutch Perspectives on the Revolution of 1688–89* (Stanford, CA, 1996), pp. 165–87.

50   On the influence of humanism see G. Remer, *Humanism and the Rhetoric of Toleration* (University Park, PA, 1996).

51   See A. C. Kors, *Atheism in France, 1650–1729*, vol. I: *The Orthodox Sources of Disbelief* (Princeton, NJ, 1990), ch. 6: 'The Ancients'.

52   See, for example, H. Trevor-Roper's remarkable essay, 'The religious origins of the Enlightenment', in his *Religion, the Reformation and Social Change* (London, 1967), ch. 4.

53   Lord Acton, 'The Protestant theory of persecution', in *The History of Freedom and Other Essays* (London, 1907), pp. 150–87.

54   A. G. Dickens, *The English Reformation*, 2nd edn (London, 1989), p. 379.

55   J. Derrida, 'Faith and knowledge', in Derrida and G. Vattimo, eds, *Religion* (Cambridge, 1998), p. 22.

56   For Diderot, see G. Adams, *The Huguenots and French Opinion, 1685–1787: The Enlightenment Debate on Toleration* (Waterloo, ONT, 1991), pp. 105–6; for Frederick II, see A. Lentin, ed., *Enlightened Absolutism (1760–1790): A Documentary*

History (Newcastle, 1985), p. 134; for Jefferson, see the preamble to *The Statute of Virginia for Religious Freedom* and N. Cousins, ed., *'In God We Trust': The Religious Beliefs and Ideas of the American Founding Fathers* (New York, 1958), chs. 5 and 6.

57 Voltaire, *The Calas Affair: A Treatise on Tolerance*, p. 98.

58 See H. Kamen, *The Spanish Inquisition: A Historical Revision* (London, 1997), ch. 5.

59 See M. Holt, *The French Wars of Religion* (Cambridge, 1995), pp. 94–5.

60 The classic study is P. Hazard, *The European Mind, 1680–1715* (Harmondsworth, 1973). One of the finest recent studies is Hunter, *Science and the Shape of Orthodoxy*.

61 See B. Shapiro, *Probability and Certainty in Seventeenth-Century England* (Princeton, NJ, 1983).

62 *The Correspondence of John Locke*, VI, p. 495.

63 Lecler, *Toleration and the Reformation*, II, p. 490; S. Taylor, 'The Enlightenment in Switzerland', in R. Porter and M. Teich, eds, *The Enlightenment in National Context* (Cambridge, 1981), ch. 5.

64 John Marshall, *John Locke: Resistance, Religion and Responsibility* (Cambridge, 1994), p. 331. Marshall's forthcoming book on John Locke and the early Enlightenment will enhance our understanding of the role played by this group in promoting toleration.

65 *Bibliotheca Furliana, sive catalogus librorum* (Rotterdam, 1714).

66 E. Gellner, *The Conditions of Liberty* (London, 1994), pp. 32–3.

67 C. Hill, 'Toleration in 17th-century England: theory and practice', in his *England's Turning Point: Essays on 17th Century English History* (London, 1998), pp. 259–74.

68 A. Grafton, *New Worlds, Ancient Texts: The Power of Tradition and the Shock of Discovery* (Cambridge, MA, 1992), p. 252.

69 D. Pailin, *Attitudes to Other Religions: Comparative Religion in Seventeenth- and Eighteenth-Century Britain* (Manchester, 1984), p. 6.

70 See P. Harrison, *'Religion' and the Religions in the English Enlightenment* (Cambridge, 1990).

71 See Kors, *Atheism in France, 1650–1729*, ch. 5: 'Other peoples'; Yeun-Ting Lai, 'China and Western Philosophy in the Age of Reason', in R. Popkin, ed., *The Pimlico History of Western Philosophy* (London, 1999), pp. 412–21.

72 See Grafton, *New Worlds, Ancient Texts*, esp. pp. 237–42.

73 E. Eisenstein, *The Printing Revolution in Early Modern Europe* (Cambridge, 1983), p. 177.

74 J. Sharpe, *Early Modern England: A Social History, 1550–1760* (London, 1987), p. 85.

75 M. Goldie and J. Spurr, 'Politics and the Restoration parish: Edward Fowler and the struggle for St Giles Cripplegate', *English Historical Review* 109 (1994), 572–96.

76 See J. Delumeau, *Sin and Fear: The Emergence of a Western Guilt Culture, 13th–18th Centuries*, trans. E. Nicholson (New York, 1990); J. Stachniewski, *The Persecutory Imagination: English Puritanism and the Literature of Religious Despair* (Oxford, 1991); P. Camporesi, *The Fear of Hell: Images of Damnation and Salvation in Early Modern Europe* (Cambridge, 1991); S. Clark, *Thinking with Demons: The Idea of Witchcraft in Early Modern Europe* (Oxford, 1997).

77 Holmes, *The Making of a Great Power*, ch. 3.

78 B. Levack, *The Witch-Hunt in Early Modern Europe*, 2nd edn (London, 1995), pp. 248–50. See also D. P. Walker, *The Decline of Hell: Seventeenth-century Discussions of Eternal Torment* (London, 1964).

79 See D. Bebbington, *Evangelicalism in Modern Britain: A History from the 1730s to the 1980s* (London, 1989), pp. 50–74. Quotation from H. Rack, *Reasonable Enthusiast: John Wesley and the Rise of Methodism* (London, 1989), p. 313.

80 A. Browning, ed., *English Historical Documents*, VIII: *1660–1714* (London, 1966), p. 399.

81 See C. J. Sommerville, *The Secularization of Early Modern England: From Religious Culture to Religious Faith* (Oxford, 1992).

82 R. Ashcraft, 'Religion and Lockean natural rights', in I. Bloom, J. P. Martin and W. L. Proudfoot, eds, *Religious Diversity and Human Rights* (New York, 1996), pp. 195–209, quotations at pp. 205, 208.

GLOSSARY

Anabaptists Radical Protestants who rejected infant baptism as unbiblical and practised the baptism of adult believers. Mainly found on the continent, though two Dutch Anabaptists were burned for heresy in London in 1575. 'Anabaptist' was also a term of abuse applied to the English Baptists.

Anglicans Members of the Church of England who resented the Puritan takeover of the church in the 1640s, and welcomed the restoration of bishops and the Book of Common Prayer after 1660.

Anti-Trinitarians Those who denied the doctrine of the Trinity. *See also* Arians, Socinians and Deists.

Arians Anti-Trinitarians who denied the divinity of Jesus, maintaining that he had been created by the Father. Several were burned for heresy under Elizabeth and James. Arianism was later embraced by John Milton and Isaac Newton.

Arminians Named after the Dutch Reformed theologian Jacob Arminius (*c*.1559–1609), they denied the Calvinist teaching that God had predestined some people to salvation and rejected or overlooked others. Arminians maintained that God's grace was available to all, and that an individual's eternal destiny was determined by their free decision to resist or receive grace. In England, the Laudians were called Arminians, though unlike the later Dutch Arminians they did not support toleration. Arminianism attracted increasing numbers of Anglicans and even Puritans in the second half of the seventeenth century.

Baptists Radical Puritans who rejected infant baptism and practised the baptism of adult believers. The General Baptists date from the 1610s, whilst the Particular Baptists began in the 1630s. General Baptists embraced Arminianism whilst Particular Baptists accepted Calvinism.

Brownists The Separatist followers of Robert Browne. *See* Separatists.

Congregationalists   *See* Independents.

Church Papists   Catholics who attended the services of the established Protestant church, whilst also maintaining links with the Catholic community.

Deists   Rationalists who rejected the authority of the Bible and traditional Christian doctrines, but continued to believe in a Deity and advocated a simple 'natural religion' shorn of the allegedly irrational mysteries of traditional Christianity. Few in number before the 1690s, but influential thereafter.

Dissenters   Protestants who were not in full communion with the Church of England. Dissenters could be Presbyterians, Independents/ Congregationalists, Separatists, Baptists, or Quakers.

Familists   Members of a spiritualist sect which followed the teachings of the Dutch mystic Hendrick Niclaes (1502–*c*.1580).

Independents   Puritans who believed that individual churches should be self-governing rather than subject to higher courts and assemblies. During the Puritan Revolution, they were heavily involved in the national church, but eventually became a separate denomination, the Congregationalists.

Latitudinarians   Anglicans who were willing to loosen the Church of England's requirements in order to allow Dissenters, especially Presbyterians, into the Church of England by a policy of 'comprehension'. After 1689, Latitudinarians were firm supporters of toleration for Dissenting denominations.

Laudians   High Churchmen who came to prominence in the 1620s and 1630s, and favoured the enforcement of rigid conformity to the liturgy and the introduction of 'the beauty of holiness' into the English church. Also known as Arminians, since they often favoured Arminian theology over Calvinism.

Presbyterians   Puritans who campaigned against the rule of bishops, and advocated a church governed by committees of lay elders and ministers. Active between the 1560s and the 1590s before being suppressed by Whitgift; re-emerged in the 1640s as a powerful movement; ejected from the established church at the Restoration but still hoped for reintegration into the Church of England; became a separate denomination after 1689.

Puritans   Zealous Protestants who immersed themselves in Bible reading, sermon attendance, religious meetings, prayer and fasting, and who agitated for 'further reformation' in England. The Puritan subculture gradually became very diverse and included moderate supporters of episcopacy, Presbyterians, Independents, Separatists, Baptists and Seekers.

Quakers   A charismatic offshoot of the Puritan movement, the Quakers grew rapidly in the 1650s, and numbered up to 50,000 by the Restoration. They stressed the inner light of the Spirit rather than biblical doctrine, and were notorious for their provocative prophesying.

Ranters   A motley crew of extreme Antinomians in the late 1640s and early 1650s, who were accused of scandalous behaviour and were said to claim that they had been spiritually liberated from the moral law.

Recusants   Those who refused to attend the services of the established Protestant church. The term was normally applied to Catholics, but sometimes included Protestant Separatists.

Seekers   Radical Puritans who became sceptical about the legitimacy of all existing forms of church government. Instead of organising formal congregations, they met informally. Many became Quakers in the 1650s.

Separatists   Radical Puritans who became so disillusioned with the Church of England that they separated from it to form their own congregations. Persecuted under Elizabeth and James, but flourished during the Puritan Revolution.

Socinians   Named after the sixteenth-century anti-Trinitarians Lelio and Faustus Socinus. More radical than Arians, but unlike Deists they continued to see themselves as biblical Christians. In the second half of the seventeenth century, a growing number of Anglicans and Dissenters gravitated towards Socinianism.

SELECT BIBLIOGRAPHY

In the notes to this book, full details of primary and secondary sources are given the first time they are cited in each chapter. This bibliography, therefore, is not comprehensive. It is intended as a guide for those who wish to do further reading on the subject.

Primary sources

The major pieces of religious legislation can be found in the following books: G. R. Elton, ed., *The Tudor Constitution*, 2nd edn (Cambridge, 1982); J. P. Kenyon, ed., *The Stuart Constitution, 1603–1688*, 2nd edn (Cambridge, 1986); J. R. Tanner, ed., *Constitutional Documents of the Reign of James I* (Cambridge, 1930); S. R. Gardiner, ed., *The Constitutional Documents of the Puritan Revolution, 1625–1660* (Oxford, 1889); A. Browning, ed., *English Historical Documents*, vol. VIII: *1660–1714* (London, 1966); and J. F. Maclear, ed., *Church and State in the Modern Age: A Documentary History* (New York, 1995). For royal proclamations see: J. F. Larkin and P. L. Hughes, eds, *Tudor Royal Proclamations*, vol. II: *The Later Tudors, 1558–1587* (New Haven, CN, 1969); J. F. Larkin and P. L. Hughes, eds, *Stuart Royal Proclamations*, vol. I: *Royal Proclamations of King James I* (Oxford, 1973); J. F. Larkin and P. L. Hughes, eds, *Stuart Royal Proclamations*, vol. II: *Royal Proclamations of King Charles I* (Oxford, 1983).

Original accounts of the experience of persecution are found in: Joseph Besse, *A Collection of the Sufferings of the People called Quakers*, 2 vols (London, 1753); *John Gerard: The Autobiography of an Elizabethan*, trans. P. Caraman (London, 1951); P. Caraman, ed., *The Other Face: Catholic Life under Elizabeth I* (London, 1960); P. Caraman, ed., *The Years of Siege: Catholic Life from James I to Cromwell* (London, 1966); Richard Challoner, *Memoirs of Missionary Priests*, ed. J. H. Pollen (London, 1924); George Fox, *The Journal*, ed. N. Smith (London, 1998); A. G. Matthew, ed., *Calamy Revised: Being a Revision of Edmund Calamy's 'Account' of the Ministers and Others Ejected and Silenced, 1660–1662* (Oxford, 1934); A. G. Matthew, ed., *Walker Revised: Being a Revision of John Walker's 'Sufferings of the Clergy during the Grand Rebellion, 1642–1660* (Oxford, 1947).

Readers who want to explore the toleration debate further can begin with modern editions of the writings of the leading tolerationists: John Locke, *Political Writings*, ed. D. Wootton (London, 1993); *Complete Prose Works of John Milton*, gen.

ed. D. Wolffe, 8 vols (New Haven, CN, 1953–82); William Penn, *The Peace of Europe, the Fruits of Solitude, and Other Writings*, ed. E. B. Bronner (London, 1993); *The Writings of William Walwyn*, ed. J. R. McMichael and B. Taft (Athens, GA, 1989); *The Complete Writings of Roger Williams*, 7 vols (New York, 1963). Some of the major seventeenth-century tolerationist tracts are also republished in anthologies: W. Haller, ed., *Tracts on Liberty in the Puritan Revolution, 1638–47*, 3 vols (New York, 1933–4); D. G. Mullan, ed., *Religious Pluralism in the West: An Anthology* (Oxford, 1998); A. S. P. Woodhouse, ed., *Puritanism and Liberty* (London, 1938).

Secondary sources

This section contains a selective list of secondary works on the subject. Essays contained in listed books are not mentioned separately. Relevant articles can be found in the following denominational history journals: *Recusant History, Transactions of the Congregational Historical Society, Journal of the Presbyterian Historical Society of England* (united since 1973 in *Journal of the United Reformed History Society*), *Journal of the Friends Historical Society, Transactions of the Baptist Historical Society* (from 1922 *The Baptist Quarterly*).

ASHCRAFT, R., 'Latitudinarianism and toleration: historical myth versus political history', in R. Kroll, R. Ashcraft and P. Zagorin, eds, *Philosophy, Science and Religion in England, 1640–1700* (Cambridge, 1992).

ASHCRAFT, R., 'Religion and Lockean natural rights', in I. Bloom, J. P. Martin and W. L. Proudfoot, eds, *Religious Diversity and Human Rights* (New York, 1996).

AVELING, J. C. H., *Northern Catholics: The Catholic Recusants of the North Riding of Yorkshire, 1558–1790* (1966).

AVELING, J. C. H., *The Handle and the Axe* (London, 1976).

BOSSY, J., *The English Catholic Community, 1570–1850* (London, 1975).

BRAITHWAITE, W. C., *The Beginnings of Quakerism*, 2nd edn (Cambridge, 1955).

BRAITHWAITE, W. C., *The Second Period of Quakerism*, 2nd edn (Cambridge, 1961).

CLANCY, T., *Papist Pamphleteers* (Chicago, 1964).

CLIFTON, R., 'The popular fear of Catholics during the English Revolution', *Past and Present* 52 (1971).

CLIFTON, R., 'Fear of popery', in C. Russell, ed., *The Origins of the English Civil War* (London, 1973).

COFFEY, J., 'Puritanism and liberty revisited: the case for toleration in the English Revolution', *Historical Journal* 41 (1998).

COLLINSON, P., *The Elizabethan Puritan Movement* (Cambridge, 1967).

COLLINSON, P., 'Ecclesiastical vitriol: religious satire in the 1590s and the invention of puritanism', in J. Guy, ed., *The Reign of Elizabeth I* (Cambridge, 1995).

COTTRET, B., *The Huguenots in England: Immigration and Settlement, c.1500–1700* (Cambridge, 1991).

CRAGG, G., *Puritanism in the Period of the Great Persecution, 1660–1688* (Cambridge, 1957).

CRESSY, D., *Bonfires and Bells: National Memory and the Protestant Calendar in Elizabethan and Stuart England* (London, 1989).

CUST, R. and HUGHES, A., eds, *Conflict in Early Stuart England: Studies in Religion and Politics, 1603–42* (London, 1989).

DAVIS, J. C., 'Religion and the struggle for freedom in the English Revolution', *Historical Journal* 35 (1992).

DURES, A., *English Catholicism, 1558–1642* (Harlow, 1983).

GOLDIE, M., 'John Locke, Jonas Proast and religious toleration, 1688–1692', in J. Walsh, C. Haydon and S. Taylor, eds, *The Church of England, c.1689–c.1833* (Cambridge, 1993).

GOLDIE, M., 'James II and the Dissenters' revenge', *Historical Research* 66 (1993).

GOLDIE, M. and SPURR, J., 'Politics and the Restoration parish: Edward Fowler and the struggle for St Giles Cripplegate', *English Historical Review* 109 (1994).

GOLDIE, M., 'The search for religious liberty, 1640–1690', in J. Morrill, ed., *The Oxford Illustrated History of Tudor and Stuart Britain* (Oxford, 1996).

GREAVES, R., *Deliver us from Evil: The Radical Underground in Britain, 1660–1663* (New York, 1986).

GREAVES, R., *Enemies under his Feet: Radicals and Nonconformists in Britain, 1664–1677* (Stanford, CA, 1990).

GREAVES, R., *Secrets of the Kingdom: British Radicals from the Popish Plot to the Revolution of 1688–1689* (Stanford, CA, 1992).

GRELL, O. P., ISRAEL, J., and TYACKE, N., eds, *From Persecution to Toleration* (Oxford, 1989).

GRELL, O. P. and SCRIBNER, R., eds, *Tolerance and Intolerance in the European Reformation* (Cambridge, 1995).

GREEN, I. M., *The Re-establishment of the Church of England, 1660–1663* (Oxford, 1978).

GREEN, I. M., 'The persecution of "scandalous" and "malignant" parish clergy during the English Civil War', *English Historical Review* 194 (1979).

GUGGISBERG, H., 'The defence of religious toleration and religious liberty in early modern Europe', *History of European Ideas* 4 (1983).

HAIGH, C., 'From monopoly to minority: Catholicism in early modern England', *Transactions of the Royal Historical Society* 31 (1981).

HAIGH, C., *English Reformations: Religion, Politics and Society under the Tudors* (Oxford, 1993).

HARRIS, T., 'Was the Tory reaction popular? Attitudes of Londoners towards the persecution of dissent, 1681–1686', *London Journal* 13 (1987–8).

HARRIS, T., SEAWARD, P., and GOLDIE, M., eds, *The Politics of Religion in Restoration England* (Oxford, 1990).

HAVRAN, M. J., *The Catholics in Caroline England* (Oxford, 1962).

HIBBARD, C., *Charles I and the Popish Plot* (Chapel Hill, NC, 1983).

HOLMES, P. J., *Resistance and Compromise: The Political Thought of Elizabethan Catholics* (Cambridge, 1982).

HORLE, C., *Quakers and the English Legal System, 1660–1688* (Philadelphia, 1988).

HUNTER, M., and WOOTTON, D., eds, *Atheism from the Reformation to the Enlightenment* (Oxford, 1992).

HURSTFIELD, J., 'Church and state, 1558–1612: the task of the Cecils', in G. J. Cuming, ed., *Studies in Church History*, 2 (1965).

ISRAEL, J., 'Toleration in seventeenth-century Dutch and English thought', in S. Groenveld and M. Wintle, eds, *The Exchange of Ideas: Religion, Scholarship and Art in Anglo-Dutch Relations in the Seventeenth Century* (Zutphen, 1994).

JONES, J. R., *Liberty Secured? Britain before and after 1688* (Stanford, CA, 1992).

JORDAN, W. K., *The Development of Religious Toleration in England*, 4 vols (London, 1932–40).

KAMEN, H., *The Rise of Toleration* (London, 1967).

KATZ, D., *Philo-Semitism and the Readmission of the Jews to England, 1603–1655* (Oxford, 1982).

KATZ, D., *The Jews in the History of England, 1485–1850* (Oxford, 1994).

KEEBLE, N. H., *The Literary Culture of Nonconformity in Later Seventeenth-Century England* (Leicester, 1987).

KENYON, J., *The Popish Plot* (London, 1972).

LAURSEN, J. C. and NEDERMAN, C. J., eds, *Beyond the Persecuting Society: Religious Toleration before the Enlightenment* (1997).

LECLER, J., *Toleration and the Reformation*, 2 vols (London, 1960).

LEVY, L., *Blasphemy: Verbal Offense against the Sacred, from Moses to Salman Rushdie* (Chapel Hill, NC, 1993).

LINDLEY, K., 'The lay Catholics of England in the reign of Charles I', *Journal of Ecclesiastical History* 22 (1971).

LYON, T., *The Theory of Religious Liberty in England, 1603–1639* (Cambridge, 1937).

McGRATH, P., *Papists and Puritans under Elizabeth I* (London, 1967).

MARCHANT, R., *The Puritans and the Church Courts in the Diocese of York, 1560–1642* (London, 1960).

MARSH, C., *The Family of Love in English Society, 1550–1630* (Cambridge, 1994).

MARSHALL, J., *John Locke: Resistance, Religion and Responsibility* (Cambridge, 1994).

MATAR, N., *Islam in Britain, 1558–1685* (Cambridge, 1998).

MILLER, J., *Popery and Politics in England, 1660–1688* (Cambridge, 1973).

MILLER, J., 'James II and toleration', in E. Cruickshanks, ed., *By Force or Default? The Revolution of 1688–89* (Edinburgh, 1989).

MILTON, P., 'Hobbes, heresy and Lord Arlington', *History of Political Thought* 14 (1993).

MOREY, A., *The Catholic Subjects of Elizabeth I* (London, 1978).

MORGAN, N., *Lancashire Quakers and the Establishment, 1660–1730* (Halifax, 1993).

MORRILL, J., *The Nature of the English Revolution* (London, 1993).

MULLETT, M., *Catholics in Britain and Ireland, 1558–1829* (London, 1998).

NICHOLLS, M., *Investigating Gunpowder Plot* (Manchester, 1991).

NUTTALL, G. and CHADWICK, O., eds, *From Uniformity to Unity, 1662–1962* (London, 1962).

NUTTALL, G., 'The English martyrs, 1535–1680: a statistical review', *Journal of Ecclesiastical History* 22 (1971).

PATTERSON, A., *Early Modern Liberalism* (Cambridge, 1997).

POLIZZOTTO, C., 'Liberty of conscience and the Whitehall debates of 1648–49', *Journal of Ecclesiastical History* 26 (1975).

POLIZZOTTO, C., 'The campaign against "The Humble Proposals" of 1652', *Journal of Ecclesiastical History* 38 (1987).

QUESTIER, M., *Conversion, Politics and Religion in England, 1580–1625* (Cambridge, 1996).

QUESTIER, M., 'Loyalty, religion and state power in early modern England: English Romanism and the Jacobean Oath of Allegiance', *Historical Journal* 40 (1997).

QUESTIER, M., 'Practical antipapistry during the reign of Elizabeth I', *Journal of British Studies* 36 (1997).

REAY, B., *The Quakers and the English Revolution* (1985).

RICHARDSON, R. C. and RIDDEN, G. M., eds, *Freedom and the English Revolution* (Manchester, 1986).

ROSE, E., *Cases of Conscience: Alternatives open to Recusants and Puritans under Elizabeth I and James I* (Cambridge, 1975).

RUSSELL, C., 'Arguments for religious unity in England, 1530–1650', *Journal of Ecclesiastical History* 18 (1967).

SCHOCHET, G., 'The Act of Toleration and the failure of comprehension', in D. Hoak and M. Feingold, eds, *The World of William and Mary* (Stanford, CA, 1996).

SEATON, A. A., *The Theory of Toleration under the Later Stuarts* (Cambridge, 1911).

SHEILS, W. J., ed., *Persecution and Toleration* (London, 1984).

SPUFFORD, M., ed., *The World of Rural Dissenters* (Cambridge, 1995).

SPURR, J., 'The Church of England, comprehension, and the 1689 Toleration Act', *English Historical Review* 104 (1989).

TUCK, R., 'Scepticism and toleration in the seventeenth century', in S. Mendus, ed., *Justifying Toleration* (Cambridge, 1988).

WALSHAM, A., *Church Papists: Catholicism, Conformity and Confessional Polemic in Early Modern England* (Woodbridge, 1993).

WALSHAM, A., '"The fatall vesper": providentialism and anti-popery in late Jacobean London', *Past and Present* 144 (1994).

WATTS, M., *The Dissenters: From the Reformation to the French Revolution* (Oxford, 1978).

WHITING, C. E., *Studies in English Puritanism, 1660–1688* (1931).

WORMALD, J., 'Gunpowder, treason and Scots', *Journal of British Studies* 24 (1985).

WYKES, D. L., 'Religious dissent and the penal laws: an explanation of business success?', *History* 75 (1990).

WYKES, D. L., 'Friends, Parliament and the Toleration Act', *Journal of Ecclesiastical History* 45 (1994).

WYKES, D. L., '"They assemble in greater numbers and [with] more dareing than formerly": the bishop of Gloucester and nonconformity in the late 1660s', *Southern History* 17 (1995).

INDEX

Macintyre, Alasdair 9
Madison, James 208
Main and Bye Plots (1603) 39, 117
Maltby, Judith 85
Manichaens 26
Marian persecution 40, 41, 80–1, 89, 90,
    92, 129, 141, 173–4, 185
Marpeck, Pilgram 52
Marprelate Tracts 95, 98
Marsh, Christopher 116
Marshall, Stephen 137, 139
Marten, Henry 139
martyrology 90, 141, 174
martyrs, see executions
Marvell, Andrew 68–9, 169, 171, 184–5,
    186, 206, 214
Marxist history 1, 8
Mary I 80–1, 82, 87, 96, 173–4, 187
Mary II 190, 209
Mary of Modena 184
Mary Queen of Scots 85, 91, 110
Maryland 123–4, 158
Massachusetts 126–7, 154–5, 177, 178
Matar, Nabil 116
Mayne, Cuthbert 88, 89
medieval period 5, 6–7, 23, 51, 60–2
Medina, Solomon de 205
Melancthon, Philip 24
Mennonites 52, 103–4, 113, 207
Methodists 201
Middlesex 187
Mill, J. S. 56
millenarianism 63–5, 115–16, 148, 155–7
Millenary Petition 111
Miller, John 183, 184, 189, 191
Milton, Anthony 16
Milton, John 2, 3, 47, 50, 52, 54, 58,
    63–4, 65, 67, 149, 150, 171,
    206–7, 208, 214
missionary priests 38–9, 86, 88–92, 117,
    123, 157, 183, 186, 183, 186
Monck, General 167
Monmouth's rebellion (1685) 39, 188
Montagu, Richard 125
Montaigne, Michel 213
Monter, William 29, 78–9, 81
Moore, Katherine 11
More, Henry 50, 56, 214
More, Thomas 48, 51, 78

Morley, George 179
Morrill, John 3, 134
Mosaic law 31, 63, 70
Moses 31, 32, 197
Muggletonians 144
Murton, John 71, 113
Muslims 30, 47, 53, 55, 62, 69, 113, 116,
    148, 214
mutilation 101, 154, 128–9, 134, 136,
    149–50

natural law 26, 27–8, 37, 56, 218
Nayler, James 26, 152, 153–4
Nederman, Cary 5, 7
Neile, Richard 112, 114, 125, 126
Netherlands 36, 48, 49, 52, 53, 79, 103–4,
    128–9, 160, 184, 211
  as model 69, 70–1, 214, 216
  as refuge 98, 104, 112–14, 126, 135,
    177, 203, 215
Newcastle 89–90
Newcomen, Matthew 34, 38
Newgate prison 88, 94, 113, 114, 175, 176,
    201
New Jersey 177–8
New Model Army 148
Newport, Countess 124
New Testament
  used to support persecution 32–3, 49
  used to support toleration 59–60, 62–3,
    211–12
Newton, Isaac 7, 204
Northern Rebellion (1569) 39, 80, 85, 92
Northern rising (1663) 39, 171
Northumberland, Earl of 110
Norwich 100–2, 112, 115, 128, 176
Norwood, Robert 150
Nottingham, Earl of 198
Nottinghamshire 174, 203

Oates, Titus 39, 185
Oath of Allegiance 118–19, 122, 124
Occasional Conformity Act (1711) 201
Ogilvie, John 110
O'Gorman, Frank 204
Oldcorne, Edward 118
Old Testament 26, 29, 30–2, 59, 62–3, 70,
    79, 147
Overton, Richard 50, 56, 58, 64, 69